More International Acclaim for Brian Keenan's

FOUR QUARTERS OF LIGHT

"With any other writer we might feel ourselves drifting into allegory and fantasy out on these frozen wastes. With Keenan, this reader believed every word because truly remarkable minds have been opened to uncharted perceptions by long silence."

—SUNDAY TRIBUNE *(Dublin)*

"Keenan has proved he is a superb writer and that his first book, *An Evil Cradling,* the story of his four years in captivity in Beirut, wasn't a fluke . . . Dog-mushing on a frozen lake beneath aurora borealis, camping in the tundra, skinning hides, boating on the Bering Sea, he has the gift of taking you along with him."

—GLASGOW EVENING TIMES

"Combines a Bill Bryson–like directness with an intimate soul-searching agenda, reminiscent in places of the introspective insights that made *An Evil Cradling* so memorable."

—GLASGOW HERALD

"The finest travel book I have read this year." —WANDERLUST

"Wonderfully evocative and at times quite extraordinarily moving. There are many moments you carry with you long after you've turned the last page. Magic." —SUNDAY TRIBUNE *(Dublin)*

"A superb travel book . . . deeply spiritual." —IRISH INDEPENDENT

D0017196

AUG 2007

FOUR QUARTERS OF LIGHT

FOUR QUARTERS OF LIGHT

A Journey Through Alaska

* * * *

BRIAN KEENAN

Broadway Books | NEW YORK

PUBLISHED BY BROADWAY BOOKS

Copyright © 2004 by Brian Keenan

Originally published in the U.K. by Doubleday, Transworld Publishers, London, in 2004. This edition published by arrangement with Doubleday, Transworld Publishers, a division of The Random House Group Ltd.

Published in the United States by Broadway Books, an imprint of The Doubleday Broadway Publishing Group, a division of Random House, Inc., New York.
www.broadwaybooks.com

BROADWAY BOOKS and its logo, a letter B bisected on the diagonal, are trademarks of Random House, Inc.

Pages 363–64 constitute an extension of this copyright page.

Map by Neil Gower
Book design by Gretchen Achilles

Library of Congress Cataloging-in-Publication Data
Keenan, Brian, 1950–
Four quarters of light : a journey through Alaska / Brian Keenan.— 1st Broadway Books trade pbk. ed.
p. cm.
1. Alaska—Description and travel. 2. Keenan, Brian, 1950– —Travel—Alaska. 3. Outdoor life—Alaska. 4. Natural history—Alaska. 5. Wilderness areas—Alaska. I. Title.

F910.5.K44 2006
917.9805'2—dc22
2006040546

ISBN-13: 978-0-7679-2325-5
ISBN-10: 0-7679-2325-1

PRINTED IN THE UNITED STATES OF AMERICA

1 3 5 7 9 10 8 6 4 2

First U.S. Edition

For Audrey, Jack, and Cal, crew of the RV Pequod.

For Debra, who guides me still.

And for Lena, who is alone now.

There is an ecstasy that marks the summit of life, and beyond which life cannot rise.　　　　　　　　　　　　　　　　—JACK LONDON

How great are the advantages of solitude! How sublime is the silence of Nature's ever-active energies! There is something in the very nature of wilderness, which charms the ear and soothes the spirit of man. There is religion in it.　　　　　　　　　　—ESTWICK EVANS, 1818

ACKNOWLEDGMENTS

* Noeleen Gernon, who typed this manuscript while setting out on a new life journey herself.
* Pat Walsh in Fairbanks, Alaska, who worked out the logistics of my trip and introduced me to many people, a special friend to Audrey and the boys. Pat Walsh can be contacted for travel arrangements in Alaska at akplaces@alaska.net.
* Debra Chesnut, my guide into the Arctic and into myself.
* Mike Davis, "the old man of the sea," who finally discovered what life is about and, like the salmon, came back! Congratulations.
* Eileen Monaghan and family, who anchored us in Anchorage.
* Clare and Tom Connolly and Noreen and Tom (the fireman), who entertained us in Anchorage.
* The Gwich'in people of Arctic Village.
* Lena and Charlie Mendenhall.
* Mike Murphy and family, Mike McCarthy and Laura, Mary Shields, John Reese, Jane Haig and John Luther Adams—Alaskans all, and all of whom enriched my journey.
* My editors, Bill Scott-Kerr and Heather Barrett, who waited until the whale came home.
* And finally my wife, Audrey, and my sons, Jack and Cal, the other anchors in my life, who never let me get lost.

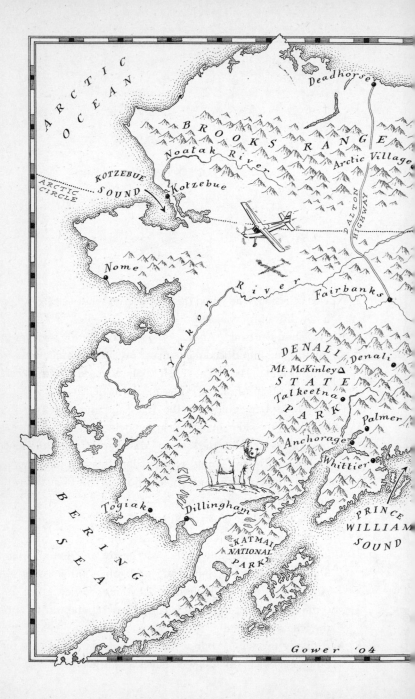

ALASKA

0 ————————— 250
miles

Demarcation Point

Kongakut River

ARCTIC CIRCLE

CANADA

Chitina
Valdez
Kennicott
McCarthy

Juneau

Sitka

PACIFIC OCEAN

CONTENTS

ONE   *Instructions and Preparations*   1

TWO   *First Footfalls in Fairbanks*   17

THREE   *Dog Mushing*   36

FOUR   *Maiden Voyage*   64

FIVE   *Ghosts in the Confessional*   74

SIX   *Road to the High One*   84

SEVEN   *Close Encounters of a Bear Kind*   96

EIGHT   *The Long and Winding Road*   104

NINE   *The Road to McCarthy*   108

TEN   *Paradise Lost*   117

ELEVEN   *A Moose Moment*   131

TWELVE   *Churchers, Birchers and Searchers*   141

THIRTEEN   *The Haul Road*   153

FOURTEEN   *Into the Arctic*   175

FIFTEEN   *Going Native*   185

SIXTEEN   *Athabascan Anglicans*   198

SEVENTEEN   *Patrick and the Caribou*   210

EIGHTEEN   *Close to the Caribou*   222

NINETEEN   *Council of the Raven*   231

TWENTY   *More Mammoths and Musicians*   236

TWENTY-ONE   *Arctic Inua*   263

TWENTY-TWO   *No Place Like Nome*   309

TWENTY-THREE   *Soul Bears*   323

TWENTY-FOUR   *The Final Quarter*   344

               Text Acknowledgments   363

＊

CHAPTER ONE

INSTRUCTIONS AND PREPARATIONS

From where I sit at my study window in County Dublin, I can see the rolling swell of the Wicklow hills. On stormy nights, if I walk to the end of the short terrace of which my house is the last but two, I can hear the sea's turbulence. As I look at the quaintly named Sugar Loaf mountain, I think that such a hill would not register in the landscape of the far Alaskan Northland. In a panorama that has one's head turning in a hypnotic 360-degree movement, in a mountainscape of fantastic dimensions such as you would only imagine in the illustrations of a mythic saga, such a pathetic headland would not even merit a nod.

Horizons are neither fixed nor finished in the Northland. Any horizon that presents itself to you only marks the limit of your vision; far beyond what you see, you know there is more. Another rugged mountain range, another somewhere, probably nameless and likely uninhabited. Only migratory birds, in their hundreds of thousands, know this landscape intimately. We poor land-bound, sight-blighted creatures can only grasp at things with our imagination and stumble over words such as permafrost, tundra and boreal forest, hot springs and pack ice, aurora borealis and midnight sun. They are all phenomena particular to the far north, but to me they are more than that: they are magic words, like a fistful of polished bone thrown from some shaman's hand. In them you might discover more of yourself than you know. Perhaps that's why I went to the final frontier—for the magic, before my own bones were too feeble for the task.

But an old man's romance is not enough for an answer; in any case, romance belongs to the rocking chair and recollection. We go places for our own reasons, even if we only half understand them. On the closing page of *Between Extremes*, an account of my travels in Patagonia and Chile coauthored with John McCarthy, I wrote, "I sensed that the only important journey I would make henceforth would be journeys out of time and into mind. There was another landscape to be discovered and negotiated. The landscape of the heart, the emotions, and the imagination had to be opened up and new route maps plotted . . . We talked late into the night arguing whether or not we, too, have journeys mapped on our central nervous systems. It seemed the only way to account for our insane restlessness."

So how could I now account for my own restlessness and my insistence on traveling to Alaska? It seemed to stand in contradiction to my deeply felt resolve at the conclusion of my South American travels. If I had determined that the only journeys I would make should be into the imagination and the landscape of the heart, then why was I thinking again of the Alaskan wilderness? For it was more than an old man's romantic folly, if not best forgotten then consigned to wishful thinking. The idea of an undiscovered country set in an elemental landscape fascinated me. It appealed to my anarchistic notions of boundless freedom. Sure it was romantic, but it was also real. Alaska was not a figment of my imagination. It existed in time and in place, and in my mind as somewhere that might test my self-assurance. One thing was for sure: it was clearly written on the map of my central nervous system.

It's a long way from Avoniel Road, where I went to school, to Alaska, where I dreamed of going, and the distance is in more than miles and physical geography. After all, what correspondence could there be between Belfast in the north of Ireland and Barrow in the far north of the Arctic Circle? But Avoniel primary school in east Belfast gouges itself up out of my memory as an original point of departure. It was 1959, and I was approaching my tenth birthday. I was a "good child," as my mother described me, quiet and untroublesome.

The school was a big, two-story barracks of a building, solid and imposing, set among the maze of back streets it served. A great lawn of two junior-sized football fields stretched out in front of it. To the right and screened from the entrance was a concrete field, and beside that the boys' and girls' outside toilets. Whatever advantage the 1947 Education Act had provided for the children of the area, it did not accommodate indoor plumbing. But then this was the catchment area of the aircraft factory and the shipyard, and me and my mates were all cannon fodder for the engineering industry. The football fields were the largest green space in the area, but they were forbidden to any of us after school hours. I was not of an athletic disposition anyway, and though I occasionally scaled the railings during the summer holidays, it was more because the place was forbidden than out of any desire to kick a football.

I compensated for my lack of sporting skills by finding a refuge in books. I excelled at reading and had finished all the "readers" we were required to make our way through long before my peers. If I was always the last kid picked to play, I was equally the first to complete any reading tasks, and I had more gold stars than anyone in my class. My special reward for being so far in advance of the rest of my classmates happened the day my teacher called me aside and suggested I might like to choose a book from the library. The library in Avoniel was an old Welsh dresser with locked doors stationed at the end of the first-floor corridor. It was also where the classrooms for the kids about to go to the "Big" school were located, and the library was exclusively for their use. The upper shelves were full with about three dozen books. I remember being quite frightened as my teacher walked me out of the class, admonishing the rest of the kids to be quiet and get on with their work until we returned. Whatever alienation I had felt from the rest of my mates, it was now compounded by this "honor." I was nine at the time and should not have been using the library for another year or two.

Standing on the rickety chair scanning the book spines in front of me, I felt like a sacrifice; these books were teeth in the great God monster that was going to devour me.

"You pick one, sir," I said, immobilized and wanting to be away from this looming altar of words.

The teacher laid his hand on my shoulder and in a voice that conveyed neither sympathy nor enthusiasm pronounced, "No, young man, you're going to read it, so you choose it."

I had never felt so alone in my life. Again I scanned the books before me. Their titles were just a jumble of words that meant little to me and only added to my confusion. Then my eyes alighted on one book; the four words comprising its title were easy for my young mind to read. The conjunction of the words were intriguing and the stark image on the dust cover of a large dog howling into a richly colored sky impressed itself upon me. I picked it out, climbed down from the chair and handed the book in silence to the teacher.

He took it from me and announced the title to the empty corridor: "*The Call of the Wild.*" He smiled thinly and continued, "So, you like dogs, do you?"

I answered him automatically, the words spilling from me. "Yes, sir. My dog at home is called Rex!"

His smile hung there for another moment, then he said, "It

may be a little difficult for you, Keenan, but it is a great adventure story. Try it, and we'll see how it goes." I held out my hand to take the book. "I'll bring the chair and you bring your dog!" he added, handing me the book.

For more than forty years I have had that dog with me, and the call of the wild echoes in me still. The story of Buck has, it seems, permeated the whole of my growing up, and here I am in my fifties still enraptured with it, the author and the landscape that gave it birth. *The Call of the Wild* is a parable about surviving and overcoming against all odds. It is about struggle and fulfillment, and it is ultimately about becoming what is in one to become. The call of Alaska's wilderness became a siren song; to resist it was to smother a vital instinct in myself. Maybe mortality and old age were knocking on my door and maybe I was not ready to let them in. There was another place I needed to go first. The last sentence of *The Call of the Wild* still speaks profoundly to me about the mystery and magic of that place, and about the torment of the author who wrote so eloquently about it: "When the long winter night comes and the wolves follow their meat in the lower valleys he may be seen running at the head of the pack through the pale moon light on glimmering borealis, leaping gigantic above his fellows, his great throat a bellow as he sings the song to the younger world, which is the song of the pack."

Still, I don't know if it was my solitary childhood immersion in Jack London's barbaric Northland that created my yearning. Isolated and barren landscapes draw me to themselves, different places for different reasons, but the one constancy is the lure of emptiness and wilderness. I suppose I feel comfortable there, untroubled. I can imagine a re-created life, and I confess a part of me is a loner. Loneliness, isolation and empty spaces are, I suppose, the preconditions of the dreamer, and I am a dreamer, unreconstructed and uncompromising. I pursue the landscape of the imagination and seek to find in the world about me some correspondence between the external and inner worlds, or perhaps a trigger for their coming together.

All journeys for me have this dual nature. But Alaska is no dreamland. It is raw, wild, primordial and uncompromising. Forsaking the holy grail of the imagination and emotion for a Klondike chronicle might be more demanding of the traveler than I could conceive. But only when you really contemplate it do you begin to slowly comprehend that Alaska is as complex as it is large.

For a start, it comprises several time zones and climatic regions. There are a minuscule number of roads for a region larger than England, France, Germany, Italy, Holland and Ireland put together. Negotiating such a vast expanse would be a nightmare of logistics, and as I intended to take my family with me I was multiplying my problems fourfold. But there was no way I could leave them behind. Maybe I was afraid the emptiness might engulf me, but my intoxication with the call of the wild was spilling over into my family life. I wanted to take my sons to see the place that had embedded itself in me when I was a child.

One belief I hold as an absolute truth is that the mind forgets nothing. I might forget things, but my mind forgets nothing. My sons were younger than I was when I was first smitten with Alaska. They might not enjoy months of living like the Swiss Family Robinson in the wilderness. I might not myself. Perhaps the illusion would evaporate there. Perhaps I had made too big an investment from my childhood in this imagined land. But that would be for me to resolve. Even if in the years to come my sons forgot their stay in Alaska, they would still have it stored in their memory bank to revisit over time, as I had done on many occasions. I only wanted to reveal to them the place that had continued to inspire me. I wanted Alaska to be more than their old man's ramblings. It could become for them whatever they chose. They only needed the seeds planted in them by exposure to the place, just as they had been implanted in me by exposure to Jack London's calling wilderness.

But there was another curious incident that swept the winds of Alaska right into my home and made my visit an imperative.

I had visited Fairbanks in central Alaska several years earlier as a guest lecturer. My stay was brief and confined to the environs of Fairbanks and its university, but it was enough to seal my long-held fascination with the place. While there I spoke with a group of students and some members of the public who attended my lecture as non-registered students about the use of the "instinct" in the creative process. I happened to mention that I had a notion to write a book about a blind musician, and as I knew nothing about music and was not blind I hoped my instinctual faculties were in good order.

I soon forgot the incident, but was brought sharply back to it while in the process of writing the book. I had spent years researching my subject and was tortuously trying to put the fiction together: I was finding it hard going trying to imagine the life of an eighteenth-century blind harpist, Turlough O'Carolan. Several months into the task I was about to give up and forget the project, though it remained very close to my heart. I was locked in one of those imaginative and intellectual culs-de-sac and was beginning to question the validity of what I was writing about. The whole thing seemed pointless.

At the very time I was contemplating this, I received a letter with a Fairbanks postmark. The letter was brief with no return address, the handwriting tiny but neat. It looked and felt feminine to me, but I could not make out the signature. It informed me that its author was aware I had intended writing a book about Turlough O'Carolan, who was a "Dreamwalker." The word threw me totally. I had not come across it before and never in reference to my subject. Mainly due to frustration with the lack of empathetic engagement with my subject, I dismissed the letter as having been written by some demented old spinster in the Alaskan outback who filled her days by writing strange letters to complete strangers.

I persevered with the book, stumbling into blind alleys and raging out of them. I wanted to get inside the emotional and psychological persona of the man I was writing about, but the fact that I wasn't blind combined with a marked musical illiteracy was making the book impossible. After months of struggle I finally came to the conclusion that I should jettison the project. Though I had promised myself for years that I would write the story of Turlough, I felt I had come to the end of the road.

Then another letter with an Alaskan postmark arrived, again with no return address, the same female handwriting and the same obscure signature. This time the letter was less brief, but the word "Dreamwalker" was back on the page and intriguingly there was an explanation of the term. I no longer have the letter, nor do I remember the exact words, but the imprint of it remains with me. Briefly, it related that the "Dreamwalker," whoever that may be (in my case Turlough), comes to visit people in their dreams. Their purpose is to give something, usually something healing and usually something that has to be passed on.

For some reason the letter seemed to take hold of me. I read it over and over again, then paced the floor trying to come to terms with the information and its relation to my work. I meticulously tried to decipher the signature and thought I could make out an Inuit name. But I could not be sure. The timing and the content of her letters seemed otherworldly. What was this strange Inuit woman from somewhere in Alaska trying to tell me? Why were her "Dreamwalker" letters always arriving at the precise moments of creative crises in my life? What was the connection between her and my long-dead blind musician? And what was my part in the weird triangle? I thought about it over and over again. It was like trying to work out some unearthly trigonometry.

Then, from God knows where, it hit me like a slap in the face. My torpor lifted and I was shown the way out of my dilemma. If my eighteenth-century itinerant musician had walked into my dreams, then I need only walk in his. In writing out his blind dreams I could convey his psychic and emotional life, thus extrapolating out of the man himself how he lived, how he composed the music he did, and why.

I finished the book with my muse from Alaska driving and directing the story. Sometimes I look at it on the bookshelf in my study and think how it would not be there, indeed how it would not exist in any form, had I not received those mysterious letters from the Alaskan wilderness. I had rid myself of my eighteenth-century musician, but a new and more prescient Alaska was calling to me with irresistible attraction. It had now given itself a voice that was separate from my own fantasizing. So I chose to return with a head full of questions about that inspiring landscape and the primitive animism that exists there.

Jack London once wrote in a letter, "When a man journeys into a far country, he must be prepared to forget many things he has learned, he must abandon the old ideals and the old gods and often times he must reverse the very codes by which his conduct has hitherto been shaped." There was something in those words of London's that excited my imagination about my mysterious pen friend, and the magic that connected us. She was not just some figment of my frustrated imagination, she was real and living out there in the boundless wilderness. Her communications had moved psychic mountains for me, and the acknowledgment on the flyleaf of the book hardly seemed sufficient reward. But could I find her in that huge country? If I was to accept London's words, what would I have to abandon, and what reverses would I have to make? For a moment I thought of Joseph Conrad's failed heroes who are devoured by the landscape they enter, and I recoiled at the journey that was beckoning me.

I thought again of London and the struggles of his heroes, men and dogs, against the forces of nature and one another. His stories embody a recognition of primal forces that can transform or crush people, at the same time hinting at something in the personality of their author, an illegitimate child whose poverty-stricken childhood taught him how to fight to survive. Like myself, the author would take himself off on small voyages of discovery, surviving on his wits and animal cunning. As a man, he was strongly influenced by Marx, Hegel, Spencer, Darwin and

Nietzsche, from whose works he evolved a belief in humanism and socialism and an admiration for courage and individual heroism. I was drawn to this complex, tragic man. A writer who wrote in the naturalist tradition of Kipling and Stevenson. A Marxist who flirted with dangerous notions of the superhero. A socialist who argued against the Mexican Revolution. But, ultimately, a man who drew his own map in life. In many respects London was like one of his strongest characters. In *The Sea Wolf* (1904), Wolf Larsen is the incredibly brutal but learned captain of the *Ghost* who is doomed by his individualism. The central character of Martin Eden was also ominously autobiographical, not only telling of an ex-sailor who becomes a writer but also of the emotional turmoil, the loss of identity and selfhood and ultimate suicide. Maybe the author's idealism was too highly pitched. He was shipwrecked by failed marriages, bankruptcy, alcoholism and suicide. Obviously there had been some dark, self-destructive alter ego that would not allow the man to "reverse the very codes by which his conduct has hitherto been shaped." He certainly had much to say about fear. He considered it mankind's basic emotion, a kind of primordial first principle that affects us all. But understood in the right way, fear need not be a harness. London's protagonists challenged it, even chose at times to forget it. Fear was a prime motivator for London the man, too: it made him shake off the shackles of conformity and achieve success.

"There is an ecstasy that marks the summit of life, and beyond which life cannot rise," he once said. I had unknowingly tasted that ecstasy as a child with my face buried in the author's epic in a tiny two-up-two-down family home whose confines smothered me. In the Belfast back streets where the only green space was locked away from me behind iron railings, I drank deeply from London's elixir and its taste stayed in my mouth. Foolishly or not, when I was younger I was a man who was afraid of being afraid. It forced me to make choices and flooded me with questions I felt only the Northland itself could answer. But I was older now and hopefully a little wiser. Maybe I was tired of being afraid of being afraid. If I was to "forget many things . . . abandon the old ideals and the old gods . . . and reverse the very codes" that had formed me, then perhaps I could only fully reclaim this lost part of myself during a wilderness experience.

Was Alaska still peopled with those quirky, eccentric and reclusive individuals that made Robert Service famous and fascinated London? Service's rhythmic and zestful poems about the rugged life of the Yukon were also part of my growing up. "The Shooting of Dan McGrew" and "The Cremation of Sam McGee" were in every school anthology and brought the Canadian outback into our mundane school days. Alaska was called the "Final Frontier" before the writers of *Star Trek* hijacked the phrase, and I wondered if it still had the same kind of allure for people as it had for its most famous writers. What impels people toward finality and the last place on earth, and what do they resolve there? Why do they stay in the seemingly inhospitable land? Have they a perverse sense of beauty akin to my own? If so, how do they understand it? These were my questions, and neither London nor Service could answer for me.

Maybe the Final Frontier is an inaccurate description, for assuredly Alaska is the Frontier of Fable. The onion-domed churches of nineteenth-century Russian Orthodoxy still break up the skyline around Juneau, Sitka and Kodiak. Further north the Inuit peoples cling to their religious beliefs with their shamanism and an animistic respect for the natural world from which we all could learn much. And everywhere one still finds those curious, rugged, idealistic individuals who have washed up in this vastness, and perhaps it's the proper place for them, for here the emptiness is big enough to contain their madness. Only a place as immense as Alaska can properly contain a fevered imagination. This is the land that Swift, C. S. Lewis and Tolkien never discovered, as fantastical as a fairy tale but undersewn with deep soul-searching.

I began to pore over maps of Alaska. But any map of Alaska

is a Spartan illustration: railway lines and road systems are conspicuous by their absence and Juneau, the state capital, is accessible only by air and sea. The state is more easily measured in time zones than miles. It contains four such zones and a total population of just over 600,000, half of whom reside in Anchorage, Alaska's largest town and port; the rest of the population is spread out across this massive, seemingly endless state in communities that make the map look more like a join-the-dots picture such as you find in children's coloring books. But this is no childhood fantasy land. The incomprehensible hugeness of the place is something to be wary of. I remember a friend I had met during my first brief visit to Alaska saying, "Be careful when you're reading maps in Alaska. Names don't always mean places and named places don't always guarantee that people live there. There are some communities in Alaska where people live so far from one another that they are all but invisible. That kind of landscape doesn't only make you feel small, it can be very scary and very dangerous too."

I thought over my friend's words as I scanned the place names spread out before me. The Inuit names scattered around the margins of the landmass were curious and almost unpronounceable; my tongue tripped over glottal stops as I tried to say them: Unalakleet, Koyukok, Umiat, Shungnak and Shageluk, Akhiok, Ekwok, Quinhaqak, Togiak and Yakutat. Then the curious European names that marked the commercial expansion and settlement: Russian Mission and Holy Cross, Valdez and Cordova, and the place names of the miners who had come in droves, desperately poor, dream-driven men whose rudimentary education made them believe their dreams and give names to places the way you would throw scraps to a dog. The names were simple, yet just reading them brought you very close to their world: Livengood, Sourdough, Chicken, Coldfoot, Eureka. Then there were the mountains, from Mount McKinley, the highest on the continent, to the permanently frozen Brooks Range, the most northerly. The Koskokwim mountains and the Wrangell mountains, and more mountains—the St. Elias, the Kilbruck, the Taylor, the Talkeetna, the Asklun, the Romanof, the Shublik—and then the great ranges, the Aleutian and the Alaskan. There were yet more mountains that no one had bothered to name because no human had ever set foot on them or ever wanted to. Obviously there were some places that refused admission to the human species.

But however brutal, imposing and empty, people had chosen to go there, and to stay. Most assuredly Alaska is not a place one simply stumbles upon. Even in the book of choices this forbidden, inhospitable emptiness would hardly rate in the top twenty of anyone's most desirable places to settle in. Yet native peoples make up only about 20 percent of the population; the rest are immigrants, or perhaps more correctly self-inflicted exiles. Who were they? Why had they come? What were they running from? And, more importantly, what had they found? How the place had transformed them to make them stay was what I wanted to know. Was there really some kind of magic here, or had the stone-cold landscape frozen their souls and immobilized them? For after Alaska there are no more choices, no more places to go. It is, after all, the Final Frontier.

Poring over maps doesn't answer questions, it only adds to them, and in the case of Alaska it only served to deepen the enigma of the place and my resolve to return. I was determined that my journey should take me through the four geographical quarters. First, the coastal southeast and the south-central region to hunt down Jack London's first footfalls; then southwest and the Bering Sea coast; then into that light-filled, enclosed world of the Arctic region; and finally into the interior, ranging out from Fairbanks on small voyages of discovery or displacement. I intended traveling only during the period of maximum light, from snowmelt in mid-May to snowfall in mid-September, for I have had more than my share of dark places, and anyway, Alaskan winters are not made for traveling great distances.

As I began to plan the logistics of trying to encompass this vast land, I was ever mindful of Jack London's advice about his Alaskan experience: "It was in the Klondike I found myself. There nobody talks, everybody thinks. You get your perspective. I got mine." I remembered too the author's imperative about being prepared to forget and abandon many things, and concluded it would be impossible and a serious error for me to try to work out a detailed schedule and timetable. The country was too big to be reduced to a precociously planned itinerary. If any journey was simply a record in time of passage between two points, then few of us would need to make such journeys; we could simply read the records of others. Rather, a journey is like a work in progress: you extract meaning and insight from the experience.

Alaska was calling me out to its wilderness. Would I be equal to it or would it be unequal to my dreams? There was only one way to find out.

Packing was a nightmare; the problem was as big as the land-mass I was venturing into. How does one wind- and weather-proof two adults and two children against climatic conditions that vary between Arctic numb and Mediterranean wet, occa-sionally bleaching into the high hot days of an Indian summer? I looked at the bags piling up: they too were mocking me. It would take a brigade of army engineers to move this lot or at least a string of pack mules. I intended traveling a lot and the idea of constant packing and unpacking was already defeating me.

I thought it through over and over again. Four time zones, cli-matic conditions so varied that nothing could be depended on. A road system, in a land of continental dimensions, that amounted to a few hundred miles rather than thousands of miles. I would have to fly long distances in tiny light aircraft, and those that know me know that my fear of heights is legendary. Also I can-not swim and much of the southeast and southwest peninsulas can only be explored by small boat. I was certainly no Grizzly Adams and the logistics of my fanciful expeditions seemed to be impossible. It was like a logarithmic problem that had its resolution somewhere in infinity, and that, seemingly, was where I was going too.

In an attempt to reassure myself and to keep my worst fears from my wife and family, I turned again to my mentor Jack London and considered how he would have handled all this. In a letter to one of his friends he writes of his first encounter with the infamous man-killing Chilkoot trail, which had to be negotiated to enter into that wildness that so fascinated the author and myself.

"The sands of Dyea resemble an invasion beach. Everywhere men bartered with Indian porters, trying to persuade them to haul their food at reasonable prices. Jack's ageing partner Shepard took one look at the glittering white wall of the Chilkoot Pass and decided to turn back. Within weeks, he would be joined by thousands more. In retreat, they would find abandoned kit littering the coastline for forty miles." Despite the Chilkoot Pass's backbreaking nature, by the autumn of 1897 twenty-two thousand men and women had reached the other side. Jack was among them. But only after a struggle which tested his stamina to the limit.

Crippled horses littered the trail, "broken-boned, drowning, abandoned by man." They died "like mosquitoes in the frost. They snapped their legs in the crevices and broke their backs falling backwards on their packs; in the sloughs they sank from sight or smothered in the same, men shot them, worked them to death and when they were gone, went back to the beach and brought more. Some did not bother to shoot them, stripping the saddles off, and leaving them where they fell. Their hearts turned to stone, those which did not break, and they became beasts, the men on Dead Horse Trail."

I looked again at our mountain of luggage and the sparse map, mulling over all the what-ifs that were niggling at me. It seemed I was contemplating my own Chilkoot Pass without having set foot in Alaska. I certainly do not possess the same "will to power" that was so much part of London the man and the writer, but I suppose I had a soul hunger akin to his, and if he could survive on that perhaps I could too.

However, no matter how I dealt with the difficulties, most of which were imagined, there were two real problems that would not go away. I was having sleepless nights about the smallest of the inhabitants of this land where everything was big, namely the mosquito and its near cousins the black fly and the suitably named "no-see-ums," whose bites are far more annoying precisely because you cannot see the creature.

Permafrost was another problem. Its constant presence just feet below the surface ensured that plumbing was more than a luxury. In many places it was impossible to install simply because it would never work. I did not dwell on this subject too much with Audrey, but simply explained that she should expect things to be very primitive in some places.

The mosquitoes eventually won out. My Alaskan friend Pat Walsh had warned us not to underestimate their number or their size. To emphasize her point, she sent me a miniature penknife, no more than an inch long, with one small double-sided blade like a paring knife. When I thanked her and queried the purpose of such an ornament she answered curtly: "It's not an ornament, it's for skinning mosquitoes!" I decided to change the order of my travels, visiting "the Bush" first, before the insects got too thick on the ground, then moving on to the Bering Sea coast and the southeast and southwest peninsular regions, where my expectation was that the open space and coastal winds would keep the bugs at bay.

Trying to solve problems before you encounter them is frequently a wise precaution but it can also be a debilitating one. Having convinced myself that it was better to confront the enemy in his own backyard, we headed north to the last frontier, come what may!

CHAPTER TWO

FIRST FOOTFALLS
IN FAIRBANKS

Fairbanks is known to many of its inhabitants as the Golden Heart of Alaska; the welcoming signs at the airport declare it with proud abandon. The origins of this accolade stem from the gold-rush industry; it also, in a self-congratulatory manner, refers to the spirit of the place and people who live there. The boom-time economies of gold and oil that created it have all but gone away and the town remains shabby but unbowed. Our taxi driver advised us not to be taken in by the remark. "In the summer this can be the sweetest town in Alaska," he said, "but the winter is when you need a place and people to be sweet. In the winter Fairbanks can be the coldest, bleakest bitch of a place. It's like a woman that's suddenly gone frigid. Man, it can get as cold as a witch's tits up here!" I liked the driver's iconic, careless manner. He was totally oblivious of the presence of Audrey and the children and gabbled on colorfully to me alone. I detected a hint of southern drawl in his voice, and when I asked him where he was from originally he confirmed my suspicions and added, "Been here more than thirty years and only been back once, when my mom died. Picked up what was coming to me and hightailed it back here faster than a fox after a hare. Hardly remember the place I come from now, don't want to neither."

I enjoyed the man's garrulous conversation and was intrigued by how everywhere else was simply referred to as "outside." For Alaskans, I later learned, everywhere that is not Alaska is "outside." In part it perhaps explained why he never went home, for as creatures we are seldom drawn in great length to what is "outside" our experience. "Outside" hints at something that is alien to our experience, and I was beginning to feel that "outside" was a place you should only visit once. So what was I doing here? Was this my "outside"? And would once be enough?

As suddenly as the question arose it dissolved, and I asked the driver, "Just how cold does it get?"

"Well," he replied, "it's been known to hit minus fifty and more here. And when you come out of a big cold like that, there's usually less people around."

"How come?"

"Some die, some take off, some freak out completely. The freak ones you have to watch out for. At first they seem normal as they always were, then one day they start acting funny, doing things and saying things that ain't like them. Then they're back to normal again as if nothing happened. You forget it once, maybe even twice, but when it gets more reg'lar than that, you know they're gone and the old dark cold has got them. They'll be gone forever, or enough so's they don't make much use anyway. It's always the loners that go first. Man needs a woman in the wintertime. Beg your pardon, ma'am!" he suddenly interjected, realizing finally that Audrey and the boys were in the car.

Perhaps all the winters he had spent there had numbed a little bit of him, but I liked him and his rickety old taxi, which as I looked closely seemed to have more duct tape holding it together than I thought possible. Our antiquated transport with its curious driver and his talk about "outsiders" and people going crazy seemed to add to my otherworldly apprehension of the place as we passed through it. I had the feeling of being washed up there, or having been uncovered in a snow slide. Fairbanks is Alaska's second city but has the feel of a dormitory encampment in the process of being abandoned. Maybe it was the grayness of the snow against a sleepy blue sky, or maybe it was me—and I was tired—but it had already impressed itself on me as a place not yet ready for human habitation. Everything hung in a murky, opaque gloom, eerily lit by wearily flashing neon. A last flickering heartbeat.

We had decided to stay the first few days in a hotel to sort ourselves out and allow the kids to get used to the place. We had been traveling for thirty-two hours on four different aircraft and we needed breathing space between our arrival and whatever departure we would determine on. The hotel was on the outskirts of the town, but as Fairbanks is so diffuse there weren't really any outskirts as such. The place was constructed entirely of pine log and heavy pine beams.

The Chena River ran alongside the hotel and made for an excellent playground. I was assured that the last of the snow had fallen, unless I intended traveling much further north. Though the snow was still lying stained and sullied on the ground, making it look like a painter's drop cloth, I was informed that summer could happen tomorrow. I believed what I was told. I had heard enough about the sudden arrival of summer in Alaska. Still, the cold seemed to be hanging in the air. It didn't really penetrate you physically but it did get under your skin, metaphorically. Its invisible presence seemed to erase the normal preoccupations that fill a day. At first it's fun—this is Alaskan snow, I told myself. This is the petticoat frill of the Arctic underskirts. This is the powder crust of the icebound heart of this great Arctic frontier. The novelty of it made me giddy, like my children playing in it. But after a few days the novelty was gone. The soft, uneven coverlet that had looked so picturesque now seemed to creep up as if to smother you. I was already trying to imagine myself living out there in the cold and dark. It was not inviting.

My first days in Fairbanks were full of this exotic contradiction. I was at the center of this northern world. Further north would be another even colder and even more enclosed world. But I was also at the between point of things. Winter was on its last legs and summer, even if I couldn't see it, was waiting out there. Maybe this accounted for my irresoluteness, but then, as I struggled with my notebook trying to find the right words to convey this place, I remembered something I had read about hypothermia. It causes numbness and irrational and sometimes violent behavior. Sometimes sufferers seem withdrawn and intense. Muscle cramps produce a morbid, introspective lethargy, and at other times bursts of ecstatic energy. I could understand how this place could cause such mercurial responses, but I wanted to believe that my own vacillation was more down to the impending summer, the life that was quietly burgeoning under the earth and in the heavens. I watched my family wrapped up against the elements, looking like Michelin men. They were enjoying the snow in the spruce woods, laughing when it slid off the branches and showered them as they charged between trees. I forgot my anxiety about bringing them here. I was glad they were with me. They were a safety net. For a man alone could lose himself utterly in this vast, cold region without having moved too far from the city. I thought about it for a while. Yes, my taxi driver was more than a cabbie. He was also a prophet!

I spent my mornings with Pat Walsh, planning and finalizing what I wanted to do, and more importantly what we couldn't do as a family. I had met her when I'd first visited Fairbanks several years ago. She had her own specialized tour business and what she didn't know about Alaska wasn't worth knowing. There were some trips it would be foolish to attempt as a family. Months before our arrival I had enlisted Pat's help to arrange a stay with the Eskimos on the Bering Sea coast. She had assured me that Eskimos adore children, especially blond-haired, blue-eyed ones, but life was very, very basic and very, very hard. There was nothing in the way of luxury or entertainment for a four-year-old and a not yet two-year-old from Dublin's suburbs. When she mentioned that sanitation would be crude in the extreme and that washing or showering, if it was at all possible, was normally a communal affair, my problems resolved themselves. Even if I wanted her to and pleaded and promised eternal, undying love, would Audrey follow me into the Arctic North under such conditions? Once the subject of native cuisine was discussed I knew there wasn't a heathen's hope in hell of my wife warming my igloo for me. Seal blubber, moose, caribou, musk ox and raw fish washed down with boiled snow was, quite simply, not on.

In preparation for our trip, Audrey had been reading *Into the Wild* by Jon Krakauer, the true story of a young man's fascination with the wilderness and his ultimate renunciation of "normal" life, which occurred in 1992. Chris McCandless, about whom the story was written, seemed a driven man. He had handed over the entire balance of his account—some $24,000—to charity, abandoned his car and possessions, burned all the cash in his wallet and simply walked off into the Alaskan wilderness alone. Such is the action of a madman, but this young man was anything but mad, at least to all outward appearances. He came from an affluent Virginian family and graduated with honors from an Ivy League university, where he was an elite athlete. "Given a few years or so and with a few minor adjustments here and there, he could be you," my wife quipped as she outlined the bare bones of the story. I disagreed, but she continued, "You're so bloody stubborn, you keep too many things to yourself. You're worse than Greta Garbo sometimes with your 'I want to be alone'!" I could only smile, but I felt the ghost of Chris McCandless closer than I care to admit. When Audrey remarked that a piece of wood carved with the words "Jack London is King" was found at the side of the young man's corpse, I was profoundly intrigued and not a little disturbed.

Chris McCandless's last words to the world were written on a page torn from a novel by Nikolai Gogol. Audrey read it to me: "SOS. I need your help. I am injured, near death and too weak to hike out of here. I am alone. This is no joke. In the name of God, please remain to save me. I am collecting berries close by and shall return into the evening. Thank you, Chris McCandless, August?" She remarked on how tragic and pathetically sad it was that he had died so young and so helplessly alone. The sadness of the young man's words struck me too, but I didn't want to show it. Instead I responded by saying that a loving wife should not be telling her husband ghost stories about people dying in the Alaskan wilderness just before he was about to disappear into it himself. My humor was lost on her. She replied pointedly, "But it's not a ghost story, it's real, and that's why I'm telling you about it!" I was unsure what to say, and to fill the silence I suggested I might read the book after her. "I'm not sure I'll let you," she declared adamantly.

"What, not let me read the book?"

"No, not let you go!"

It was the same stern voice, but this time I thought it coldly authoritative, not wanting any argument or humor from me.

That night I thought about McCandless and his fatal exile in the wilderness. He was a highly intelligent and committed young man inspired by Jack London and the great nineteenth-century Russian writers Tolstoy, Dostoevsky and Gogol. Asceticism and moral rigor would certainly have been principal psychological characteristics of a young man steeped in such literature, and such qualities could, to a mind so disposed, be perfectly suited to the wilderness landscape. The lure of such a place could become irresistible, and if the young man were such an athlete, then the challenge would be doubly hypnotic.

As a young man I suppose I had drunk from the same cup as young McCandless, but I was older now, if not wiser, and I had brought my bonds of love and affection with me. I had burned no bridges in the fires of renunciation—quite the reverse. I hadn't intended to leave Audrey, Jack and Cal for any longer than I had to. But at the same time I'm sure I both sensed and was looking for what McCandless was seeking—self-affirmation, a new compass bearing from which to set out on life, something profoundly fulfilling and maybe even life-altering.

The Alaskan wilderness is just another desert, and like the desert it is an environment of extremes. In substance and in form it is alien and austere, inimical to human presence. In such a wilderness the mind expands in new vistas of light and space. The northern sky is enormous, awesome and threatening, yet intoxicating. The architecture of the earth and the expansive heaven diminishes you, yet allows you to see further than is possible for the human eye. In this landscape you may discern more clearly that map imprinted on your nervous system. In such places men can be caught up in strange rhapsodies, and may be transformed. Such places have spawned the leaders of great religions. But, I told myself, those who choose the wilderness retreat do so not to escape reality but to find it. I think it was Dostoevsky who wrote that to fall into the hands of the living god was a powerful and dreadful thing, and maybe that is what happened to Chris McCandless. For had he kept his eyes firmly on reality, however flawed, he might have made the journey back, for that is the important one!

I thought again of the words carved on the scrap of wood, the word "King" underlined, and wondered what that meant. It was an exuberant statement from such a well-trained and disciplined mind. What did he mean? Was London the king because he understood the dreadful nature of the world he had entered into? In *White Fang* he wrote:

Dark spruce forest groaned on either side of the frozen water-way. The trees had been stripped by a recent wind of their white covering of frost, and they seemed to lean toward each other, black and ominous, into the fading light. A vast silence reigned over the land. The land itself was desolation, lifeless, without movement, so alone and cold that the spirit of it was not even that of sadness. There was a tinge of laughter, but laughter more terrible than any sadness. A laughter cold as the frost, and partaking of the grimness of infallibility. It was the masterful and incommunicable wisdom of eternity laughing at the futility of life and the effort to life. It was the wild, the savage, frozen-hearted Northland Wild.

That dark spruce forest remains on the hills around Fairbanks, and even in the first days of summer there was nothing pretty about it. It was old and unsightly, and the trees looked more dead than alive. They could have been fifty or sixty years old, but they looked like saplings. Because the ground they grow out of is permanently frozen there are insufficient nutrients to allow them to gain any real bulk or to spread. I was told that only the black spruce can grow on such ground, and as I looked at them their blackness was pleasant enough against the late snow, but nearer the town, where they aged long before their time, they were antagonistically ugly.

Then again, as we drove around Fairbanks trying to make purchases for our excursion, Audrey and I agreed that the town was a contradiction in terms. The word Fairbanks suggests a pleasantly situated environment along the banks of the Chena. But this is far from the truth. The banks of the river are built up with offices and small factories long since closed up with the decline in gold mining. In the outskirts private homes are built in a variety of styles and materials and many of them have their own private seaplane moored on the water at the end of their well-manicured lawns.

Overall, the town would not score any points for architectural or cultural merit. It is constructed on a grid system so typical of Middle America, and such simple expediency does not encourage artistic evolution. But even with this ordered constraint, the town seemed to be thrown together the way boom-and-bust frontier towns of necessity usually are. The charm of Fairbanks has its origins firmly in that era, for Fairbanks is indisputably a blue-collar town. It may be the second city in the state, yet it has the feel of a town. The people here are open and friendly in the extreme. All the airs and graces of a cultured European capital would find no place here.

The atmosphere of a frontier town still hung in the air. This was a place where people came to work out dreams and found they had to spend nine months of the year simply trying to survive. The winters here favor no one person above another and everybody ultimately depends on everyone else. Just to underline the fact, there were no designer shops of any description. Wind- and weatherproofing are essential elements of clothes design in Fairbanks; color, texture and cut are only meaningful if they enhance these first priorities. Men and women alike dressed like lumberjacks in flannel shirts, workmen's overalls and sturdy boots. "Dressing" to go anywhere meant no more than exchanging one pair of jeans for another, or a pair of boots that hadn't been clean for months for clean ones. Still, you knew that nobody would bat an eyelid if you walked into an opera performance at the university in full bush gear, caked with mud, wet with snow, smelling of the great outdoors and perfumed with perspiration, blood and offal from the moose you have just finished skinning.

In the gray morning light and half light at dusk, Fairbanks looked like an expansive container yard with acre upon acre of rectangular clapboard buildings and square, rough-hewn log cabins. It is down-in-the-mouth stubborn, and persistent. It hangs on like grim death against all the odds. In the afternoon, while walking downtown where every other building was once either a bar, a brothel or a gambling parlor but was now boarded up, empty or demolished, you sensed that the winter winds had blown the place clean of this sordid but ebullient lifestyle. In the daylight the buildings seemed impregnated with amnesia about the past, as if they had forgotten why they were there in the first place. The bars that remained were rank with the smell of stale beer, tobacco and urine. There were a few native people in them too sick to drink anymore. Their eyes were full of anger and emptiness. It was not a pretty place, and the reality factor was cauterizing my romantic imagination. The men who stared at us with their ghoulish eyes were indeed ghosts. This was their land, by birthright and inheritance. They were born into it, were taught about it, understood its ways, yet here they were washed up in these soulless back streets existing on a daily round of alcohol, vomit and the sleep of stupor.

During the day I kept most such thoughts to myself, allowing Alaska to pose its own questions, which I might or might not find the answer for. But it was early days yet. We were still busy planning, shopping for clothes and equipment and making occasional forays into the bush before the plagues of mosquitoes and no-see-ums made it impossible. In the meantime my friend Pat had arranged for us to have the use of a log cabin in the hills above the town. We had been to view it a few days previously, and to me it seemed idyllic. It was set well back off the road a good half mile and nestled snugly under its own growth of white spruce and birch; thankfully, the gloomy black spruce was not in great abundance in this particular area. All around us were stands of aspen and poplar. Pat informed us that Russians had a name for this type of woodland—"taiga," meaning "little sticks," because the trees, which were maybe more than a hundred years old, rarely attain more than a few inches' girth. The nearest cabin to our new home was a few hundred yards through dense scrub and alder thickets.

Audrey saw the drawbacks that I impatiently dismissed. Staying in the cabin meant fetching our own water, and if there was no running water that of course meant there was no flushing toilet. A neatly constructed log outhouse with an acceptable chemical toilet and mechanical shower for which you could pump waste water from a storage tank and heat it by compressor seemed perfectly adequate to me, but my wife and mother of two children had reservations and frowned on my enthusiasm.

I could see her point. The place was, in fact, in chaos. My forays around Fairbanks had confirmed to me that there was an excusable slovenliness about Alaskan homesteads. The front yards or back plots of most were littered with the detritus of several winters. Carcasses of old cars and trucks, some of which would make a vintage collector's mouth water, were strewn here and there. Snow machines in various stages of disrepair seemed obligatory. Coils and coils of rusted chain and bright orange or blue nylon rope of varying thicknesses lay like somnolent snakes among the wreckage. Piles of blue tarpaulin that had been intended to protect some of this "gear" from the winter snow had been blown into corners where they served no useful purpose. Snow tires and winter wheels were stacked in short, squat columns. Stockpiles of lumber waiting for an intended or unfinished addition to the cabin were commonplace. And everywhere boxes and boxes and more boxes of God knows what. Snowshoes and skis, life belts and buoyancy jackets; aluminum canoes and deflated rubber rafts—the proliferation of stuff was interminable and every home had its own peculiar and unique collection. I loved these fabulous accumulations and played games imagining who might live in such a place. I had once queried this phenomenon with Pat, and she'd explained it with simple logic: "In Alaska you need a lot of stuff."

"But what about the things that are either completely obsolete or beyond repair?" I persisted.

"Well, the permafrost doesn't allow us to dig great garbage dumps so we stockpile it. You see, most Alaskans believe that even the most useless piece of equipment will someday find a purpose, or that someone else will find something to do with whatever it is."

I couldn't argue with that and I didn't want to: these "middens" were a place of endless fascination.

"Do you know," she continued, "that the most popular place at the weekend is the district dump? People meet up there every Sunday just to see who doesn't want what, and to exchange rubbish. There is always somebody who will need something that I don't, and vice versa. Makes sense, doesn't it? And another thing: few people up here lock their doors."

When I looked at her quizzically she explained that there were lots of stories of people getting lost or having a breakdown in the below-freezing temperatures and they had had their lives or their extremities saved from frostbite by finding an open cabin.

"What about valuables?" I asked.

"Well, not a lot of people have valuables in the sense you mean, and in any case, if your open door has just saved someone's life or even their fingers or feet, they simply aren't thinking about stealing from you, are they?" The pragmatic simplicity of Pat's explanations to my questions became a trait of hers.

As I sat on the raised porch that provided a sheltered entrance to our dacha I wondered at the skeletal trees all around us. They seemed greener than I had seen them a few days ago. Maybe it was because there was less snow and more light, or maybe it was because I was actually taking time to absorb rather than just looking and taking notes—or maybe I was already finding the boreal forest less intimidating now that I'd actually moved into it and become part of it. I could imagine this place in the autumn, the declining sunlight and the glistening tinge of frost creating its own kind of Halloween. All around me the tamaracks, alder birches and willows would send up amber and golden flares clarioning the winter; in the undergrowth, blueberries, cranberries and kinnikinnik bushes flaming red, amber, gold, salmon pink and high bright yellow. It would be a sea of glowing fire before the soft white mantle of frost and snow extinguished them. Amid such a vista you could excuse the black spruce its wretchedness. I looked around me again. Yes, everywhere the green serge of summer seemed to be bleeding out of the woodlands. Beyond that the winter silence of the sub-Arctic horizon lay motionless, waiting.

I was more than a little content with my cabin in the woods. I breathed in the air, intoxicated. In the outskirts of my imagination I was beginning to see more than my eyes uncovered. My thoughts were an elixir, fulsome and seductive. "Oh, what I could do here!" I thought, and this was immediately followed by an avalanche of exciting ideas and projects. In this welter of self-indulgence I began to wish that I had left my family behind and that I could remain here by myself creating my own perfect world in my beehive of a cabin. Wilderness to the creative mind is like a blank canvas to a painter: it is full of possibilities. Here is perfect peace and absolute freedom; here too may be the prologue of melancholy or bliss. In the wilderness, there are no ready-made roads; you make your own and go where you choose. I loved this undeclared absence of prohibition.

I thought of Chris McCandless and his fatal walk in the wild. My wife was correct: in my youth I was very like him. His rapture with London, Thoreau and the mysticism of nature was my own, and even now I felt it. But age tempers you. That crackling static of reality short-circuits your dreams more and more.

The next morning Pat arrived with a companion following her in another vehicle. They parked at the end of the path and picked their way through the muck toward the cabin.

"I brought someone I think you should meet," Pat announced.

There was a hint of Inuit about the woman. Her face was round and almost copper-colored, her hair long, straight and shiny black. Before Pat could say more, the woman introduced herself. "Hello, my name's Debra Chesnut. I'll be your guide when you head north to visit with the Eskimos."

There are times when seemingly insignificant events, such as a casual introduction, open up doors to the most intriguing and scary panoramas. This was one of those moments, but I barely felt the tremor of it.

"I am sorry," she continued, "I really have to rush off, but we should meet up soon, to discuss travel arrangements and other things."

"Yes, of course," I said. "Patricia has spoken to me about you."

Jack and Cal were nagging at me to be taken inside, and Debra turned and walked away without saying another word to me or anyone else.

"Call me," I shouted after her, a little anxious and embarrassed at the brevity of our encounter.

"I will, soon," she said, turning her head in my direction. Her voice was soft and confident, as if she had already determined to do what I had only just asked her. And then she was gone. Pat was also in a hurry and explained that she had brought Debra along just to ensure that we wouldn't be strangers when we met to arrange travel details. Then she, too, was gone.

We waved to Pat as she roared her old Plymouth down the rutted track that led to our cabin and quickly tumbled inside. The blast of heat from the log oven was instantaneous and we all slumped onto the sofa. Cal was soon asleep, and Jack wouldn't be long behind him. Within minutes we had both lads snugly wrapped up in their beds.

Over the last cup of coffee, Audrey and I discussed how the long hours of daylight confuse the senses. Your mind seems to be fooled and remains constantly in daylight mode, and then suddenly weariness slams into you. I loved this constant light and the cabin we were in seemed to energize the sleep out of me. After a brief discussion about some of the people we had met and our plans for the next day Audrey surrendered to the demands of sleep, but I wanted to sit up and see if there was any noticeable difference between the end of night and first light. I couldn't discern any noticeable change, and after a while I too went to bed, thinking about Debra and another woman, Jane Haig, whom Pat had arranged for me to meet.

Jane was a community activist with strong liberal views. She had all the makings of a politician, and when she told me about her book *Women of the Yukon*, a collection of biographical vignettes on famous females from Alaska's pioneer era, and about how the real economy of the redeveloping frontier was more due to feminine enterprise than to macho exploitation, I was intrigued. But when she confessed that she hadn't always been a writer and was in fact a house builder—not, she emphasized, an architect—everything seemed to fall into place.

I talked to her about the fascinating array of different homes I had seen and suggested that maybe that was part of the attraction of the place. Building your own home with your own hands and taking most of the material from the land itself is, I supposed, everyone's dream at one time or another. She agreed. There were few rules or regulations and no planning permission to be obtained, and that inspired lots of people. Sometimes, she thought, living here reopened other doors in ourselves. "Everyone can be something of a visionary up here and it can sustain you for a very long time." She hesitated briefly, then continued with her voice lowered, almost sighing out the words. "But nothing lasts forever."

I looked at her and wondered if today's women in Alaska had inherited the spirit of the women in her book.

"They were quite singular women and it was a very different "time," she said. "I suppose there's a bit of them in all of us who came here."

Jane seemed unsure so I redirected the question to her. "Well, how do you feel after a quarter of a century?"

She answered without hesitation. "Oh, I think I'm slowly turning into a snowbird."

I was puzzled. "A snowbird?"

Jane smiled and explained how sooner or later the "SADs" got everyone in Alaska. I spoke English, but I was having trouble understanding her. Snowbirds and SADs were beyond me. "Seasonal affective disorder," she explained. "When the long winter dark sets in, so does depression. Everyone up here suffers from it one way or another, but particularly women."

"Why?" I asked.

"Biology," she answered. "The prolonged darkness really affects women's irritation levels, and women's lives are more enclosed here anyway."

I noticed she emphasized the word "enclosed." "How?" I asked.

"Well, most women's lives here are involved with looking after the home and kids and spending a lot of time preparing for the winter. Hunting, shooting and fishing is not a big part of a woman's psychology, so they can't get out from the pressures of the dark." She hesitated again. "Unless she becomes a snowbird—someone who migrates out of Alaska for the winter months and returns when the worst is over. But 'snowbird' is a term of mild abuse up here."

"Why? Birds migrate, animals hibernate, or migrate themselves. It seems entirely rational to me, so what's the problem?"

Jane Haig smiled wistfully and simply said, "Tell my husband that."

Over the evening we discussed how difficult it had been to have her books published. Many Alaskans, she thought, were poor historians of their homeland. Some of them, when confronted by the reality of the place, admitted they knew very little about it. "Unless you are really into it, many Alaskans don't travel much outside their backyard." I commented on the emptiness of the town, and Jane explained that the town didn't really function as a social center. "Alaskans might get worked up about the big issues but they are not really civic-minded. We don't even have a proper city police force here because no one wants to pay for it."

Jane gave me a few of her books when we parted. I watched her as she walked toward her car and wondered if she would ever fly off from this place. I looked at her books about women and sleigh dogs and asked myself whether people who write social histories about a place ever leave it. Perhaps Jane's books were her way of dealing with the SADs and her increasing urge to become a snowbird.

Sitting on my porch, well past midnight, I thought again about her words and looked at the spindly trees all around me. They were withered, shriveled and feeble, and I wondered if that was what happened to your soul up here if you subjected it to years of long, cold darkness without some kind of nurture. I knew what it was like to be trapped by malign and dark forces, and I also knew that being fettered and controlled by something dark and unknown is the deepest irrational fear in all of us. Yet some of us are forever drawn to its edge. We want to look into it, maybe to diminish its hold on us or, perversely, because it excites us. Was that why I came here? Was that why young Chris Mc-Candless died here?

I looked around again. The night had come and gone with no perceptible change of light. Time, it seemed, had stood still. I could cope with the everlasting light but the silence was something different. Somehow it seems to exaggerate the bigness of the place. You wait and you wait, yet nothing stirs. Even the wind is noiseless. It moves through the spindly landscape leaving no visible sign of itself. If you dwell on it, the silence is disturbing, as if there is something out there waiting, motionless, breathless and invisible; for a moment the chill on your skin seems to come from an anxiety within rather than the dropping temperature of the early morning. It was time for bed, I resolved.

The cabin was bathed in a soft aura of light as it filtered through the worn curtains, and the incense of pine resin accompanied me to bed, where I suspected my mattress would be stuffed with more imaginings than my head could hold. After all, here we were right in the middle of a forest that was home to hares, lynx, squirrel, moose and a host of other animals that must sooner or later get curious. I took a last peep through the curtains, hoping something would stir in the clearing around the cabin. Nothing moved.

I remembered it being explained to me why it was necessary to create a big clearing around one's house. Apparently the bush receives more lightning strikes during the summer months than it has people living in it and it is wise to put some space between your home and forest fire. When I asked how come the forest cover remained so extensive, the curious phenomenon of how the black spruce cone can remain unopened for many years before it explodes and the ash and sunlight fertilize it was explained to me. I noticed the close proximity of the aspen and birch behind the cabin, and then I noticed how the tree line to the front was several feet inside the stumps of the original clearing. If lightning struck anywhere near us the whole place would flare up like a roman candle! In Alaska you had to survive more than the cold, it seemed.

The following morning I examined my map of Alaska. The green patches marked the numerous natural parks, but around them and holding the place together was a vast expanse of white. There were a few place names at the intersection points of rivers, but the further north you looked the more unrecognizable these place names became. They were Inuit names, full of the strangeness of an old race and a language system at the very edge of extinction. Further south the names were Athabascan Indian and European. Takoma, Tanana and Galena mixed with names such as McGrath, McCartney, Georgetown and Crooked Creek. Lots of the European names had a strong Irish influence, but even this did not ease the apprehension I was desperately trying to hide from myself as much as from my family. After all, I was taking them into a land about which I was becoming increasingly confused. I had pored over these strange place names before departing from home. Then they were tinged with magic and adventure, but now that these names had become a reality I was less intrigued and my anxiety level soared. Alaska was not the edge of nowhere, Alaska was what you fell into when you were over that edge. Alaska was uniquely its own place, and that's why I was drawn to it. It challenged you in the deepest parts of yourself.

I looked again at the map and noticed how the few familiar names were obliterated by Indian and Eskimo words with their abrupt closed-vowel endings. I was entering into a world where there were no roads to or from such places, and I thought again of Conrad's expeditions into dark landscapes where all the self-assuredness of European civilization was worthless and washed away in a moment. I scanned the names, trying silently to get my tongue around them and by doing so dispel some of the mounting worry.

"Do many people live in these places?" I asked Pat awkwardly later that day.

"Hardly," she answered, "a few families perhaps. Some of them are only names, left over from the early exploitation of the place. But I can't really say. In any case there are a lot of reasons for not going to a lot of places."

As instantly as she said it I wished I had not asked her.

"What time do I have to be at the dog musher's tomorrow?" I asked.

Pat replied, "People up here don't tend to watch the clock too much. He'll expect us when we arrive, in the afternoon."

Later, I looked again at the extensive white expanses on the map. It did not signify snow but emptiness; the strangeness of the "Great Land" roared out at you. I thought of my young sons, especially Cal, who had not yet learned how to walk, and a small part of me somewhere felt that my own first footfalls in the remoter corners of Alaska might be just as momentous as his.

✳

CHAPTER THREE

DOG MUSHING

The dog musher's cabin was a short drive out of Fairbanks and I knew we had arrived before the homestead came into view—a continuous howling announced the fact to everyone for miles around. The cabin was a small log-built construction with a smaller outhouse some thirty-five feet from the main house. In the foreground, squat wooden boxes and upturned barrels were splayed about; each had a dog sitting beside or a few feet from it and all were chained to some fixed point driven deep into the ground beside each of these kennels. Some of the animals had jumped on top of their kennels, others strained at the full extension of their chain, but all had their heads tilted fully back and their jaws partly open as they caroled to the heavens that I had arrived. I looked at Pat. "It's okay," she said, "they're just saying hello and welcoming you." I accepted her word without question, telling myself that if I was going to get on with these creatures I had to convince them I was not afraid. I have had enough dogs in my life to know that animals can sense fear in an instant, and it disturbs them, perhaps because it touches something primitive buried deep inside them.

"What's our musher's name?" I asked.

Pat smiled at my question, the guileless smile of the innocently dumbfounded. "I'm not really sure. You see, I don't know him too well. In fact, I hardly know him at all. I only know of him and got directions here from someone else, another musher. You'll meet her sometime during your stay. She's a lovely woman and a real Alaskan."

I quietly registered the fact that mushing was not a male preserve, then queried, "But didn't you ask what his name was?"

Pat explained that she had met the man briefly some years ago; she remembered his name as Dan. But in trying to make contact again through other mushers who knew him and could explain how he might be found, she'd been confronted with the fact that not everyone knew him as Dan. Some called him Luke, others Mike, and some knew him as Ben. None of them could agree on a surname.

"So what do I call him?"

"Dan should do, unless he tells you otherwise. Mushers are a special breed." Pat laughed at the unintentional pun before continuing. "They are quiet, even reclusive. They can be quirky, occasionally bad-tempered, just like their dogs, but most of them are pleasant and if you can get past all the quirkiness they are quite likeable."

I could do nothing but take her word for it.

As Pat was driving off she advised me not to wait on ceremony. "Just stamp the snow loudly off your boots, give the door a good bang and go right in." For a moment I remembered my own instinctive thinking about showing fear in front of animals and decided that this was also the best policy to adopt for Dan the dog musher.

The ferocity of the stamping of the snow from my feet on the cabin porch must have clearly declared to whoever was inside just how apprehensive I was about this first meeting with a stranger with so many names. The cabin, however, was completely different from my expectations. The place was warm and comfortable and very practical in every way. In the center of the far wall of the main living area was a great log-burning fireplace, and to the side of that a pile of logs and an assortment of newspapers—my eye caught a pile of *National Geographic* magazines. In the center of the room was an old settee and on either side, cozily embracing the fireplace, stood two even older easy chairs. The proper state of their dilapidation was hidden by the fact that all three items of furniture had either a tartan throw spread over them or what looked liked ex-army blankets. A big TV and an expensive hi-fi glowed amid this coziness. The kitchen was an open-plan affair on a raised platform leading from the main living area; it too was unexpectedly tidy. I'd been anticipating the kind of comfortless disarray that marks a single and reclusive male living on the outskirts of the Alaskan wilderness. I couldn't help but be confused by the casual order that confronted me.

Dan the dog musher spoke up. I had not seen him as he was standing behind the place in the kitchen where he seemed to have hung all his bulky coats and overalls. His voice simply said, "Hello, I've been expecting you." He said little more beyond suggesting that I should get myself a seat by the fire. He moved about swiftly and silently after that. The minutes seemed protracted by my own anxiety about whether I should stand up and say, "Hello, my name is Brian Keenan, what should I call you?" Instead I watched him move about the kitchen, presumably making coffee and something to eat. He was tall and lean and wore the proverbial checked shirt and braces, which held up a worn pair of denims. He sported a well-kept beard beneath which I fancied I might find the remnants of a young James Dean, a middle-aged Clint Eastwood and a mature Gene Hackman, if such movie icons could be mixed into one person. Dan the dog musher seemed at every point a classical Alaskan male.

I sat a little nervously on my easy chair waiting on Dan to make the next move or at least to say a little more to ease the logjam of the silence. As I waited, part of me became aware that men like Dan are part of the silence of the place, as if they had subsumed a greater silence into themselves and words only cluttered up the cleanness of it. I tried to occupy myself by taking mental notes of the cabin I was in and looking inconspicuously at Dan. My first impression, on arrival, had been that the cabin and its environs had all the possibilities of being the perfect location set for an early John Ford western.

In a country where distance frequently makes even your nearest neighbor a stranger, or at least someone who lives twenty miles over the rise and whom you rarely see, I expected our conversation to be forced and filled with more of the kind of silences I had already encountered. But when it came, conversation was slow and easy. It was the sort of exchange I suppose travelers at an airport might share before they set off to their different destinations from the different places they had come from. I answered his questions about Ireland and he talked about life in Alaska. Dan, it seemed, had had many jobs since leaving the army but nothing particularly skillful and nothing that fired his enthusiasm enough to stick with it. His longest stint was working as a carnie, a casual laborer with a traveling circus-cum-carnival. As I listened to him talking about his life with the carnival folk I thought that perhaps the seven or eight years he had spent traveling around America working at the canvas rigs and living with these people who exist at the edge of normal society, even if they bring some curious entertainment with it, had predisposed him, in a way, to Alaska. I suppose if you live with a bunch of people whose life and work are carried on at the very margins of normality, you become part of that and find day-to-day existence in a normal lifestyle hard to deal with. I talked over these thoughts with Dan but he seemed unimpressed, though not uninterested.

Our conversation continued, and became easier as he got a hold on who this stranger was in his cabin. I thought I would dare to do what I had been advised not to do. I explained to him how people didn't seem to know his name and how Pat, when trying to locate him, had called around to a few other dog mushers and had been given different names. Dan listened and laughed unself-consciously. "Many people arrive in Alaska and change their name as soon as they set foot in the place, or as soon as someone asks them who they are," he answered by way of simple explanation. I pushed him on the subject, trying to burrow my way into his personal story. He laughed again and shrugged his shoulders, saying once more, "Nobody cares up here too much anyway." I thought about what he said, and part of me agreed. After all, it's not so much why you come to a place but what you do with the place when you get there, or what you do with what it does to you, that matters. So I left him with his past. It didn't really concern him, so why should it concern me?

Soon we were talking about his dogs, the two dozen or so animals he kept outside. They had gone quiet over the time we had been together, almost as if they had accepted that I was here and that there was no need for any more uproar. Dan had drifted into dog mushing like everything else he had done, but now he enjoyed it to the exclusion of everything else. I wasn't convinced by the exclusion-of-everything-else bit and pointed knowingly to his expensive hi-fi equipment. "Maybe dogs and music are a way of dealing with this country," he said. There was almost a wink in his eye. "Mushing helps you get into the country. When you are behind a team of dogs you can go anywhere and there is nothing your team won't do for you."

"And the music?" I said, pushing the question.

"Sometimes the weather gets wicked up here so you turn on some heavy rock or turn up some Beethoven and you can blow the whole friggin' place away."

I sensed that maybe Dan was making up some sourdough story just to keep me amused, but the idea of a blizzard blowing outside and Beethoven, Bach or Led Zeppelin breaking decibels inside while Dan's two dozen dogs howled their own accompaniment seemed to me absurdly honest.

Whether Dan realized I was genuinely laughing at his story or whether he wanted to encourage the fantasy, he decided then to pour us some whiskey. I explained I didn't drink spirits and he looked at me with mock surprise, said there wasn't an Irishman alive who didn't drink whiskey and proceeded to triple the amount of the stuff in my tumbler with the remark, "Nobody up here cares too much what you do or don't do, and anyway, once you've drunk that you won't impress me about saying you don't drink spirits." I shrugged my shoulders in compliance. Part of me thought that Dan was just being macho again. He must have read my thoughts. "You'll need something warm inside you if you are going out with the team," he said. "Coffee's fine, but it doesn't sustain you out there." There was something solicitous in the remark. Dan was after all as practical as his comfy cabin had presented itself to be.

I suggested that he play one of his favorite classical CDs. He laughed. "Oh no," he said, "music is for listening to when everything else gets done and there's nothing else to do but listen."

"Okay, that seems fair," I said.

Raising my overfull tumbler of whiskey, I dashed off as much of the three swallows I could without gagging and choking and suggested we make ready with the dog team. After all, that's why I was there.

What I wasn't expecting was the amount of preparation one has to do before going out to hitch the team. Dan rummaged through the gear hanging up in the kitchen, pulled out an old box of more gear and threw clothes at me like a rag picker, saying, "Put that on, that should fit, if it doesn't roll up the sleeves, it doesn't matter if the gloves are too big," shouting orders at me while I just stood in obedient silence trying to fit on all these clothes.

"What's all this for?"

"It gets very cold out there, very cold, and when you're charging through the bush the cold doesn't care too much for you so you need plenty of layers, plenty of thermals."

Soon Dan had me dressed in an outrageously sized pair of waterproof and windproof leggings, a topcoat to match a huge pair of fur-lined gloves, a pair of his own special boots, a cap with fur muffs to cover my ears and another coat with a hood to tie around that again, a scarf to ensure my mouth and nose were covered, and finally a pair of sunglasses. I looked in his small kitchen mirror at my bulk and size and said, "How are the dogs going to pull all this weight?"

Dan's answer was quick. "A dozen of those dogs in front of you will pull faster than the same number of elephants. Remember, you ride on top of the snow, not through it, and you'll have to learn to hold on tight."

On the porch I stood and watched like the abominable snowman in secondhand throwaway clothes. The evening was chill and there was a sense of a new crispness because of the snow that lay all around us. The dogs silently watched for a very brief moment, but as soon as Dan laid out the tracelines and guidelines they jumped up and began howling, yelping and barking with great excitement. The noise was deafening. There was a kind of ritual to this preparation, Dan explained. The dogs get very excited and want to run all the time. You have to be careful to put them in order to stop them bolting off before you are ready to go. You always choose first the older, wiser and calmer dogs, who know how to sit and wait; put the younger dogs in last and always put your guide dog in after everything else is done—he will determine the pace and the line you take. I watched amazed at the dexterity of his fingers in a cold I knew to be bitter even in my well-wrapped-up condition. Not once did the dogs stop yapping. This is what they lived for, and I could understand that after sitting half the day in the cold and snow suddenly having this opportunity to go racing off would certainly excite any creature.

When Dan had finished attaching all the dogs to the sleigh he invited me to climb in. I thought the contraption was ridiculously small and equally ridiculously frail, but I settled myself in. There was a thick kind of tarpaulin that was secured around the incumbent's waist the way it is done in a kayak to stop the water flowing in. The purpose I suppose was the same here—to stop the spray of snow falling off trees and bushes as you passed from settling in around you.

"We only really use this for cargo, it's really a cargo sleigh," Dan explained. "The tarpaulin is to keep everything dry and everything safe, but for today you are the cargo."

I watched as Dan finished his own preparations—fastening and zipping up his ancient anorak, pulling down the fur over his face and pulling on his long, filthy-looking mittens. I thought how ridiculous we both looked. I suppose in a way he looked like a deep-sea diver; all he really needed was one of those brass helmets. Then I thought of my own position, strapped into this sleigh; I felt like a child of about two years sitting in one of those ancient Pedigree baby carriages you used to see children wheeled about in during the fifties. I was so enclosed and encased in clothes and the greasy old black tarpaulin that not one piece of my flesh peered out. Dan had made sure that no skin was showing, giving me a meticulous once-over.

Then, without warning, we were off with a sudden jolt. Before I had time to realize what was happening we were tearing through the bush. Dan was right: these dogs could pull a sleigh faster than my imagination had thought possible. Pieces of bush and twig slapped into my face as we careered helplessly through the countryside. I now understood why Dan had been so insistent that no part of my flesh or face show: had one of these twigs caught me in the eye or in the face it would have left a scar I would have remembered for a long time, and not with much gratitude. Dan seemed to use only three or four expressions of encouragement to the dogs, directing them left or right as the trail opened up, then for long periods he would run, jumping on and off to negotiate the sleigh without a word of direction to the lead dog or any of the dogs in front of me. The lead dog seemed to know when to turn right or left and when to charge on bull-headed, and instinctively when to slow.

I clung helplessly to the low side rails of the sleigh waiting to be tossed out as the dog team charged into a sharp right or left turn, but it never happened. Trying to be helpful, I occasionally leaned into the turns as they came up or sometimes leaned back against them. On one such occasion Dan commanded me not to roll with the turns or resist them. "I'll carry your weight," he said gruffly. I could not for the life of me understand what he meant by that, for how could he, but then I really was an infant at this game.

After some fifteen minutes of charging through the bush I was becoming accustomed to the experience. I relaxed back, did what I was told to do and let Dan carry the weight. I began to enjoy it, quickly understanding what Dan had meant by needing some-thing to sustain you, something stronger than coffee. Without all this wet gear and wind- and thornproofing I could not have lasted more than a few moments in the bitter, bone-shattering coldness of the bush. This was my first ritual experience of the Alaska we know about—panting dog teams and snow and cold too fearful to contemplate—and I was enjoying it the way my sons enjoyed me racing them in their buggies.

Soon the adrenaline rush translated into a strange kind of im-patience. I wanted to be physically part of the thrill of this ritual ride. I really was just another piece of cargo and felt a bit like a dead log being hauled back for Dan's magnificent fireplace. I wanted more than this. I wanted my arms and legs to be em-broiled in the experience, to be working like the team charging with exhilaration in front of me. After what seemed like half an hour I raised my left arm in the air and made a circle, signaling to Dan that we should turn back. I hoped he would understand, and he did: with a few commands the whole team circled in a great arc, bumping over ditches and dead logs, and then started their excited charge back again. After some minutes in more open territory where I was taking fewer blows to the head from bushes or low branches, Dan reined in the team with a single command.

"We're two miles out," he said. "Do you think you could manage the team back?"

I wasn't sure if Dan was reading my mind, but the musher and his dogs had already got to me and I was already unbuckling my sleigh pram. The words tumbled out of me: "If you want to put your life in my hands, let's go for it."

Dan just smiled, and with a nonchalant "okay" began giving me instructions on how to handle the team. "Remember, these dogs can sniff out every nook and cranny and everything that's buried beneath the snow before you and I can see it or sense it. Their nose moves faster than your eyes or mine." There was something in Dan's own eyes that impressed me. I was being taken for a ride, only this time it would not be in the smothering safety of my Alaskan baby carriage sleigh. I was full of questions, to which Dan seemed oblivious. "Here's your riding platform. When the going is easy stand here and let the team do the work. If the ground is rough and the dogs are straining, jump off and I'll encourage them. Once they are moving, get on quick or you'll fall flat on your face and this bunch won't wait for you. When you come to a turn, lean against it; it stops the dead weight going to the dogs and stops the thing going into a roll, otherwise we will have to pick ourselves up, unhitch the teams and start unraveling the lines and harness. The dogs don't like that, and boy, do they let you know." Dan's words were no longer genial; there was a stern warning in them. As I listened, my enthusiasm quickly became sheepish. "You don't need to use your weight much. There's enough between the two of us, but you can slow the sleigh as it comes into a turn. Reach out your foot, dragging the snow as you come into the turn. It will stabilize everything without losing the drive, and when we get back to the cabin throw out this anchor." Dan lifted up a small object that looked like a boat anchor only several sizes smaller. It worked on the same principle of dragging and biting into the ground, where it locked itself on a pivotal spring so that even if the dogs wheeled about they could not uproot the empty sleigh and go charging off again.

Dan's instructions were curt, but their brevity emphasized how absolutely fundamental they were. He left me in no doubt that this was a once-only lesson and that apprenticeships in running a dog team lasted as long it took to explain these simple rules.

I tried to absorb what I had been told in the same manner as I had been told it. Dan's words had implied but left unsaid something that was now echoing in my ears: in the bush you learn fast or you get left behind. However, my tutor didn't leave me much time to dwell on this unspoken speculation. Like an eel he was inside the tarpaulin, fidgeting himself into a comfortable position. In no time his face disappeared behind the thick fur of his parka, his eyes hidden behind the shiny blue-black lenses of his sunglasses. Squatting against the whiteness of the bush, he looked like a hideous insect newly emerged from its chrysalis. I quickly jumped behind Dan and his dogs, took a firm grip on the sleigh rails and hung on like grim death.

"Mush" was the word to say to get us moving, but it felt so foolish and so childish an expression, which indeed was exactly how I was feeling at that moment. I was master of nothing. No part of me was connected to the animal engine that was driving us. My hands held me to the sleigh, but that's all they did. There was no "hands on" manipulation from me. I had no steering wheel to direct our passage, no clutch, gearbox or accelerator to control the speed. A pilot in the air has his joystick and a whole bank of computerized controls to draw on. I had nothing, not even a pair of reins to connect me and give me power over the creatures that were now charging ahead at breakneck speed. Even a sailor in his small yacht has more control, for he can shed sail or manually position himself against the wind. I had nothing but a pack of mad dogs working with one mind, setting its own course to the tune of Ben the lead dog, and plunging precariously through this snowbound outback. I was simply hanging on to their tails, letting them drag me where they wished. Stupe-fied, I clung on, trying to replay Dan's instructions, but my mind could not compute as fast as the team could pull.

Then Dan roared out something short and inarticulate to the dogs and almost simultaneously rotated his head in a half turn and told me to "Lean hard left, Brian, lean hard left!" Without questioning him I squatted on the runners and pitched my up-per torso as far over to the left as I could. I dared not be too in-hibited. In Dan's language, hard left meant hard left, so that's what I did. Part of me imagined a downhill slalom skier weav-ing between markers down a sheer slope. It worked! My weight-bearing lean seemed to correct the rolling tendency of the sleigh as the dogs made a hard right. I was mesmerized and flushed to self-congratulation, but had little time to relish it. Dan was roar-ing orders again.

"Two more turns. Wait till the lead dog has made his move and drop your foot to slow us into the turn. After the second turn it's open country. They will see it before us and go into a fast run. Make sure you give plenty of foot brake and then lean, then brake, but lighter this time."

The instruction, as always, could not have been simpler. I did as Dan demanded and we traveled in and out of the turns with an effortlessness that made me feel like grace revealed. The dogs must have felt it too, at least I wanted to think so, for they ate up the open ground as if each of them had grown another set of legs. I was riding on the crest of their enthusiastic yelps, wanting to yelp myself. Then the cabin loomed and in no time we were sliding up to the dog enclosure with my foot and sleigh anchor guiding us up to the porch. Dan soon had the team tied up se-curely.

I watched, wanting to pat some of the dogs, but that seemed as silly as wanting to shout "Mush!" at the team. Dan called out a few words of praise to two of his dogs, Samson and Caesar, then ushered me into the cabin. For a second I wondered about these names. I only knew of the lead dog, but to me Samson and

Caesar were characters out of a childhood memory of history, and I wondered if the names Dan had chosen indicated something about the man himself. Inside the cabin I suggested to my host that he might have named some of them Beethoven or Bach. In response, Dan explained that most of the animals had come to him with those names. "Just like you," I remarked, hinting at Dan's secret past. He just laughed and answered, with good-natured dismissal, "Just like me!"

I moved out onto the porch again, not sure whether I had been probing Dan's past a little too much. He joined me and didn't seem bothered by my remarks. We both stayed on the porch for a while musing over nothing of significance. The dogs sat and watched us without making a sound. Only a few of them displayed the classic husky-like appearance.

"Few mongrel bloodlines in some of them boys," I said, feeling comfortable and familiar.

"Yeah, just like me," Dan said again, looking at me with the same wry smile on his face.

I smiled the same way and looked out at the timberline, thinking to myself that whatever I might learn about Alaska and Alaskans, Dan was a closed book. He was enjoying his evasion too much, and anyway, I was fast coming to the conclusion that his past didn't really matter much and could not be half as interesting as his present.

"Well, what did you think about your first sleigh ride?" he asked.

"Wee buns," I said. Then, noticing his perplexed expression at my Ulsterism, I translated it into his own vernacular: "Piece of cake!"

"Oh, yeah," Dan said, wanting a little more.

But it was my turn to tease, and I could not resist. "I really enjoyed that, but I reckon I could do it blindfolded."

I thought Dan would enjoy my cool-hand-Luke approach, but his response completely stunned me. He turned his head toward me and with a throwaway smile said, dryly, "You got a deal." It was the first truly serious expression I had heard from my friend in the time we had been together.

I was busy trying to work out just what Dan was thinking, and more importantly just what I had set myself up for, when he said, "You go and pour us both another drink. There's coffee on the stove and whiskey in the bottle. I'll hitch up the other team." I thought he was joking until he got up, went around to the rear of the cabin, pulled another sleigh from under a great sheet of heavy-duty plastic and dragged it round. The sight of the second sleigh sent the dogs into a howling cacophony. I wanted to believe he was bluffing, but his dogs knew he wasn't. I was intrigued, but more than a little worried. Dan ignored me and disappeared into his cabin, returning with an armful of harness. He walked to the front of the new sleigh and led out the line in obvious preparation to hitch up the new team.

One by one he detached the dogs from their kennels and brought them to the sleigh, and after some gruff words and a lot of pushing, shoving and cursing, his fresh team was hitched to the second sleigh. He removed two dogs from our original sleigh of eight and looked at me. "Think you can handle a team of six on your own with no cargo?" Before I could answer, he informed me he would take the fresh team and lead and I would follow with the second team, and there shouldn't be any problems. "The sleigh will be a lot lighter, so you will only have to worry about yourself. At least you won't have to do any running." There was a pause. "Unless you fall off, that is. Come on, let's get some coffee and a warmer."

Without responding I followed my companion into the cabin. "I'll pass on the whiskey," I was about to say, but realized it was useless as Dan had already fortified my steaming mug. Instead of returning the bottle to the table he packed it into an ex-army canvas bag, informing me that we might need it later. I was too unsure of what was happening to ask anything except where the bathroom was. Nerves always activate my bladder at the most inconvenient times, but I was hoping that Dan would not realize the cause of my urgent need. If he did he didn't show it; instead he remarked how dogs have to do their business on the run while we two-legged creatures are a bit more fussy. He pointed to a small shed about ten or twenty feet from the cabin with the words, "Can't put much plumbing in the permafrost, you'll have to take us as you find us." Feigning macho indifference, I replied that I had been in some shitters in my time so nothing would surprise me. Dan passed me a roll of toilet paper, explaining that he didn't read many newspapers so he didn't keep a ready supply for the "bathroom," he said, mocking the use of the word. He concluded with the remark that it was always better not to be carrying more weight than is necessary.

I returned from Dan's primitive amenity, which was little more than a few planks of broad timber with a hole cut in them and an even bigger hole underneath them. As I reentered the cabin I placed the toilet roll near the kitchen counter but was too shy to ask about hand-washing facilities, having already convinced myself that real men would shun this, and anyway, in a place with no plumbing water was not to be wasted on such trivial matters. I could have saved my embarrassment. Dan had already gone outside again to put the final touches to our sleighs. I still wasn't sure what he was planning but felt I needed to confess some anxiety on my part.

"I wasn't really serious about doing it blindfolded, you know," I said, half sheepishly.

Dan continued to make further adjustments to the two teams' harnesses. "Didn't think you were, but we still get a few hours of night light up here. It's the best time to see the country. No snow glare from the sun and the moon lights up the place in its own peculiar way. Now, listen." He ushered me over to the team of six. For a few moments he rehearsed what he had already explained about using my foot as a brake and leaning on the turns. "Remember, you have no ballast on board, which makes the sleigh very light, so you are going to have to create your own traction. You are traveling over the snow, not through it, and don't forget this." He placed the small anchor within easy reach. "Now, don't lose it." It was his final command.

He maneuvered his team in a direct line in front of my sleigh. "We'll take the first few miles easy so you can get a feel of it, but remember, save the sightseeing until we stop and you'll do okay."

Dan lifted his anchor and was about to set off when I called out, "How do you get them to turn?"

Dan stood still for a few moments trying to make out what I had said from behind my muffled mouth. "Gee for the left and haw to turn right, that's all you need to know, but call it out clearly and repeat it until the lead dog begins to turn."

"What about stop?" I asked, my panic rising.

"Don't worry, they'll stop when I do."

Dan suddenly remembered something, fumbled around in his sleigh, then turned and threw something in my direction. It landed at my feet. On retrieving it I saw it was a headlamp like the type you see cave explorers wearing as they climb through their gloomy enclosures. "Don't put it on in case you lose it," Dan said. "It's only for emergencies, in case we get separated. There's also a whistle in your breast pocket for the same purpose." And with no more fuss, Dan called out to his lead dog, "Away, Cou-caisse!"

I ran the first few yards, following Dan's example, then jumped onto the rear running board. The dogs barked and snapped to assert their position and then we were gliding easily over the snowy tundra. The concentration had quenched my excitement, and I had already forgotten whether haw or gee had meant right or left. I would listen to Dan's first command and that should sort out my confusion.

Everything at the beginning was perfectly pleasant, and I couldn't understand why I shouldn't sightsee; after all, there is no more original way to see Alaska than from your own moving sleigh behind a panting dog team. But once we'd left the clearing behind Dan's cabin I quickly forgot about looking behind me. The land began to undulate and break up and all my attention was given over to avoiding being whacked by low branches. I quickly learned the importance of leaning gently to the right or left so as to glide the sleigh easily at the most appropriate moments. Just as I was becoming assured and was greatly enjoying my mastery of this primitive transport, Dan hurried the pace. I thought it was about time; I was eager to be flashing over the snow. Then, as suddenly as Dan had shifted up several gears, I wished he hadn't.

There were fewer trees now, but the terrain was rougher and filled with sudden crevices, then short but steep slopes. The dogs were in their element and charged on regardless. As we banked and rolled and plunged over this white nightmare I became all too aware just how light the sleigh was under me. Dan raced ahead heedlessly, his body as fluid as hot gelatin. I was dreading the growing distance between us and my team seemed anxious yet encouraged by it. They charged harder and faster, trying to lessen the gap. The sleigh bucked and leaped into the air, banging back into the land and causing the dogs to strain and snarl at my incompetence. I had not forgotten to use my foot as a brake, or about the necessity to lean, thus displacing weight and creating traction on turns, but the terrain was too rough and the obstacles came at me too suddenly. All I could do was hold on and hope. Within the space of a few miles I was bundled into the snow several times with no hope of tossing out my anchor. Every time I took a spill my team barked and yelped as if they were a team of hyenas and my comic performance was to their liking. It was a clear signal to Dan to come back and wait for me.

"Do this blindfolded, can you?" he asked with gleeful sarcasm after my fourth tumble.

It was pointless to try to reply with any type of macho excuse. I picked myself up, dusted off the snow and got back behind the sleigh with the words, "I'll get it, I'll get it." I don't know if my feeble affirmation convinced Dan, but he tried to be helpful, explaining that everything was about coordination and compensation. I understood what he meant, but that did not automatically provide me with the skills to perform the bodily contortions demanded by the landscape. Dan suggested that if I could persevere for another few miles, we would then travel down a snow-covered riverbed that would be a lot easier to ride on. Otherwise we could double up on his sleigh, towing my sleigh behind. Defeat at this stage of my Alaskan adventure was too devastating to contemplate. "No," I stated. "It doesn't hurt much, even if my ego does."

"Okay," said Dan, and we were off again without another word.

Whether it was stubborn determination or the ignominy of returning "in the baby carriage," as I had come to think of it, I stuck at it, trying to worry less about myself and somehow marry myself to the movements of the sleigh. After all, it was only a piece of wood and I was the brains in the operation.

Dan, of course, had lied. It was more than a few miles to the riverbed. Indeed, it felt like a few hours, but in that time I achieved some measure of accomplishment with only two minor falls that didn't require Dan's assistance. I was again becoming quite assured, but this time it was accompanied by an awareness that in this outback world you really have to survive alone, and will was just as important as skill. Sometimes one was the teacher to the other. And so I persevered, always watching the lead dog to see if it would disappear down a crevice or make some sudden turn to avoid what might be a deep snowfall. I was constantly trying to ride the tossing currents of this whitewashed land rather than fight them.

The snow-covered riverbed was a dream to travel down. My sleigh could have been a canoe. The large rock formations and accumulations of fallen timber were easily avoided with my new-found skill of leaning and dragging. Now I could gee and haw and my dogs were happy to oblige. Dan, too, seemed happy to allow me to chart my own course. Part of me wished that Jack and Cal were bundled up in the sleigh in front of me, but they would probably have deserted me for the certainty of Dan's sleigh after my second tumble. I would not have liked that at all. I watched the dogs charge ahead joyously. These animals seemed to show little in the way of genuine affection. For these dogs, it took a long period of mutual trust, forbearance and appreciation to make a workable partnership. I wanted to think that maybe they had accepted me, or at least wanted to give me a second chance. Somewhere inside me I was sure that by seeking to overcome the failures in myself and accepting that they were in charge, I had been allowed to become one of their team.

Dan was right about the moonlight on virgin snow; it adds a lunar luminescence to the lift and fold of the land. In a way it had all the pristine quiet of an old Japanese print in black and white. Behind all the intimate softness was that immense sky, just beginning to color up with approaching night.

As I continued to ride uncomplaining into the great white eiderdown of the river valley, I heard Dan call out to me. Obviously he wanted me to stop but I remembered he had not given me the word for this command. I let the dogs drift, desperately trying to think what the word might be. Then suddenly, I said, "Easy, Ben, easy, boy. Slow up there." I called out as clearly and as comfortingly as I could. Ben was a true leader, and the sleigh began to slow, allowing Dan's sleigh to overtake and stop in front of us. I explained that I had no command for stop and Dan simply stated, "Well, you managed it more or less. The old Eskimo words for right and left are part of the tradition of dog mushing. Everybody uses them to honor that tradition. When you are out on the tundra you only need to instruct them right or left; anything else is straight on and sleighs and dogs don't do reverse. You don't need much else except stop and go." Having communicated this Spartan logic, he announced, "It should get just a little darker very soon. But like I say, the darker it gets the brighter it gets. We'll want to get down across the lake by then. Stick behind me from now on, I have a feeling you might enjoy this."

As always, there was something in Dan's words that left out more than he told me. I wasn't too sure what it was, or whether it was simply my imagination breaking free in the limitless landscape, but something in me was thinking how difficult we sometimes find it to trust the moment. It was the way Dan said things, emphatically yet incompletely. There was no time for questions anyway. He was soon off at a gentle trot and I fell in behind, accepting that he too was part of the spell of the place and I shouldn't question what I didn't need to.

I wasn't sure exactly when we reached the lake, but when the low banks of land defining the valley seemed to get further and further apart I sensed we must be near. In front of me stretched a great white plain, a phosphorescent quality about it. Dan's sleigh stopped in front of me and he began checking his harness. "I really want to run this one hard," he announced. "We are probably on the outer edge of the lake now. It's hard to tell, the wind keeps shifting the snow. The dogs know, and sometimes it spooks them a bit, but it seems to be okay. It's only when they get really spooked that you need to worry."

I don't remember being so suddenly terrified in my life. "You mean we are on the lake already?" My voice was beginning to quake with incredulity.

"Oh yeah," said Dan. "In the summer there will be thirty feet or more of water below where you are standing."

Somewhere, an inner voice was screaming that summer was almost here. Suddenly I was remembering all that I had heard about how summer arrives almost instantaneously in Alaska. Dread spilled into my head faster than I could control it. I couldn't swim. What if I went through the ice with the sleigh and the dogs? I could already envisage the scene in horrifying slow motion: dogs splashing and howling, me hopelessly flailing around for a firm ice hold, the weight of my layers of clothes and the freezing water seeping into my skin, numbing me, the dogs strangling in their struggle and then everything drifting away like an old echo. What if Dan's team went down too? How would anyone know what had happened to us? What would Audrey and the kids do? That thought sent another terrifying shard through me. I thought of the spooked dogs. Were they feeling the animal equivalent of what I was going through?

"Stick close now," Dan demanded as we moved off.

Contrary to my rising anxiety, the teams moved easily. Their demeanor was one of relaxed enthusiasm, and I was glad of it. My attention was focused on Dan and his team. If anything were to go wrong, they would be first to encounter it. Another part of me was telling me that this was foolish. Ice breaks when you are on top of it. There are no prior warnings. Yet another part of me chastised such foolishness. Dan was a dog musher of long experience. He had been living in the wilds of Alaska, and much of that time in the company of dogs. His laconic attitude to my naive questions confirmed him as a man who knew what he was about, and he was certainly not about drowning me, himself or his dog team on a whim. "Anyway," I kept telling myself, "this is something special. Here you are, Brian, driving your own dog team across a frozen lake in the Alaskan outback on a night that's glowing like a million candles under the snow." The thought warmed me.

The basin of the frozen lake seemed to enclose the silence and draw everything into itself. Only the noise of the dogs padding across the dry white snow and their panting could be heard. It was comforting. My fears of drowning were subliminally being replaced by something softer, something childlike. I was thinking of a warm soapy bath and hot milk; I was thinking also that I didn't care how long it took. The pleasure was intoxicating.

Suddenly Dan shouted and waved both his arms in the air in front of me. "Look up, look up!" he was calling as his team came to a slow stop. So I looked up, like a man who has just woken up in a strange room, not sure where he is or how he got there. Above me the heavens were opening up in a luscious harmony of color and form, like a sensuous curtain blowing in the breeze; I could almost feel the texture of it on my face. At first it was a distant glow on the horizon that ringed the lake bowl. It was like being out at sea and seeing the echo of light from three or four different lighthouses fusing in the sky. Greens, blues, yellows, ambers, oranges and purples, like a rainbow in a melting pot before it has been stretched into its glorious arc.

Quietly, my team came to a halt and laid themselves on the snow. They seemed to know instinctively how to worship and receive what I could only stand and gape at, half afraid and half amazed. The aurora got bigger as I watched, transfixed. It seemed to come toward us with inconceivable momentum. I stood helpless, half expecting to be swept away to God knows where. Yet there was nowhere to run to and nowhere to hide on the white expanse of this frozen lake. It was as if it had waited for us. Now it was swooping down on us with monstrous magnificence.

To me, it was as if the universe were a mass of colored cells merging and differentiating, growing and multiplying. My ears were whirring, and a quote from W. B. Yeats was in my mouth before my brain could articulate its own thoughts, something about "The heavens' embroidered cloth, inwrought with gold and silver light, of the night, and the light and the half light." But the poet's eloquence could not contain the Elysian orchestra that was now hovering and enclosing me in the fantastical dome.

I got off my sleigh and walked the few feet to where Dan stood, drinking in the wonder. I didn't want to speak to him, nor him to me, but I wanted the comfort of another human being to share and be witness to this seduction.

"I told you you might enjoy it, but I didn't expect this. She's big-mouthed and brazen tonight!"

I hardly heard Dan's words. If I had been initially a little frightened by our escapade on the ice, I was immune to such fear now, though the hair was standing on the back of my neck for different reasons. Had the ice opened up beneath me that very moment I would have felt nothing, for I had already been lifted up into that mysterious, ineffable miracle that was happening in the skies around us.

Dan tore me from my rapture by elbowing me with one arm and holding out the whiskey in the other hand.

"No thanks, Dan, there's more than enough stimulation for me up there," I said, darting my eyes from the bottle to the sky.

"You never know when she's going to show up," he said. "You can sit and wait for weeks and weeks, watching and waiting, and you never see even a distant glimmer. There are lots of Japanese who come here just to see what you are seeing tonight, Brian. They believe that the lights increase fertility."

I laughed at the image of thousands of naked or semi-naked couples sitting in precoital readiness for the first signs of the aurora rushing out of the horizon.

"What do you think about it, Dan?"

"Haven't really figured that out yet, though I've seen lots of nights like tonight and some much, much better than tonight. But if you take the time to watch it—not study it, I mean just sit and watch it, like letting yourself drift into it—you come out of it after it's gone like you've been kind of cleaned out or something. It's like it cleans out all the garbage and nonsense and all the old worries that have been getting up inside you, unknown to yourself. You feel easy and relaxed and I suppose sort of happy with the world for a while. I don't rightly know what to make of it. It's an omen of some kind, that's for sure. But it means different things to different people. The people of the Tlingt tribe believe that the lights are dancing human spirits. They are dancing in celebration of some event or coming event directly related to the tribe's people. But the Inuit peoples spread out on the Bering Sea coast believe they're walrus spirits playing with human skulls. I don't really know what that is supposed to mean. An old Finnish musher friend of mine told me that the Lapland natives call them foxfires and said that it had something to do with an arctic fox starting fires or spraying up the snow with its tail."

Dan looked at me and added quietly, "But like all good omens it can mean many things or anything you want."

Dan handed me the bottle again, and this time I took it, drinking down the burning whiskey in long, slow sips, and at the same time drinking in the blazing heavens.

"Maybe it's come here just for you," said Dan as he stashed the whiskey back into his sleigh holder and gestured for us to head back. "A kind of omen for your travels."

I'm not exactly sure how long the journey back to the cabin took. I know that I braked in and out of turns and rolled up and down gullies and crevasses with the luxurious ease of Rudolf Nureyev. I really don't know how, for my eyes were fixed on the skies. Above me the celestial orchestra continued to play, and I danced all the way home. I could do nothing else, for the whole world was enchanted and had wrapped me in its spell.

Back at the cabin, I helped Dan unhitch the dogs, return them to their boxes and chain them for the night. Dan patted each and every one as if to thank them, and I followed suit. The dogs accepted the affection without much fuss, and settled down. I asked Dan why his lead dog had such a weird name. It was a way of returning myself to reality. "Cou-caisse means 'broken tail' in French. A French-Canadian musher gave her to me as a pup. Don't know how she broke her tail, but there it is." I looked at the distinct kink in the animal's tail. I hadn't noticed it before. "The Frenchman had some crazy idea that she would not make a good working dog. But she is one of the best lead dogs I have had."

Without further prompting, Dan introduced me to the rest of the pack. The names were as varied as the ancestry in their bloodlines. Some were simple, like Ben my lead dog; some were elaborate, like Cou-caisse; others were humorous, like Big Foot and Professor, because the animal had curious ring marks on his eyes as if he was wearing spectacles. These animals were Dan's heroes and he spoke of them with real devotion. I ventured to suggest to him that he loved the creatures more than he showed.

Dan's answer was as honest as it was simple. "There ain't no medicine like a dog for cabin fever. Keeps away the crazies better than any medicine, though some of them can get a bit crazy themselves, especially this one," he said, wrestling with Coucaisse.

The animal, as I recalled, had been the soul of discretion throughout our trip, never yelping, never barking, never getting excited, always performing with sure-footed determination like the thoroughbred bitch its mongrel features declared it was not. It had sensitive ears that hung down from its head, eyes that looked at you with bright intelligence, and legs that seemed madly disproportionate to its body. Altogether a queer character, odd, conceited, fiercely independent, a quiet creature who could do crazy things.

"You know, Dan, I think you are a lot like that dog," I said as I walked into the cabin.

"Howzat?"

"Well, a little bit bent maybe, but not quite broken."

Dan smiled uncomprehendingly, not quite interested enough to pursue the matter. I should have known better. Dan, like Coucaisse, gave nothing away.

As I changed out of my trail gear, Dan spoke animatedly about his dogs—buying and selling them, the cost of feeding them, how dogs probably had saved more lives than doctors in Alaska, and how sometimes the best-trained dogs could do inexplicable things totally out of character, never to be repeated again. I asked Dan why he thought the team had got a little spooked at the lake. Was it the ice, I wondered? Dan just shrugged his shoulders; no, he didn't think it was the ice. "Maybe they just knew Old Aurora was coming up." I looked directly at Dan to see if he was sending me up, but I could see he wasn't. He was telling me something I already knew from Jack London. Dogs represented the spirit of the place. They were an incredible part of the folklore of Alaska. They were the ultimate survivors, the link between humans and the wilderness. Jack London had first introduced that to me some forty years ago, Dan had shown me the reality of it on the trail, and that night I had tasted some of it hands on.

There was little time for more chat. Dan knew I had to be back and offered me a lift in his truck.

"Which one?" I said, looking at the three vehicles outside.

"The only one that runs!" came the answer.

It was a quick and uneventful trip back to Fairbanks, and I spent most of the time pondering over Dan's image of the aurora as a kind whore. Though it did not leave that kind of impression on me, I could see how Dan, who had had many encounters over the years, would look on it like some old seductress with whom you consort out of affection, not desire. Old Aurora had the capacity to awake and stir up powerful emotions, as I had found out myself and as Dan had testified to when he had told me of the Japanese belief in the association of the aurora with fertility. But whatever the nature of the powerful emotions, Aurora still made you feel warm and safe like a lover does and a whore cannot. But still she came and went at her own whim. She gave herself to you only when she wanted to, and left you breathless and panting for more.

At the end of the track leading up to our cabin, I bade Dan a grateful farewell and casually promised to meet up for a beer.

"Sure thing," he said as he drove off.

As I walked up to the cabin I knew it didn't matter whether or not we ever had that beer. There are chance encounters you should never attempt to repeat. It puts a veneer on things and dulls the power of the moment. For a split second I wondered once more what Dan's surname was, then just as quickly decided I never wanted to know.

Everyone was asleep when I entered. I was glad. I could not have begun to explain the events of the last few hours. I had only been away six or seven hours in all, yet on coming home I felt I had been away for years. On the lake I had been snapped up out of time and had entered another world outside time; how could I explain this to my family when I could hardly explain it to myself? I was too restless to sleep. I thought I should make some notes by focusing my mind on the temporal reality I had come home to. In preparation, I took up a book on the phenomenon of Old Aurora.

I have not a scientific turn of mind, but I sometimes find the explanation of scientific fact as wonderful as, if less momentous than, the event itself. Auroras, it seems, are caused by electrically charged particles blown from the sun and attracted to the earth's magnetic poles—hence the presence of the aurora borealis in the northern hemisphere and over Australia, as the aurora australis, in the southern hemisphere. The dancing lights and the extraordinary shapes in the night sky are due to the bending of the earth's magnetic field by gusts of these electrically charged particles. As I was digesting all these facts and simultaneously trying to replay in my imagination the sights I had experienced, I kept thinking of some of the fabulous seascapes by Turner. He too would have loved the magical interaction and fusion of color I had witnessed. The colors in the auroras, however, are from a palette of gases rather than paint: the green and red come from oxygen in the ionosphere, while the blue and violet come from nitrogen. The green, it seems, is a result of oxygen glowing about sixty miles above the earth; the red glow, on the other hand, is caused by oxygen reacting to the sun's particles at an altitude of about two hundred miles. They appear along ring channels known as auroral ovals, which hang particularly over Alaska and Antarctica in the south.

As I completed my notes, part of me mused on the fact that though science can explain the facts of something it can never explain its effect. The isolation on the lake no doubt added to the drama, just as my initial fears heightened the unreality of the moment. But the marriage of science and psychology was still not enough for me. The essence and effect are only partly revealed by them; the backwash takes longer to work out. The naturalist John Muir, an explorer who traveled through the Alaskan wilderness in the 1880s, wrote, "I have been one thousand feet

down in the crevices, with matchless snow and sculptured figures and carved ice work all about me. Solomon's marble and
ivory palaces were nothing to it. Such purity, such color, such
delicate beauty! I was tempted to stay there and feast my soul
and softly freeze, until I would become part of the glacier. What
a good death that would be!" For me, Muir is nearer the mark.
I too, in a moment, had sensed a similar feeling. The lure of
wanting to stay, to remain, to become one with the earth and the
inspiring heavens—it's a profound seduction. It enfolds you
completely. But it is dangerous, because you cannot remain. Dan
was right to befriend it like a comfortable old whore, not to let
himself become utterly beguiled by it.

CHAPTER FOUR

MAIDEN VOYAGE

The *Pequod*, as I had chosen to call our twenty-six-foot RV (recreational vehicle), had arrived. The name Herman Melville gave to his tragic ship in *Moby-Dick* seemed somehow appropriate to our own vehicle of exploration. It was, after all, going to help me find my own white whale in this massive expanse of Alaska. Initially I loved its compactness, but as soon as we began to load it with all the gear we had brought or bought in Fairbanks, it became unattractive. But we made several day trips out into the bush to get the hang of the vehicle.

So when Mary and her husband Pat, a retired lecturer at the University of Alaska at Fairbanks, asked me to go canoeing on the Chena with them, I agreed readily. I remembered both of them from my visit a few years back when I was a guest speaker at the university. Mary was then married to a history professor and Pat was single and a science teacher. I was happy to meet up with them again and plan a short trip down the Chena into Fairbanks.

Mary had advised me over the phone that long outback trips took lots of planning and preparation and you were ill advised to undertake such a trip unless you were well versed in survival skills; Pat had concluded that survival skills were fine, but you had to be fit enough to apply them in the first place. I presumed Pat's remark was a way of reminding us that he was now retired and not up to the rigors of a trip like an enthusiastic younger man or even a curious writer. I was happy to comply with Pat's thinking. Both he and I were about the same age and trials were not something I was looking for. Trials, at my age, were situations that unfortunately happened to you, and were to be avoided at all costs. With this unspoken agreement we loaded what little kit we had, strapped the aluminum canoe to our roof and drove off beyond the city's reach.

During our journey Pat explained to me that it was a good time to take to the river, as the glacial meltdown had already begun, though it was much earlier than in previous years. He insisted that just because it was mild outside I shouldn't be fooled; the rivers were always cold when they were swollen with glacier melt. "If you fall in and are not hauled out within four minutes, you're gone," he said. "You've a four-minute life expectancy in the water."

It sounded drastic. "That's like a three-minute warning before a nuclear holocaust," I said.

"Yes, except there are two differences: one, you've got a minute longer in the river, and two, you are the only one who is going to die."

I looked at both Mary and Pat. Their faces were noncommittal, as if they had just explained to me the recipe for a blueberry pie.

"Well, four minutes will be more than enough for me. I can't swim," I said equally noncommittally.

They both smiled, and replied, "That's okay, then."

In the Athabascan language, the suffix "na" simply means "water" or "river," and my frequent studies of Alaskan maps revealed that practically all the named rivers carried this suffix—Chena, Tanana, Nowitna, Susitna, Lake Minchumina, and hundreds more. This was the land of water, yet curiously the native mind had not invested it with any elaborate religious or spiritual significance to anything like the same degree they had the other elements of earth, air and sky, and every species of plant and animal life. I was beginning to understand. Water was God here; it needed no explanation, only to be respected and feared.

Our conversation had opened up another interesting topic. Many people during our stay to date had commented on the early arrival of summer, and how generally summers were arriving earlier and winters were arriving later. The phrase "global warming" was offered by way of explanation by many to whom I had spoken. Pat was quick to take up the question. He explained that if it was global warming there was little Alaskans could do about it, but they should be aware of its effects. The greater part of the Alaskan landmass resided on permafrost, and if that started to thaw, Pat declared, "We've got real big problems, bigger than probably all the gold and oil revenues could cure." As Pat explained it, part of the problem was more than just the physical one of permafrost thaw; it was just as much to do with a way of thinking and an attitude to the problem. Scientists thought in terms of centuries and large-scale catastrophe; engineers, politicians and big business had a habit of thinking in shorter increments, such as decades. As he was explaining, Mary winked slyly at me, letting me know I was about to get a lecture.

"Long-term projections don't really inject the right degree of urgency into the matter," Pat said. "But it's a bit like falling into the river. If we don't take care of the thing today it will be too late tomorrow. The facts as far as they already exist should inform our politicians about the urgency of the problem. Currently, the state spends over thirty-five million dollars a year on permafrost repairs to our roads. When you drive down that roller coaster between Delta and Valdez you'll see what I mean. And the Leaning Tower of Pisa can't hold a candle to the buckled and decayed houses in the Farmers Loop area. People fail to grasp the larger picture. Global warming means more frequent storms and more tidal waves. Already there are several villages along the northeast coast that have had to move. Relocating a whole village and reinvesting in its infrastructure can cost anything from fifty to a hundred million dollars. Now, that's not petty cash." Pat stopped abruptly and looked at me. "You sure you want to listen to this?"

"All grist for the mill," I answered, encouraging him.

"Okay then. You see, the problem is as much under our feet as it is above us. One of its characteristics is that permafrost literally freezes carbon in place. Carbon is a greenhouse gas and is responsible for global warming. More than one seventh of the earth's carbon is stored in permafrost. Unfreeze that and climate warming will escalate. Accordingly, the tundra will become grasslands more common to Alberta than to Alaska."

"And Fairbanks sinks into the sods," I added.

"No, Fairbanks is on the Tanana River floodplain; gravel-laden permafrost will thaw in a more stable way. But out there, wet, silted soils will repeatedly thaw, jumping and dancing like a bucking bronco. On your travels you'll see lots of telephone poles zigzagging along the roadside like they were tipsy. Well, if you could speed up a series of time-lapse photos taken over the last thirty or fifty years, you could literally watch them jerk right out of the ground."

"Okay, Pat," Mary interjected, "you keep talking and we'll miss our set-down point. Look, there it is. Pull in."

"Your lecture was delivered with perfect timing, professor," I said to Pat.

He smiled as he hoisted the canoe from the roof. "That's the core problem, time. How much time have we got?"

Again Mary interjected. "Enough to paddle our way back to Fairbanks. Now hurry up, Pat."

Within minutes we were on the river, with Pat steering from the rear, Mary in the middle and me paddling downstream like an enthralled Chingachgook, last of the Mohicans. After our discussion in the car, floating down the Chena was like looking through the long viewfinder lens of a millennium camera. Pat had spoken in terms of evolutionary ages, centuries of change and glacial speeds. Now it was as if the lens had been jerked back into tight focus. From a global contemplation we were thrust into this up-close image of three insignificant individuals in a tiny canoe floating easily down the Chena in its first glacial swells. I mumbled to my friends some inconsequential remark about the silence. Mary's voice answered from behind me. "You don't really hear the silence until you are up in the northern reaches of the Yukon. Out of nowhere you hear the sudden cracking and thundering and then this terrifying hiss as the glacier breaks up. You could be hundreds of miles from it, but you hear it, like it was only around the next bend. For a split second you half expect a wall of water to come down on you. But there is nothing, just pristine silence. Like you never heard before."

Mary's words seemed entirely appropriate and did not require an answer. I let the echo of them float into my senses as we drifted on to the soft splashes of the paddle, like hands clapping in the distance. The overriding impression was one of watchfulness, as if I was being watched and even weighed up by the land I was moving through. The forest I was looking at was in fact a forest of eyes looking back at me. I don't know if it was the silence of the place or if it was some kind of an inverted echo of my night on the frozen lake, but here everything was aware, sensate. Nothing was inanimate.

I could rationally understand the indigenous peoples' insistence that nature had a persona, as had every living thing in it. It must not be offended and must be treated with respect. Even at this short distance from Fairbanks, nature, the natural environment and the endless unforsaken outback, was in control. In Europe the countryside is controlled by civilization; wild places, such as they are, are protected by communities of men and the laws of government. Man is in control. We pass through countryside en route to another part of human civilization, another time or another city. Here in Alaska you realize very, very quickly that it is the reverse. Man is the alien species here. The outback has neither been conquered nor been controlled. People survive in the outback only to the extent that they live in some kind of harmony with it.

I remembered standing in a wooden cathedral in Chiloe, an island off Chile. The entire structure was made of meticulously carved tree trunks. All the adornments, the altar and the Stations of the Cross were constructed of hand-carved wood. The whole place was an homage to the god in the wood. In that place I had felt the same sensation of being watched by every artifact in the cathedral, just as now, in this blown-away wilderness, I was being observed. But more than that, it was as if I was being measured for my suitability to enter into this living place. I remembered thinking as I stood in the church and absorbed this watchfulness that perhaps Christ didn't die on the cross; perhaps his spirit was received into a tree and something of that powerful spirituality was radiating back at me from the tree-framed walls. Though I was thousands of miles away from Chiloe in geographical space and millions of miles away in cultural evolution, and though my present surroundings were wholly different, the sensation was so alike. But I didn't dwell on the comparative facts of my thoughts; instead I accepted the coincidental reality of my feelings, and with that the watchfulness wasn't threatening anymore, or at least it made me feel less apprehensive.

I was dragged out of my reverie by Mary poking me in the back with her paddle. As I turned to her she pointed upward. Above me I saw the almost vaporous V of some twenty or so geese moving in the luminous sky. They were turning at an angle away from us and were soon gone. Mary and Pat were trying to decide whether they were geese or swan. Mary resolved that they were trumpeter swan, and that was a sure sign that summer would be with us in less than a week.

As we continued I would occasionally catch a glimpse of

something in the distance, and when I questioned what it might be I was informed it was "the pipeline." I had been contemplating a few minutes earlier how everything in nature had a personality, but the manner in which my question had been answered confirmed that the pipeline also had its own separate existence.

"Oil and Alaska are synonymous terms to the outside world," I ventured.

Pat was quick to respond. "The pipeline has funded almost single-handedly, directly or indirectly, the development of Alaska. But the relationship of Alaskans with the pipeline is an uneasy one. As I see it, there are two major problems to be resolved." I had begun to notice that, like all scientific minds, Pat thought in lists of facts to be examined. "How much oil is there left on the North Slope? Some say another thirty years, or more if Bush's government opens up the Arctic Refuge to exploitation. And secondly, can the existing structure withstand another thirty years? If permafrost thaw is to continue at an accelerating rate, then the seventy-eight thousand structures that carry the pipe some eight hundred miles to Valdez are in serious danger. The cost of constant renewal would be astronomical. And while these short-sighted engineers and politicians who are in the pockets of the oil company continue to insist that things won't happen overnight, they are only adding to the catastrophic dimension of the whole thing."

"Okay, Pat, we want you to steer us back before you have a coronary," Mary shouted. Nevertheless, she continued trying to explain to me just how hot a potato the pipeline was with everyone in Alaska.

"Yes, and with a lot of know-nothings who don't live here," Pat injected, refusing to allow the subject to be put to bed. But neither his wife nor I was prepared to pursue the matter. Permafrost, global warming and a devious but all-powerful oil dollar were bigger issues than the three of us could resolve. The river course was, in any case, bringing us into Fairbanks again.

Chena riverside land is prime real estate, and the size and

flamboyance of the homes confirmed it. Many of them had their own small jetties, and the others, not to be outdone, had small sea planes moored at the end of their properties. It was an astonishing change from only an hour ago in the wilderness, where everything was so sensual and mysterious. Here, the senses became cluttered with mundane things such as the backyards of these solid but sumptuous homes.

As we paddled on into the heart of the city Mary confessed that she was a writer herself and had penned several short stories but was now working on a novel. I was keen to know what an Alaskan writer has to write about, and asked her. Her best story was the tale of an old Indian woman looking back on her life. The novel, which Mary was still working on, had as its overall theme the emergence from loneliness and finding a new sense of purpose. Listening to Mary and quietly comparing my own limited experience of Alaska, I could well understand how a reflection on a life lived, loneliness, and finding renewal and redemption in a new, unexpected relationship were themes that seemed somehow synonymous with the expanding emptiness outside the townships and the cities.

But in another way they also seemed close to Mary's own personal experience. I suppose all writers consciously write out of their own life as a way of fixing it or loosening the hold of the past to renew and secure the future. I was sure it was so with Mary. But the thought caused me to ask of myself what I might be writing had I lived here as long as Mary. I was sensing the smallness of the huge place. In winter, especially, it physically forces you to live a confined life. Eight months of darkness must take its toll on one's emotional growth. People are forced together as a survival strategy, but if they had no well-developed cultural code and relationship with the living environment as the indigenous peoples had, then existing here could be precarious indeed.

I took the moment to ask Mary, "If it was possible, how would you sum up Alaska?"

She turned to me, paused for a moment, then said, "Everything survives and exists here on a very thin foundation." Her eloquence was profound, yet I knew it wasn't a phrase learned from some book. There was a ring of quiet authenticity about it.

That night, with the kids in bed and our cabin humming with heat from the great log fire, Audrey and I discussed my trip down the Chena. Audrey had been spending much of her time playing fetch and carry back and forth to the town with the boys while I was off on my excursions. We had not had a lot of time to talk until now, but I wanted to keep her filled in. I spoke about the trip and my companions, explaining what a pleasantly odd couple they were, the scientist and the writer. Inevitably we moved on to discuss the bush, particularly my feeling that something other than the trees existed there and that you could feel its presence. Surprisingly, Audrey concurred with me. "Sometimes I hate this place," she said. "It's those black spruce. They're creepy. There's something very deathly about them. They remind me of that horrible part of *Sleeping Beauty* where the castle is surrounded by an impenetrable wall of vicious black thorns. But it's not just that you don't know what's out there watching you—a bear, a wolf, a bull moose, anything. It's like you're always looking over your shoulder. It gives me the heebie-jeebies."

Without mentioning it, I picked up on her sense of being watched. "Do you think it's only animals that might be watching you?" I asked.

Audrey returned my question with one of her own. "What else are you thinking of, weirdo ghosts?"

I wasn't sure how to answer. I didn't mean a ghost, but I did mean something else, beyond empirical definition. Audrey was curious and pushed me on the subject. As I wasn't sure of the ground I was standing on, I began by explaining how the native peoples believed that the natural world and the supernatural world were one, and that they had a set of beliefs and concepts for explaining the supernatural world and even manipulating it. Men could form a partnership with these spiritual forces.

"What are you trying to say, Brian?"

I confessed again that I wasn't sure, but emphasized that these same beliefs were logical, consistent and powerful. "Maybe I mean it's that power our cultural upbringing denies that we sense out there," I said. "And we are apprehensive because we don't know how to respond to it." I knew I wasn't unearthing the answers we were both looking for. For a moment I related how Pat had talked to me full of facts, figures, scientific data and logical projections. Pat's world was explained through rationalist and scientific means. He had been paddling the backwaters of the outback for years, but he had no concept of the mystery of the prying eyes that make your hair stand on the back of your neck, and if he had it didn't seem to have expanded his scientific mindset. "I'm not saying he was wrong, he simply understands differently. But his logic doesn't have the power that the native believes in and chooses to cooperate with."

My mind was still turning over its impressions of the boreal forest from my aluminum canoe. My innocence and optimism about tracking down the ghost of Jack London had so far only provoked an encounter with some other kind of ghost, which I had weakly described as some kind of powerful presence. Perhaps I was learning my first lesson about Alaska, that things are not always what you have chosen to see. The problem with trying to encounter a place vicariously, through the artistic impressions of someone else, is that you sometimes discover that their imagination creates an articulate world, all neatly mortised together in their fiction. The reality is always less well finished. Mary's statement about things in Alaska existing and surviving on a very thin foundation was echoing in my head. Expectation, I resolved, was a dangerous thing.

*

CHAPTER FIVE

GHOSTS IN THE
CONFESSIONAL

That night I went to sleep expecting to dream of monsters in fairyland and those deformed black spruce trees with skeletal boughs and gorgon-like black limbs constantly pointing me in the wrong direction and whispering all sorts of curses and ill omens on me. But it didn't happen. I slept dreamlessly. The forest, it seemed, had not turned against me but smothered me in the lullaby of its embrace.

Whatever trepidations and dangers I had avoided in my sleep Jack brought to me in the morning. "Dad, are we going on a bear hunt?" he repeated as he jerked me out of my forest of the night. I had read Helen Oxenbury's story *We're Going on a Bear Hunt* to him many times in preparation for our departure to Alaska, hinting that we too were going on our special kind of bear hunt. Jack adored the story, but by now I was utterly tired of the book's journey to discover the bear with the shiny wet nose, big furry ears and two goggly eyes, and then having to do the whole trip in reverse with the bear tearing after us. But I had always insisted that the bear was not a scary bear. In fact, the bear had pursued the family not to frighten but to befriend them. Because they allowed themselves to be frightened, they didn't understand the bear. The closing illustration in the storybook reveals a lonely bear walking dejectedly along a dim foreshore with the midnight sun creating a shimmering path out into the sea and the waves lapping like liquid silver around the creature's feet. I had become weary of the book, but reading it yet again now to Jack as we both curled up on the big settee, it came alive, for we were in the land of the bear and the midnight sun. Soon we too would be traipsing through all kinds of wilderness, searching for something as benign as a mystical bear just waiting to become our friend. Already I was beginning to believe that *We're Going on a Bear Hunt* had become our totem story. I wanted to think that for Jack it had a similar significance as *The Call of the Wild* had for me. Certainly I could see it now as an extended fairy-tale metaphor of Jack London's man-killing Chilkoot Pass, which had to be conquered through a terrifying ordeal before Alaska could be felt and understood.

After breakfast we got ready to go into town, climbing into the *Pequod* and rolling down into Fairbanks. Audrey was going to drop me off and we agreed to meet up back home. As I got up to leave, I explained to the boys that I was going to meet a friend and would see them later.

"When are we going to find the bears?" Jack asked.

"Soon," I said. "We'll begin our bear hunt very soon."

"In the car-house?" Jack quizzed.

I smiled at Audrey. "Yes, we're going on a bear hunt very, very soon . . . in the car-house."

While walking toward the restaurant where I planned to meet Debra, my guide into the far north, I thought over how my son's innocent lack of vocabulary had rechristened the *Pequod*, erasing all its dramatic and portentous import. It struck me then how his young instincts received the world as it was, without overloading it with all kinds of imaginary clutter. Something in me told me that Jack and Cal would not be as apprehensive about the wilderness as both Audrey and I were, though we only hinted at it to each other.

Debra drove me to a restaurant outside the city on the banks of the Chena. I sat and watched the heavy mass of water, remembering how our canoe had moved in it, dreamy and idle. I thought of Baudelaire's contemplative lines, "When shall we set sail for happiness." Yet the moment the lines came into my head I rejected happiness as totally inappropriate to my sense of what was waiting out there.

As strangers do at a first (proper) meeting, Debra and I exchanged banal conversations about books and travel and writing, and obviously about Alaska. I confessed I wasn't exactly sure what I expected from this place. I had a head full of half-baked notions that were pressure-cooking away inside me. She had spent many years working in hospital and community health projects in the north of the country and expressed a real affection for the Eskimo people and their way of life. She spoke without a hint of romanticism or naïveté. I studied her as she spoke.

Her face was round and her coloring sallow. Her skin was smooth and unmarked and showed no signs of the years she had spent in the outback of Alaska. Her voice was soft by nature, I thought, rather than disposition. But another part of me suspected that she lived a life less hectic than others and therefore didn't have to project her personality onto the world. I found it very difficult to put an age on Debra, but her mane of raven-black hair, flowing straight and shiny over her shoulders and down her back, compelled me to wonder if she herself was part Inuit or had some indigenous Indian blood in her. I didn't ask if it was so, and I'm not sure why. There was something mysterious about her, something hidden or perhaps withheld, that intrigued me. I didn't know what it was, so I couldn't address it either with myself or with her. It was as if a memory of something or someone was surfacing and submerging as our conversation evolved.

"We will have to cross the Kotzebue Sound, then snake in and out of the sloughs and inlets along the Bering Sea coast toward the Chukchi Sea until we find Lena and Charlie, the old Eskimo shaman we shall be staying with," Debra informed me. "It would be hopeless to try this on our own."

Suddenly I was drowning in the strangeness of the places she mentioned, their extreme remoteness and isolation, the fact that I would be living at close quarters with people I knew nothing about and whose world was so utterly alien to my own. My un-spoken panic must have signaled itself to my guide, and she threw me a lifeline. "It's a very different life than that which most of us are used to, but after what you've been through things shouldn't bother you."

I grasped the lifeline quickly, and nodded, full of mock macho indifference. "I suppose not!"

Before I could take a breath she asked simply, "What is it you're looking for anyway, Brian?"

Maybe it was the way she used my Christian name, combined with the starkness of the question, but her words caught me completely off-guard. I looked at her coppery face and her placid dark eyes. There was neither animation nor a hint of a question in her eyes. It was as if she hadn't asked it, as if it had come from somewhere else, or maybe it wasn't a question but rather a state-ment. In any case she had caught me adrift and I answered like a stranger in a strange town who has been asked for directions. "I don't really know!" I spluttered. Then, to cover my confusion, I stumbled through my lexicon of interests, finally homing in on the world of the Eskimo and the Alaskan landscape, with its mercurial climate, its vast emptiness, its eternal beauty and its ever-present silence. It must all lead to a contemplation of some-thing other than the world we saw with our eyes. How closely did the lifestyle of the Eskimo relate to their spiritual under-standing? She informed me that native peoples rarely talk with outsiders of such things, partly because they feel outsiders would not understand and they do not want to offend, but mainly because the spirit world is an everyday reality directing and informing their lives. "Anyway," she said, definitively moving the discussion on, "the spirit world is something you find for yourself and you share with them if you can, and if they will." I listened, spooked by how intuitively she had honed in on what I was stumbling around.

I was expecting more tangible information but was surprised by the next shift in our conversation.

"Before I forget, it is customary to bring some gifts as well as food," Debra said. "Remember, whatever food you bring must be shared. In a sense it is communal property. So don't bring any weird or fussy foodstuffs, or that's what they'll think of you."

"Okay, no pig's feet or gorseflower wine," I joked, trying to sound unperturbed. "What type of presents?" I added, admitting that I wouldn't have a clue what to bring an old Eskimo shaman living in the far reaches of nowhere.

"Tins of salmon for Charlie and bolts of cloth for Lena," Debra confirmed.

I was dumbfounded, as if the joke had been thrown back in my face. I looked at Debra in disbelief. Tins of salmon to the Eskimos had the ring of coals to Newcastle about it, and as for bolts of cloth, I kept thinking of old B movies which portrayed the white man giving gifts of blankets and beads and all manner of colorful gewgaws to the natives. It was all too much of a cliché, and seemingly absurd.

"You must be joking. Salmon to an Eskimo? The whole of Alaska is coming down with salmon. And tinned salmon? I mean, why would he want tinned fish of all things?"

Behind the smallest hint of a smile, my guide explained. "Tins keep for a very long time, and in the winter when there isn't much food about you need to have a store to draw on. Charlie also has a sweet tooth, and the oil the tinned salmon are pressed in is a lot sweeter to an Eskimo than seal oil. As for Lena's bolts of cloth, the summers are long and hot and you have to work hard to prepare for the winter. Light cotton is more comfortable and more colorful, and Lena is a very colorful woman, as you will see."

Debra's explanations only compounded my puzzlement. It really was that simple, but I would never have guessed it. I was learning my first lesson about Inuit and subsistence living. Subsistence means survival, and that means doing what is easiest and obvious, not making life difficult by cluttering it up with a host of unnecessary complications. While I was mulling this over, Debra chose to put into practice what she had been explaining and suggested she would order in the provisions and presents as I would be too busy traveling; I could pay her my share when we set off in a few weeks' time. It was sensible and simple and I concurred, returning her half smile and implying that perhaps there was more Inuit blood in her veins than she knew. I couldn't be sure how she took my throwaway remark, as she was busy making some notes to remind her about what to purchase for our trip. She turned her head from the table and stared into the slow-moving Chena River, doing a mental calculation about numbers of people multiplied by the number of days divided by the number of locations. I sat watching, doing my own calculations and feeling comfortable, relieved that my guide was a woman rather than some macho frontiersman who was out to impress. I was now feeling very safe with Debra. She knew which things were important.

At that moment something flew into my head and was out of my mouth before I had time to consider it. "Debra, did you ever write to me several years ago in Dublin?" I was about to leave the question there but carried on, overwhelmingly convinced that Debra was indeed the mysterious woman who had twice contacted me to explain that the musician I was attempting to write about had been a "Dreamwalker." Before she could answer I was moved to turn the question into a statement. "You are her!" I said, with the calm assurance of absolute enlightenment.

A brief silence passed between us, then Debra said, "You didn't reply."

Her face, vacant as a snowdrift, contrasted with the torrent of words that poured from me.

"I couldn't because there was no return address on the correspondence. I couldn't make out your signature. But I did much later. About one month after the book was published I broadcast a message on the BBC World Service to the Inuit woman in Alaska. It was broadcast at Christmas. Do you get the World Service? I have never mentioned those letters or you to anyone in Alaska, and here you are. I mean, here we are. This is just too much of a coincidence!" I paused, breathless at the speed of my chatter. Then, with the same calm assurance, I stated, "But it's not a coincidence. I don't believe in coincidence, only in significant coincidence."

This time I turned and stared into the Chena. Debra, I know, was looking at me. I was thinking harder than my face showed. I wanted to say that if nothing more came of the encounter and our travels together, then so be it. We would have a meeting of minds; somehow we would share the magic of this moment.

"Nothing in this life happens by chance, Debra," I continued. "There's a route map laid down for us all to follow if we will and if we can. I didn't only come to Alaska to write a book about this place, I came to find something else. I'm not sure I know rationally what, but whatever it is I have a very strong instinctive sense that I may find it here, or at least discover the next signpost along the way. I didn't come to the ends of the earth to write a travelogue. There is another agenda at work here, and I am not the author of it."

I turned to my guide and looked into her face, part of me demanding an answer and wanting that quiet, dark demeanor of hers to be gathered up into my own excitement. But her face remained unmoved. "Jesus," I thought, "the woman thinks I'm nuts and is contemplating how the hell to extricate herself from this situation." But when she spoke her voice was soft and untroubled. "Yes, I have felt the same thing very strongly for several days. That's why I thought we should meet. But I also needed to hear and understand your thinking."

I thought my excitement had peaked, but then Debra said, "Perhaps we should go somewhere less busy." I agreed, but insisted on saying something before we departed. While we waited for the bill I told Debra how important her communications had been and how they had arrived at a significantly troubled time during the writing of the book. She could not possibly have known that they had provided the key to unlock profoundly difficult parts of the novel, but I was deeply indebted to these "missives from the Alaskan ether," as I called them, and I wanted her to know it.

"Things happen," she said as we rose to go. It was as if I had told her nothing more significant than the time of day. But both of us knew better than that.

We drove to Creamers Field, once the most northerly dairy in North America, now a protected nature reserve and stopover for thousands of migratory birds. There were three well-laid-out nature trails that within minutes allowed you to depart from Fairbanks environs and submerge yourself in the wilderness. Only some waterfowl and cranes hunt at the periphery of this forest. Inside, it's the stalking ground for moose and a breeding ground for mosquitoes and a million other kinds of fly and insect that thrive in the wet heat of the place. As we entered into its shadowy depths I understood why the wildfowl remain on the outskirts. The temperature of the place seems to shoot up, and the heat rising from the melting permafrost and the remnants of the last snowfall changes the very texture of the air in the place. You feel as though you're steaming over a dark cauldron.

It was an otherworldly place indeed for two seeming strangers to come and talk of their separate understanding of what had propelled them together. But paradoxically, the deeper we walked into this infested confessional, the more unencumbered our conversation became. I was entranced as I watched how the flies, mosquitoes and moths seemed to be drawn to us both. Debra remained unperturbed by them; I, on the other hand, punctuated my conversation with wild swipes as I tried to keep the creatures from me. I was quite taken by Debra's equanimity, as were the insects themselves, who seemed to alight on her hair only momentarily before disappearing. It was as if they came solely to acknowledge her presence and welcome her, and then took their leave. I didn't think much of it at the time, as I was too busy trying to protect myself from the ravaging creatures, but the recollection has struck me often since. Part of me does now believe that these creatures came almost to give homage. If not the queen, Debra was an honored guest in this humming hive of the wilderness.

I don't precisely recall how we got to the subject, but I found myself speaking about my incarceration and, paradoxically, how I had never before felt so free, so much at peace and with such clarity and lucidity of mind. They were subjects whose complexity and depth and perhaps strangeness I have never sought or been inclined to share with anyone, much less a stranger. But my guide to the Inuits did not seem like a stranger; in this strange cathedral of trees humming with an unearthly chorus of insect sounds, I felt at ease with her. Confession seemed effortless. It was as if Debra had been delivered to this place for this purpose. She listened in intense silence, intuitively understanding what my words seemed to stumble over. During lapses in my conversation, as I struggled to communicate, she spoke of her encounters with worlds that are hidden from the eye. Such worlds are often difficult to reveal, and many a life is lived in the shadows from a lack of such validation, but when we live close to our intuitions and emotions we can if we wish find companions in the strangest of places. The whole tenor of our shared exchange was one of support and deep mutual understanding. It would be foolish of me to attempt to record here the things we spoke of. I couldn't anyway. For it was not so much the topic of our conversation but the emotional and psychic correspondence behind it that was significant.

When we emerged out of the forest it was as if we had made another level of contact. We had been to a place that takes some people many years to come to. As we parted, Debra confirmed that we would speak again soon, but between times she needed to make some journeys and speak with some people. I understood without another word that these journeys would not be to any place on a map, and that whatever information she sought would not be in this world.

As I wandered home from our encounter, I contemplated where my guide might take me. A part of me has always been looking for a place of belonging, a spiritual homeland that has nothing to do with ownership but a place where authenticity can be found and affirmed. Carl Jung called it a "psychic observation post" from which we might understand the deepest parts of ourselves and recalibrate the trajectory of our life. Would my Inuit guide help me find such a place?

CHAPTER SIX

ROAD TO THE HIGH ONE

Bolstered in the *Pequod* RV and loaded to the gills with all manner of supplies, we set out to navigate along the Alaska highway, stopping where we could before entering into the far reaches of Denali National Park, whose wilderness features had been praised by everyone we had met. On my map I counted more than two dozen "protected wilderness refuges." I love the reference to such remote places as refuges. I had intended staying in several of them throughout the state but was rapidly becoming aware that these places were huge. Yukon Flats Refuge, for instance, is larger than Ireland, and several of the other two dozen are larger than that. But Denali was supposedly famed above the rest. "It's like nothing you've ever seen," people had said. "When you arrive, be prepared for the ultimate Alaskan experience."

So we set off full of expectation. Adventures, we assume, are for children, but part of me believes we leave our childhood too soon for the disappointing El Dorados of adulthood. I had to admit I was more excited than I could comprehend. I looked at Jack and Cal strapped into the dining area of the RV. I wanted desperately for this adventure to work at a level they could understand so that it might better inform me.

It's only when you are on the road that you can begin to form a response to the phenomenon of "breakup"—when the melting ice swells the rivers, signaling that summer has arrived. Outside the enclosure of the town it begins to strike you like a candle that has just been lit, then swells up to its full brilliance; that seemed exactly how the forest floor appeared when the first sun flooded it. As if by magic the dark-green foliage of plants such as the cranberry and Labrador red contrast with the brilliant green of the moss carpet that seems to be burning chlorophyll amid this first prolonged saturation of natural light. The fireweed was out and already marking time. The first blush-red and green shoots would grow up to half an inch every day, reaching some six feet by September. Like red-hot rods pulled out of a furnace, they burn in a fusion of red, orange and yellow. Summer is over, Alaskans say, when the fireweed blooms to its top in September. Wherever you are in the state, look to the fireweed and it will tell you unerringly just how far off winter is. This same fireweed would mark the duration of our stay. We set off as it was just emerging from the frozen earth, and would be departing when it reached the apex of its growth.

Now, journeying south and away from the northern ridges, we could see the effects of the winter snow's dissolution into the thousands of rivers and streams. It is not impossible in the space of one day to stand at any creek bank and witness this surge in the water volume. The rising tempo of the cascading rivers is an acoustic background to the powerful forces moving across the land.

Of all the elements, none is more important than water. It dominates all other things. It shapes the land, creates habitats for wildlife, makes obstacles or avenues for travel, threatens or sustains human life. A watercourse fed by snowmelt and breakup ice floes can create the kind of havoc that cannot be contained. For some communities it is a time for prayer: that the ice may make a safe and peaceful journey to the sea. Such can be the fury and suddenness of these surges that in some areas it is not uncommon to see young moose stranded on loose ice floes, being swept down the raging torrents. If they are lucky the ice raft that carries them might be swept onto the nearby remade banks, where they can scramble to safety. But for the majority, the torrents defeat them. We were too far south to witness such an event, but I had seen and heard the mood music of the water and could well believe the tragedy that awaits the innocent and the unprepared.

We had to keep a watchful eye on Jack and Cal. The floodwaters of these rivers take no prisoners. So I made my own obeisance to the spirit of the rivers that its passage through the land would be untroubled and that it would protect me and mine as we traveled across or on it. Even as we were careful of the creeks I could not but be aware how the orchestra of the water's movement echoed out across the land. Everywhere the silhouettes that were trees had burst into leaf, as if offering up an uncontrollable, roaring applause. The urgency of everything around us made us more anxious to get off the road and further into the bush. Already on our sight line we could see the snow-capped peaks of McKinley or, to the native inhabitant, Denali, an Indian name meaning "the High One."

Denali National Park is about 120 miles south of Fairbanks on the main route to Anchorage. Although we were on the major heartland motorway, the *Pequod* felt as if she really was at sea on several occasions. As had been explained to me, the concrete carpet of road had collapsed in several places into axle-breaking ruts, or had buckled into sudden ramps as the melting permafrost had allowed. But we were on the borderline between spring and summer and the road had not yet acquired the usual volume of traffic. By high summer there would be a wagon train of RVs congesting these highways, and if the surfaces got much worse

many of them would be laid up by the roadside, having acciden-
tally driven into the permafrost shifts.

In front of us Mount McKinley's snow-encrusted summit
filled every vista, no longer a shadowy hulk in the distant horizon. At over twenty thousand feet it's the highest mountain in
North America. But then I joked with Audrey that everything
was big in Alaska. "It has the biggest oil field, a glacier bigger than
Rhode Island, the biggest bears, the largest expanse of emptiness
anywhere in the world . . . some Alaskans on the Pribilof Islands
even live nearer to Japan than their own state capital Juneau!
Now you can't get anything much bigger than that." Audrey was
unimpressed and rolled her eyes slightly as if to say "Really!"
then quietly pointed with her finger toward me and back to her
mouth, her eyes all the time wide with emphasis. I took the hint
and turned my attention back to the road rolling out in front of
us. "Aye, aye, Starbuck," I answered.

I liked it that Denali was a being revered perhaps for more
than its height and strength. It looks like the ghostly head of
some ancient warrior, its stone face staring out from the shadow
of its tarnished helmet. The native peoples believe the mountain
was created during a battle between two magical warriors. The
raven chief, Totson, pursued his enemy Yako down a river. Totson threw a magic spear, but Yako threw up a gigantic wave of
stone to deflect the arrow, and Denali was born. In another story
Denali is called "the home of the sun." During the longest days
of summer the sun makes almost a complete circle in the local
sky and disappears for a few hours below the horizon. From certain angles it appears that the sun rises and sets behind the
mountain, and an old Athabascan legend testifies to this with the
words, "Surely we found the home of the sun and we saw with
our own eyes, the sun goes into the mountain, and leaves its
home in the morning."

Somehow, as I looked out on this panorama, I was drawn into
the story of the warriors and the specific reference to the fact that
they had performed magic deeds. For me, magic seemed to be

spilling out of the mountains. I knelt down to my two sons and pointed. "Do you see those silver-white mountains? Well, they're magic, and that's where we are going. To see the bears and the big moose and the foxes and the wolves." I knew it was Disneyland talk, but maybe Disney and Denali were not so far apart in terms of magic, and maybe Cal and Jack were looking on this fabulous landscape with the same sense of awe and wonder that a young native child might have as he goes on his first hunt with his father.

So we set our sail and drove the *Pequod* into the wilderness to berth somewhere in the lee of "the High One." But because the park is a protected area, the traveler is restricted to a series of camping grounds which move deeper into the wilderness. Still, much of the park is restricted from any form of human activity as it's a critical habitat for wildlife and plants. Here the dynamic of nature unfolds according to its own laws and the way of life is left unmolested. Author Wallace Sterner wrote of such places, "We simply need that wild country available to us, even if we never do more than drive to its edge and look in. It can be a means of reassuring us of our sanity as creatures, a part of the geography of hope." I wasn't too sure what that last sentence meant. It shadowed my own feeling that wilderness places can affect us profoundly, but I wanted more than reassurance. I wanted to know how this Alaska might change people.

At the campsite's check-in that evening we were informed that some of the furthest campsites were now closed and only vehicles were allowed to go and stay at the furthest available site; back-packers and overnight hikers were forbidden from large tracts of the park. Foodstuffs of any description were not to be carried into certain areas, and all food waste was to be stored inside vehicles and brought out of the park on departure. I was more than dismayed as the list of prohibitions continued. There was a curfew on people detouring off designated trails, and all animals had to be kept in their owner's vehicles or walked on a leash within the campsites. The exasperated look on the other visitors' faces mirrored my own. What had happened? Was it a sudden epidemic or earthquake? Alaska, I remembered, had had several in its history. When I asked what the problem was, I was told, "Wolves, sir." In the past few weeks it had been reported that a wolf pack had taken to raiding some sites, particularly those in the more remote areas. The ranger explained that no one had been attacked and wolves coming anywhere near campsites or humans was most unusual. "Wolves do not like people and always keep well away from them," he emphasized.

His words reminded me of the electric tension in Jack London's take on the confrontation between man and beast. At ten and eleven years old my imagination had no knowledge or interest in the symbolic or metaphorical significance of the author's work, but for a few seconds I was back in my childhood with London's snarling, salivating wolf pack.

The ranger was unaware of my momentary lapse and was patiently explaining the necessity of such precautions. "This behavior is so unusual that we need to nip it in the bud before something really bad happens. We do not want the wolf pack to consider the campsites as easy pickings, so we are making sure we eliminate any such behavior from becoming established. If the wolf doesn't react to you like a real bad smell and want to avoid you like the plague, then we've all got problems!" The ranger's final comment might have had a folksy ring to it, but his face displayed serious intent.

There was nothing to be done but accept the limitations. Having purchased what we required, we headed along the prescribed route to the furthest campsite allowable. It was almost full when we reached it, but we soon reversed into an empty bay and had supper cooking on the stove.

I turned my thoughts again to the wolves. After all, this was their place, and the early-evening dog show outside my window was poor compensation. What seemed to disturb the rangers was that the wolf pack's abnormal behavior disturbed the critical balance in nature that makes wilderness unique. What had caused such a drastic change in their normal pattern I could not ascertain. Neither were the rangers sure. Trying to apply my human, city-bound logic would be useless. I had a notion that the only way I could begin to understand was somehow to shed my preconceptions and merge my mind with the wilderness itself. And even if I was cribbed and confined in the *Pequod*, I was determined the wilderness should not be denied me.

When the coast was clear and I was assured I would not be accosted by some fellow traveler with a menagerie of miniature canines, I decided to go for another walk, only this time well outside the confines of the camp. I took my camera as an excuse. Audrey seemed hesitantly content, but warned me not to go too far and not to stay out too long. She knew my predilection to "go into solitary mode" when I got restless, but this time there was a genuine hint of anxiety about my going. "I'll not be long and I will be careful," I assured her.

The camp had acquired an almost unreal silence. Apart from the occasional yapping dog, as I passed there was little to suggest that there were probably sixty or more people squeezed into this tiny half acre. The intermittent flash of TV screens or a sighting of people reading in the curious evening light simply added to the emptiness of the place. It was actually more sterile than empty, I thought as I passed the last camper van. It was from upstate New York, and I heard faint traces of what I thought was Ravel's *Bolero*. I thought of Dan, and Johann Sebastian Bach or maybe Black Sabbath blasting out against a howling whiteout. Maybe the *Bolero* was better. I wasn't sure, but it seemed to swell my somber mood for a moment, and my desire to get away. Within minutes the camp and its occupants were gone.

The camp was located by a small stream, and as I followed it I soon found it was a tributary of a larger river, one of many, I suspected, that shift and remake themselves as the waters swell after the glacial meltdown. The river would give me a bearing and its clear banks would reveal any creature I preferred not to confront, in time for me to make my exit. I was relieved to be gone and trudged on glad-heartedly. I had noticed as I was leaving that a few more campers had arrived. They and several others had window stickers declaring "Jesus Saves" or imploring me to "Seek ye the lord while he may be found," or some other variety of biblical text. I was doubly glad to be away from them. "Why do these salvation merchants come here?" I asked myself again.

Then the noise of the water and the amplified silence of the outback dispelled such thoughts. I walked on, leaving everything else behind, and absorbed the world around me. A few mosquitoes disturbed me, but it was still the subarctic and the chill breeze soon blew them away. The riverbank was dotted with aspen, larch and poplar, and beyond that dwarf birch, blueberry and stunted willow, which seemed to be everywhere. Young snow-shoe hares also seemed to be everywhere, and not the least bothered by my presence. I stopped after some twenty minutes and climbed onto a huge boulder. Some dried-out trunks of trees from last year's meltdown were still trapped under it. The bulk of the stone and the size and number of the tree trunks told me all I needed to know about how powerful these waters could get at the height of summer.

I sat down and let the wilderness wrap itself around me. But this trance-like torpor lasted only a moment, and then my senses seemed suddenly and simultaneously alive, pushed by some kind of automatic adrenaline into new levels of alertness. Perched on top of my solitary rock, I experienced the same feeling I'd had on the Chena River—a feeling that it is not only creatures that inhabit the outback. It felt as if I had been stalked to this very rock, that all around me a thousand eyes were squinting and bearing down on me. "Wolf pack," I thought, panicked by the sudden sense of estrangement. But there were no wolves, not real ones, just my imagination creating them. But imaginary wolves are still real enough, and though they were only in my head they still meant something. And anyway, I cursed, isn't that why I came here? Damn Jack London and his wolf pack!

I reflected on what my guide Debra had explained to me about Inuit people and their worldview. To their mind there is always something in the air that watches. However remote a place one finds oneself in, one is never truly alone. But if my sense of dislocation when sitting alone was real, I was certainly no happier in the community of the campsite. If I had been born here I would surely conceive the world differently; even my imaginary wolves would have more significance. To the Inuit mind the invisible and real worlds are one and have a meaningful relationship.

Their "Distant Time" stories, an extensive coda which outlines and defines the proper relationship of everything in nature from the minute to the cosmological, begin with the wonderfully liberating premise that in a time prior to our present order of existence animals were humans. At some stage certain humans died and metamorphosed into plants and animals while retaining human qualities and personalities. It is almost the vision of Darwin in reverse. In this cosmology the wolf is one of many significant beings, along with the bear, wolverine and lynx. Such spirit beings should be treated with great respect, for not to do so could bring serious harm. Consequently, hundreds of tales and taboos have evolved around the treatment of these creatures. To offend an individual animal is to offend against the species.

Because of their mutual origin, the distinction between animal and human is obscure and the two orders coexist with unique empathy. The creature has all the qualities of the human and can even understand human behavior. In this belief system the wolf is considered most like humans. They possess intelligence and strength, and live communally. Even today it is believed that wolves will leave fresh kill for humans as a repayment of service in a bygone age.

I had unearthed much of this material when my love of Jack London's books had made me look for an imaginary prototype for the wolf-dog–man nexus, something that was clearly derivative from the native peoples' belief system. Jack London's stories were fables, and in their own modern way were themselves "Distant Time" stories with their own expostulatory critique.

But all this thinking had not cleared my focus but rather brought me to a crossroads. Yes, it had helped clear away the panic and fear that accompany being alone in a desolate place. I was comforted by this belief in the empathy between man and beast and the spirit world; I was intrigued by the notion of transmutation between man and creature. The whole fabric of traditional belief was about honor, respect and shared understanding. It was also about harmony, balance and order, and how things only become calamitous when the relationship between all these things is somehow broken. To the traditional mind, the body of a creature in death should be as revered as at any human passing. Those sightless eyes still see, lifeless ears still hear!

If the wolves were not savage beasts but rather my brothers, then this "living" wilderness was here to receive me. If my sense of dislocation and fear was the problem, not the place I was in, then the wolf pack's "aberrant" behavior was not "aberrant" but rather a reaction to some fault or flaw in the system. The wolves had attacked no one; they need not have ransacked campsites. Indeed, they could have stayed in the wilderness where no human entry was permitted. Wolves have their territory and remain in it for life. A few isolated campers could not force a whole pack to break with long-established instincts. It was whelping season—could that have contributed to their behavior? I remembered the serious urgency of the ranger's face when he explained the complications of the pack's behavior. Whatever the cause, it was an irrational act. The wolf pack had come to tell us something, something important, and it was communicating its urgency to us. The wolf's power was not only in its physical presence; it was spirit power of the first order. We need only listen to it to understand. I was new here, even if I felt I had been somehow brought here. I asked the wilderness to forgive me and to be my guide.

It was time to return. There were the remnants of a trail running at right angles to the river. It would take me deeper into the bush, but should, I thought, bring me out somewhere near the road which would lead back to the camp. I felt easier with the land now, not feeling the need to cling to known features such as the river course. The night light was softer, but with that wonderful brightness that comes from nowhere specific but seems to radiate out from the land itself. The clarity of the light and the silence lent a sense of austerity to the world I was walking in. The landscape features on my horizon stood out in high relief. In this light I could scan distances that at other times would have been impossible. The vista across the tundra was giving way to the burgeoning summer. The tussocks of sedge and cotton grass were shedding their russet and ocher hues; the dry yellow of winter grass against the dark beech green of alder, dwarf birch and willow blended into brown and black. To my imagination the whole color scheme was like a wolf skin. They were the passing colors of winter.

The reds, oranges, bright greens and early blues of mountain aven, fireweed, moss campion and various species of saxifrage were breaking out. The tundra birds were settling into their ground nests, full of eggs. My approach neither stirred nor fussed them. If I came near they merely eyed me with curious intent. I returned their stare, wondering what communication might be passing between us. It reminded me of the way people look at one another at funerals, half recognizing a face you look at directly in the eye, the solemnity of the moment excusing the intrusion. In that exchange you ask questions, seek recognition and share something that you both know might never be spoken. I passed them by and they acknowledged me as if I were just another lone caribou.

Around me, as I neared the end of my walk, my eyes discovered more remnants of the changing season—pieces of bone and animal fur, fluffy fledgling feathers and the light flight feathers of more mature birds. Everywhere, it seemed, spiders' webs were shining like crystals against the refracted light. It felt as if the whole landscape were opening itself up to me. Maybe it was the silence, maybe it was the acknowledging stare of the birds, maybe it was the glow of the evening, but the bright night seemed filled with beneficence and the final passing of winter.

Without understanding where it came from, I began to sense another passing. What if one of the wolf pack had died at this time of change? The corpse of such a creature would embody great spiritual danger and should not be tampered with but left within the omniscient domain of nature. Only then could such a powerful spirit be appeased. Maybe that was it; maybe the pack was preparing their own funeral rites. Perhaps they were ritually cleansing the hunting grounds in proper observance, and those raided campsites were part of this, and also partly a way of communicating this powerful occurrence. I walked on with silent reverence, not wanting to offend. Maybe I had instinctively stumbled upon what it was that had thrown the whole functioning of this wilderness park into disarray and had so utterly perplexed the rangers.

*

CHAPTER SEVEN

CLOSE ENCOUNTERS
OF A BEAR KIND

Perhaps it was the prohibition the wolves had indirectly placed upon us or maybe it was the incessant yapping of the miniature dogs that spurred my desire to move on. Certainly the prospect of a long drive to a destination called Wonder Lake deep in the Denali parkland hastened our decision to up anchor. But the "Wonder Lake" experience was anything but wondrous, and only whetted my appetite to experience something less controlled and organized.

The bus trip took us some ninety miles deeper into Denali's parkland. We were advised to bring food to sustain us and enough wet gear to protect us, though there were only two stopping places where we could disembark and make short sorties into the landscape. We decided it was better than nothing. If we were going to have any chance of escaping from our camp compound, then this was the only option. We were also assured that it was the best way of viewing the park and its wildlife.

Our bus might have come from the same conveyor belt as the

original model T Ford, with its wooden-slat seats, aluminum sliding windows and plasticized, lino-like floor. Overhead storage, which comprised a two-foot-wide section of cord netting, stretched the length of the bus. The vehicle was green with a brown and dull gray interior. Maybe the landscape we passed through was meant to be the inspiring thing and our means of transport was designed not to detract from that. But, by God, it was bloody uncomfortable for five hours on a mountain road that had seen little more than essential safety maintenance.

Yet, as our ranger driver had promised us, it did afford us a fairly in-depth, if brief, experience of Denali. I guess our score sheet for the day's outing was pretty good. We spotted porcupine, red and gray squirrel, a red fox vixen and her cubs, and beavers repairing last season's dams at the Wonder Lake. The twenty minutes or so that we stayed there did not reveal to me why anyone would have given it the name it possessed. The only sense of wonder or relief I experienced was when I heard it had toilet facilities. After a long journey in a bumping bus with two small children, that's wonder and relief indeed.

The trip back was a monotonous repeat of the outward journey, the tiresomeness of it eased only by two incidents. We did encounter bears. The grizzlies out foraging for berries and roots were making their way from the riverbed to higher ground and had to cross our path en route. It was as if we were not present. They paid little heed to us staring at them wide-eyed. It was our first sighting, but like the lake it was uninspiring. My son must have thought so too. Recalling the bedtime story I had read him many times, he said that he didn't think the bear would come home with us as he already had a friend with him. The larger of the bears ambled past our bus and climbed onto a rock some twenty-five feet from us. He collapsed onto his vantage point with slothful grace. I watched him from the rear of the bus while the others concentrated on the smaller bear, which was approaching the bus. He surveyed us with an air of ponderous disdain. Nothing about our presence moved him; our excitement had obviously not radiated itself out of the bus. His demeanor declared nothing more than that he had seen it all before. I could imagine him thinking, "Here they are, back again, those strange creatures that stare out of their metal box like the arctic grayling fish that stare out of the Toklat River. Like the fish and the berries and the caribou, these creatures will come and go again, but only I remain."

"He's very grumpy looking!" I heard Audrey say behind me.

"Yes," I answered, still lost in my own thoughts.

"I think he's still not woken from hibernation yet. Look at his big, sad, sleepy face!"

I looked at him again. Maybe Audrey was right. Maybe bears aren't cursed with the need to think or philosophize too much about the meaning of life.

"Anyway," I said, "let's leave him to whatever his thoughts are. I'm not so sure he would take too kindly to our idle speculation."

Audrey began settling the boys as the other passengers reclaimed their seats and we set off again. I tried to imagine how our tiny little green safari bus must have looked passing through the bush. The immensity of the empty landmass roaring at us through the bus window was astonishing. There are places out there, I thought, thousands of valleys and creeks and high plateau lakes, that no human being has ever set foot in. Only bears and wolves and dall sheep with their bleached white coats and their magnificent upturned horns have ever been to those empty places. From the map on my knee, I counted eighteen glaciers flowing out of the immense Alaska Range of mountains that I could see through my bus window. I could take in the huge sweep of their fearsome summits. I looked again from the window to the outspread map and back to the window, unable to resolve the stupefying calculations my brain was struggling with.

I thought back again to the big brown bear sitting aloof and uncaring on his stony throne. He was part of it all and didn't have to rationalize it. Whereas I could only look from my map to the window and gape uncomprehendingly, he sat and shrugged indolently at it all. "Do you know," I said to Audrey as our tiny green slug of a bus crawled its way along, "I don't think you should be so critical about the old bear!"

She looked at me with an expression that said, just what is he going to say next, and is it really worth my while listening to him. Her look was a challenge.

"The proper attitude to adopt is one of awe, especially if you are a woman." Audrey's countenance immediately changed. "Only men can hunt them and eat them. In fact it is a great offense for men to speak of the bear in front of women. It's even forbidden for a woman to touch the hide of a long-dead animal!"

"Is that why you didn't want to humor me when I came over to talk to you about the bear?"

Now I looked at her with the same kind of puzzlement that she had earlier fixed on me. I had not thought of the bear as an avuncular old man who had just woken up. As I considered it now I said, "Maybe I was just picking up something from the bear's spirit."

"You're not the only one who has been reading about bears," Audrey said, opening up the park brochure about these creatures. "It says here that hikers should have great respect for the unpredictability, aggressiveness, tenacity and power of the brown bear. No wonder you're picking up things from that old bear, you and him have a lot in common!"

I looked at her, asking if I should regard that as a compliment.

"Maybe," she answered inscrutably.

The bus drove on back to our camp. My thoughts were less and less directed out of the window. Audrey's tongue-in-cheek remarks had thrown another gloss on my thinking and I wasn't too sure where it was taking me. At that point the bus stopped and the driver pointed out some dall sheep. He informed us we were exceptionally lucky, as it was most unusual to get so close. I looked and saw we weren't that close. One of the passengers heard me remark how I admired their mantle of horns and lent me his binoculars. I focused on one animal standing proudly with its head and chest facing the wind. For a moment it seemed to be looking directly down the tube of the field glasses. It stared fixedly at me and then abruptly jerked its head back and just as abruptly fixed its stare on me again. I set the glasses down for a moment and thought. Was that sudden tossing of the head a kind of acknowledgment of my presence, a gesture of welcome? But the figure that the upturned horn made as his head flicked back could also have been the animal equivalent of a two-fingered gesture that simply means "up yours, pal!" I had a feeling that the sheep and Audrey were inscrutable companions.

When we were about some twenty-five miles away we were flagged down by three hikers. They had been camping and hiking out on the back trails of the mountain range but had decided to cut short their stay. The problem, as each of them complained bitterly, was the mosquito swarms. They had hoped that by staying in the high trails and crisscrossing the snow line the chill factor would keep these pests at bay. But summer had set in early and with more intensity than they had expected. They could just about cope with the creatures by staying on the move, but rest periods and sleep had become impossible. They had decided to give up and replan their route after stocking up on supplies of repellent and mosquito nets. One of their parting phrases remained with me: "Summer's moving in hard and fast this year and you've got to stay ahead of it if you really want to see anything." Denali's six million acres might make it larger than Massachusetts, but it was still the size of a postage stamp on my Alaska map. In any case, no matter how big the place was these tiny mosquitoes had ganged up on the seasoned hikers and put them to flight. I certainly had no intention of remaining to be eaten alive. Having completed what seemed more like a Sunday-school safari to the wholly inappropriately named Wonder Lake, there was little else we could do given the limitations of wolves, park regulations and now mosquitoes. When I suggested to Audrey that we should think about moving on the next day, she seemed relieved.

The next morning we walked to the camp's entrance. The yapping of dogs met us as we passed each vehicle. A few owners were already out walking their delicate pets. Here were these people, in the wilds of Alaska, thousands of miles from their own homes, doing exactly as they would at home. At the entrance to the campsite a large bulletin board had been erected and on it was a largish poster informing the traveler about what to do if they encountered a bear.

Rule number one: Do not run! Bears, it explains, can run faster than thirty miles an hour.

Rule number two: Back away slowly, which I thought was reasonably sound advice. But what followed puzzled me. "Speak in a low, calm voice or sing softly while waving your hands above your head." I suggested to Audrey that if a bear was charging me I don't think I would want to wave at him and sing him a lullaby.

Rule number three: If a grizzly makes contact, play dead! For sure, I thought, if a coronary hadn't already dispensed with the need for playacting. This rule concluded with the strong advice, "If the attack is prolonged, fight back furiously!" Now that was real Alaskan mountain-man stuff.

Rule number four was even more macho: If a black bear makes contact with you, FIGHT BACK! There was no suggestion here of waving, singing or reciting poetry, or even playacting and feigning death. No, sir. When it comes to black bears it's a case of getting stuck in with fists and feet flying and no quarter given. Both Audrey and I laughed nervously. The wilderness was more ominous than we cared to imagine, and I thought about the bears we had encountered yesterday in a different light.

One of our fellow campers joined us to check some notices and I asked him why it was necessary to react differently to a grizzly and a black bear. He explained that the black bear was smaller and with a determined effort can be scared off. But in the case of the grizzly or brown bear, fighting was a last resort to save your life—but, he added matter-of-factly, "If a big brown decides he's gonna attack you and he gets hold of you, you'd be better praying than fighting because he's gonna kill you and you're gonna hope it happens real quick!"

We drove out of the campsite at Denali with no clear idea of where we might head. Circumstances beyond our control seemed to be forcing us to make changes in our planned schedule. Audrey drove while I studied the map. I remembered the hikers' remark about keeping on the move and trying to stay one jump ahead of the elements and the insects. We were on the main road to Anchorage and it seemed best to carry on in that direction, stopping at a place called Talkeetna to fill up on supplies, then onward toward Anchorage but swinging left at Palmer and motoring hard along the Glen Highway to Glenallen. There we could turn south once more and take a secondary road toward a place called Chitina, following the road until it stopped. Audrey listened, then asked pointedly just where the road did end and why we were going there. I began to explain that mostly we were trying to avoid the mosquitoes, and also to get to a wilderness area that was less controlled by rangers and the national park regime. Audrey thought I should be less critical of the rangers.

I changed the subject. "It also says in the Denali information pack that caribou are the animal most plagued by mosquitoes. At this time of the year they frequently head into the hills, where the colder atmosphere and the mountain breezes keep the insects at bay. The snowbanks and the wind-blown ridges protect them from mosquitoes, and they calve there. At these higher elevations their young are safe from bear and wolf predators. So we are heading into the hills between the Chugach mountains and the Wrangell and St. Elias mountains. I think Jack and Cal should be safe from predators there and hopefully we should have left the mosquitoes behind us."

"Yes, Brian, but *where* exactly are we going to end up? I don't want us camping out in the wilderness alone." She paused for a moment. "What would happen if this vehicle broke down or something?"

"Well, the road ends at a place called McCarthy. One way in and no way out!"

Audrey's response was less anxious. "I knew it, I just knew it. When I looked at the map two nights ago and saw the name of the place at the end of that road to nowhere I said to myself, I bet we end up there. I just knew it!"

CHAPTER EIGHT

THE LONG AND
WINDING ROAD

Audrey was doing the driving and the boys were strapped into the dining-area bay seat playing with some plastic dinosaurs we had bought for a few dollars at an open-air market in Fairbanks. I sat up front trying to catch up on some reading and making notes. I had grandiosely inscribed my notebook with the words "Captain's Log" and underneath had printed "The RV *Pequod*: Star Date 2001." The mongrel mix of Herman Melville and the *Starship Enterprise* had not lost its quirky appeal for me. For some reason I was humming the Beatles song "The Long and Winding Road" to myself as I scanned my notebook making amendments and adding afterthoughts to my observations. The song, Melville's book and the TV series have the common theme of a journey and they had tied themselves together subliminally in my mind. But it was a particular kind of journey, a journey in search of resolution, revelation and perhaps paradise.

I suppose it could be summed up as a spiritual quest that

would hopefully conclude in some kind of personal transformation. Such quests have a long history, but in contemporary times such transformations are linked to a spiritual homeland where the weary old rationalist and traditional ideas of self and salvation are cast off as powerless impediments. This search for a renewed experience of authenticity was the objective of writers such as Richard Burton, T. E. Lawrence and Gertrude Bell, each of whom found in their desert landscapes a sense of beatitude and timeless quiet in which their spirit was cleansed and nurtured anew.

My favorite travel writer in this genre is Freya Stark. Her book *Beyond Euphrates*, an autobiographical account of five years' traveling and living in Iraq and what was then Persia, is a vivid example of finding a place of belonging, somewhere that was totally alien to all her European upbringing. Beyond the great Euphrates lay the uncharted mountains and valleys she mapped for the British Embassy. Freya found her soul-home there, a place and a people that inspired and stilled her. Many of these writers found their cathartic home in the Islamic world. But in my own mind, if there was such a place that could heighten, enrich and ultimately transform my understanding, I was sure I would not find it in those parts of the world where religion had deeply embedded itself. I wanted to discover somewhere that still might be pristine and elemental, untainted by well-wrought belief systems, dogmas or regimented codes of ethical and religious observance handed down by religious elites. Yes, I wanted paradise without proscription, liberation without a leash. I felt I might find it in the wilderness, where the law was not man-made and enlightenment was not revealed in a holy book—in short, in a living encounter.

Samuel Johnson defined "wilderness" in 1755 in his *Dictionary of the English Language* as "a desert; a tract of solitude and savageness." But wilderness has a dual aspect, as recorded in fairy tales. I remember particularly from my childhood the stories of the Brothers Grimm. Their woodland wilderness had a twofold emotional tone: on the one hand it was inhospitable, alien, mysterious and threatening; on the other, beautiful, friendly and capable of elevating and delighting the beholder. Involved in this second conception is the idea of wild country as a sanctuary in which those in need of consolation can find respite from the pressure of civilization.

This was near to my own understanding of the place. For me, Jack London's books had only extended this sanctuary metaphor of wilderness. Dictionaries and logistic analysis are only holding pens for language. Ultimately an understanding of wilderness is as complex as it is partly contradictory. It elicits instinctive responses, can awaken feelings that are preternatural and emotional. It can reveal a new psychological persona and a more expansive communion within its quiet. It disinters parts of ourselves that domesticity has consigned to some dusty attic of our being. For wilderness is primarily a state of mind, a response more than a place apart. But whatever it was, it was out there waiting for me to enter into it and to draw from it whatever authenticity it offered me. My cerebral musings were in any case creating their own kind of wilderness, and I was happily ready to jettison them for the real thing.

Our arrival in Talkeetna brought me back down to earth. The small town apparently took its name from a Tanana native expression meaning "river of plenty," and it turned out to be just that after our Spartan experience in Denali. It had retained much of its frontier character with small log and clapboard cabins lined along narrow dirt roads. The main street, which is no more than about 150 yards long, boasts a sign which reads "Welcome to downtown Talkeetna." Downtown comprised a handful of coffee shops and restaurants and a gem of a general store called Nagleys, which hadn't changed a lot since it was built in 1921. Inside, huge rusty bear traps lined the walls along with an assortment of bric-a-brac from the early establishment of the town as the engineering center for the railroad north. The assortment of rusty iron railroad fittings made for a curious accompaniment to the piles of fresh bread, baskets of berries, jars of homemade preserves and sacks of dry beans. At the other side, across from the food, were stockpiles of everything a homestead community would require, from hatchets to headgear. There was even a display case full of handguns.

The other principal commercial enterprises were a filling station with a mechanic's work bay, and adjoining that a laundry with shower rooms which Audrey was especially relieved to find. "Civilization!" she sighed at the discovery. I nodded in silent agreement. A hot shower and fresh clean clothes were the nearest thing to civilization I might encounter over the next few months. Across from the store was the unimaginatively named Fairview Inn, which was as original as the store and would have made a perfect setting for a saloon scene in any Hollywood western. Even the customers had that "howdy, pardner, give me three fingers of red-eye whiskey" look about them.

Within minutes we had walked to the end of downtown Talkeetna and were standing on the banks of the Susitna River. "Civilization doesn't last too long in Alaska," I said, reminding Audrey of her joyous remark on seeing the laundromat. She laughed, stating that she was only too happy to take whatever was on offer, and with that we made our way back to the RV and found ourselves a campsite only a mile or so from the main street on the banks of the river.

*

CHAPTER NINE

THE ROAD TO McCARTHY

The following day, a few hours' driving had us passing through the sleepy little village of Willow, and then Palmer. They had developed out of one of Roosevelt's New Deal relief programs. Approximately two hundred farming families devastated by the great depression of the Midwest had been transplanted to the Mantanuska and Susitna valleys to raise livestock and cattle. The scheme was only a partial success, but the present inhabitants, grandchildren of the original settlers, had maintained a quiet, unexcitable air about the place.

Apart from purchasing some foodstuffs we kept on the road to McCarthy. Though the route was scenic, abutting the Mentasta and Wrangell mountains with long wide valleys of spruce, birch and alder, it didn't have the raw-edge sense of isolation Denali had offered. It was "settled country." I was beginning to miss Talkeetna but then decided that too was a kind of halfway house, a patched-up romantic idyll on the edge of wilderness. It had all the color of a frontier town and the mountain men looked as though they had been or were about to go over the range. But in the end I was left with a sense that they had merely stumbled to the edge of the wilderness and somehow their vision had stopped there. Maybe I was being unfair. They had, after all, created their own world, and there was only one Talkeetna. I had noted that on the fifteen-mile drive from the town to the main highway into Anchorage there were at least seven small Nonconformist churches. They were evidence to me that the world they inhabited on the fringe of the wilderness was the escapist world away from urban America. But maybe that was enough. Within a few miles of these townships you could hunt across enormous areas where a no-trespassing sign could never be erected—not that anyone would take heed of it. You could drink from the wilderness cup as much as you wanted and as often as you wished and return when you'd had your fill of it.

Way out here, beyond the finite roads of civilization, was the isolation, a condition uniquely Alaskan that bore no comparison to anything imaginable, something you would have to be born into in order to survive in permanently. I thought of the taxi driver in Fairbanks and his remarks about the winters making people go crazy. I could believe that out there lay a kind of psychic crossroads where the worlds of humanity and nature elide and metamorphose into each other. All the way along the road Mount McKinley overshadowed us, changing slightly with the distance and the quality of sunlight but always a perfect enlargement of the Paramount Pictures logo—that industry which projected fantasy onto film.

Finally we reached Glenallen, though we were not encouraged to stay there. It was little more than a service station for people heading north to Fairbanks and beyond, or for those wishing to get into the Wrangell and St. Elias mountains. It was quiet at this time of the year, but I could well imagine that in a few weeks' time Glenallen would be no more than a glorified RV car park.

I looked at the map. We had another few hours to go on a poor secondary road to Chitina. I remembered Pat, who had planned this trip for me, telling me that the road from there to McCarthy was hazardous even at the best of times, and that we should check conditions for ourselves when we arrived in Chitina. The alternative was to fly from Chitina to McCarthy in a small four-seater aircraft; the twenty-five-minute flight could save maybe five or six hours' driving. My fear of heights did not make her sensible proposal very persuasive and I was determined to tough it out, not realizing just how hazardous and dangerous the journey from Chitina could be. Pat had also advised us to take whatever essentials we needed with us. McCarthy had a general store, a restaurant and a few very small hotels, but because of its remoteness everything was expensive and might well be in short supply.

The supermarket we visited in Chitina was certainly not in short supply of anything. We seemed to be the only out-of-town shoppers and the place had an oppressive atmosphere. At first I wasn't sure what it was. It was gaudy and bright, and the piped music was dated. It felt like it was being squeezed through the PA system like cheese through a grater. Then I noticed the other customers. None of them revealed any marked ethnic features of the Eskimo or the Indian. It was the manner in which they were dressed that set them apart. The young girls wore long floral print frocks and short ankle socks over very plain shoes or converse high-tops. Their hair was pulled back off their heads and tied in a tight bun at the back. Most of them wore round-neck cardigans buttoned right up. Their mothers were dressed almost identically. The few men who were there seemed to have shopped at the same outfitters. All wore jeans or dungarees with working men's boots and plaid shirts. I got the feeling they were not dressed this way simply because it was a rural community where style was irrelevant. The charity-shop hand-me-down appearance of these people had much to do with poverty, but it was also a cultural expression. The children followed their parents around the store subdued and obedient, which seemed a perfect reflection of the sullenness on the faces of their parents.

I remembered my discussions with Jane Haig and what she had told me about the reason for the plethora of small dissenter churches that sprawled around Fairbanks. She had suggested that the poor Protestant whites of the southern Dust Bowl communities had been attracted by the homestead ethic that the Alaskan frontier offered. Consequently they brought their various hues of Christian evangelism with them. The "mission ethic" that was central and common to all these churches was, she said, drawn to the lawless, amoral townships of gold rush Alaska, where there was a multitude of sinners as well as savages to be saved.

At the entrance of the supermarket, one family was gathered. The children had constructed a counter out of empty cartons and were selling small parcels of cakes and cookies. Their father stood behind them in his patched overalls and threadbare shirt. He had a young man's build and face hidden behind a long beard, but his eyes were watery like an old man's. Looking at them huddled together, trying to make a dollar or two, I felt I could have been looking at an old, yellowing photo of a family in the Ozarks over half a century ago. In my imagination, these were the descendants of Steinbeck's "Dust Bowl" people, the people Jane Haig had spoken of and the New Deal plantation of Palmer had confirmed. History and geography had eroded nothing from them, but neither had it given them much. I was sure that there was no wife for this man or mother for his four young daughters. Maybe she had died, or maybe she was a snowbird who had neither the courage nor the energy to return. I decided it wasn't only sullenness I could read on the adult faces, it was desperation, rejection and maybe even anger too, subdued under the weight of the effort to survive. There would be work on the farms and on the land for two, possibly three months in the year—hard work, with long hours; any spare time was given over to preparing woodpiles for the winter, and hunting moose and duck to provide sustenance, and then comes the long, dark winter when you just hang on with what you've got, hoping it's enough. In their own way, they were the living inheritors of *The Grapes of Wrath*.

Many people make fun of Alaska's national cuisine of spam and pilot bread—a type of ship's biscuit containing neither oil nor eggs to make it go rancid and little water to discourage mold. It has a shelf life of years, some say. Spam, that chopped-ham-in-a-can, has similar qualities of longevity. The bread may be as tasty as a bowl of toenail clippings and as mouthwatering as old plaster, yet together they have held back hunger pains and the worst of the long winter when the cupboard is bare.

I looked again at my family in the aisle and threw some pilot bread and spam into our trolley.

"What's that for?" asked Audrey.

"You never know when we might need it," I answered, having already decided to leave it in the miner's cabin we would rent at Kennicott, in the hills beyond McCarthy. It was an act of acknowledgment and empathy. Maybe it salved my conscience. Whatever had brought me to Alaska, it wasn't driven by the same desperation that had washed these people up here and still held them.

Maps of Alaska can be misleading things, especially when it comes to revealing small areas of roadway on an otherwise massive landmass. Such roads look relatively straight and unencumbered, as did the seemingly short route to Chitina. But such was not the case. The old roadway hacked its way over lakes and meandering rivers and skirted endless forests of spruce and birch, its course dictated by the lie of the land. It rolled languorously. The bedrock and permafrost were resistant to dynamite. Nowhere was there a straight line between two points. Nature determined everything here, and all around us the mountains, still dusted with snow, seemed to melt in and out of the azure sky.

The further south we headed the worse the road became. The

softening permafrost had buckled and left craters in the road that had only been temporarily filled with loose screed. We rolled in and out of them frustratingly and the *Pequod* began to lurch dangerously like a sailboat caught in a crosswind. Audrey had to dash back to Jack and Cal to prevent them falling out of their chairs (luckily they were asleep). The large culverts under the road had been crushed by the shifting permafrost and the road had had to be dug up to replace them, so every twenty to thirty yards a trench had been loosely filled with small stones where the drainage pipes had been replaced. Travel was frustratingly slow, and the *Pequod* was swallowing petrol at an astonishing rate.

At last we reached Chitina, which comprised six buildings, all of which looked as though they were about to collapse. The clapboard structures had not seen paint for years, and most of them were empty. Inside the rickety café the owners lazily watched us enter. They were neither surprised nor interested; we were just some more flotsam that had been washed up at this end-of-the-world place. Over a cup of coffee we quizzed the owners about the state of the road to McCarthy.

The road was only seventy-five kilometers long but had been the original rail line (minus the sleepers and rails). It was too soon after meltdown to be sure that it had not been washed out completely. We were warned about debris and sharp metal leftovers from the road's previous life. We were also told the trip would take up to five hours. Having already driven for ten hours, we were not encouraged by this. We decided to call Wrangell Air on our mobile phone, but the café proprietors told us that cell phones don't work in Chitina; in fact, they elaborated, nothing worked in Chitina. We used a portable landline and rang Anchorage, only to be told that it would cost $140 per person to fly the twenty-five minutes to McCarthy. I complained to Audrey and said I would ring back. Over $500 was robbery, and I was determined to drive. In the meantime, we ordered some food.

While we were there two new visitors entered, an old man

and his daughter who had just driven back from McCarthy. The journey had taken over three hours in a four-wheel drive, and they'd sustained three punctures. It didn't seem as if we had any option. After five minutes or so the airline rang back to confirm that the plane would come from McCarthy to meet us at eight p.m. I complained about the cost and pretended I would rather drive. The lady in Anchorage wavered and confided that she would not charge for Cal. I remained unhappy. Audrey was signaling with her hand for me to keep cool, but the choice between five hours of hazardous driving (after ten hours of driving on a crater-filled highway) and flying at exorbitant prices made it beyond my capacity to be reasonable. I stated that I would ring her back as our supper was being served.

The proprietors, the couple who had just returned from McCarthy, and a few locals who had come into the establishment were silently engrossed in the exchange between myself and the airline operator in Anchorage. I couldn't be sure, but I felt they were enjoying my obstinacy. The truth was, I didn't really have an option. Even if we drove carefully and made it to McCarthy without mishap, we would still have to make the return journey. We could not be in luck twice! While I was considering this, the phone rang again. It was Anchorage for Mr. Keenan. They offered to charge only for Audrey and me, which effectively halved the price. With pretended uninterest, I accepted.

We hurriedly finished our meal and asked for directions to the airstrip, which was apparently only ten minutes back along the road we had come in on. There would be a small sign pointing out where we should turn off the road. What we discovered was that there were many signs, and they were warnings, not instructions. Everywhere we found evangelical injunctions declaring the need for salvation and the dreaded consequences of refusal. Placards on trees roared out that "the wages of sin" were death, that "God would punish the ungodly," or to "Get ye the lord while he may be found," and reinforcing these dire proclamations were "no trespassing," "private land" and "keep off" signs. Collectively they gave off the impression that the whole place was somehow contaminated and under some kind of prohibition.

Inevitably we missed the sign we were looking for and resorted to stopping at one of the homesteads to ask for directions. Our reception could not have been colder, nor the directions less helpful. At a small roadside teahouse I approached the only occupant, a small woman wearing a straw hat, long purple blouse buttoned at the neck and wrists, and a long floral dress down to her ankles. Her demeanor, too, was distant and cool. She told me in as few uninterested words as she could manage that the airstrip was a few miles along on the right, but when I asked if she could be more specific she said I should ring and pointed to the phone. Above the phone was a framed embroidery of a biblical text declaring that I needed to be washed in the blood of the lamb, and across from it was another assuring me that only the redeemed shall be saved. I chose not to pursue the admonishment and rang the airstrip, informing someone there that we would be a little late arriving. As I left, the woman emerged from the room she had disappeared into and began to wipe the telephone.

"Jesus," I said to Audrey as we drove off, "you'd have to hit her in the face with a hammer to crack a smile out of that one! This place is beginning to give me the creepy crawlies!"

When we eventually found the airstrip we saw a lone man walking around a small yellow plane pointed out along the runway for takeoff. The tiny four-seater Cessna did not look encouraging, but Mike McCarthy, the pilot, was so relaxed and accommodating about our being one hour late that we loaded up the tail of the plane in relieved good humor, joking with Mike about his surname and our destination. Then we loaded ourselves: Audrey and the kids got in behind Mike and I went up front, which was not where I wanted to be.

I bit down hard as Mike fired the engine and within seconds we were scooped up into the air. Mike explained that our ascent would be bumpy, as there were strong winds blowing up the creek. I whispered "okay." I hadn't meant to whisper, but rising panic had choked my words. "How long?" I managed through clenched teeth, trying to sound calm.

"Forty minutes or so, depending on the winds," Mike answered, unaware that every time he mentioned the word "wind" he ratcheted up my panic levels. Though it was a several-million-to-one chance that anything would happen during a half-hour flight, my imagination created several scenarios for catastrophe. Fear is usually irrational, and if you cease to believe in it you can make it disappear. It's a matter of telling yourself lies and believing them.

We made it. After reloading our baggage into Mike's very dilapidated flatbed truck we rattled, bumped and collided our way along the last few miles of the old railway road I had considered driving on from Chitina. I concluded then and there that we would never have made it. The *Pequod* would almost certainly have floundered, and us with it. I turned to acknowledge to Audrey that she had been right about flying after all, only to witness her furious attempts at beating off mosquitoes. The cab was full of them!

*

CHAPTER TEN

PARADISE LOST

I knew nothing about where we were going and had entirely open-ended expectations about what we might find there. Telling Audrey we were trying to stay ahead of the mosquitoes was a half-truth, and now she knew it. At least Pat Walsh had spoken highly of the couple we were going to stay with.

Outside the town of McCarthy the road bifurcates, and we traveled for little more than a mile up a steep, washed-out, boulder-strewn passage enticingly named Silk Stocking Road before we came into the town of Kennicott. Yet to apply the title of "town" to either McCarthy or Kennicott is more than a misnomer, for the permanent population of both rarely exceeded more than two dozen; Mike McCarthy informed me that during the summer months that figure quadrupled, swelled by hunters, hikers and the extended families and friends of its permanent residents. But that fact seemed insignificant set beside the name of the road we had bumped and swatted our way over to get here. A Silk Stocking Road joining up two ghost-town communities somewhere at the end of nowhere between the Chugach, Wrangell and St. Elias mountains was an unexpected anachronism that tantalized more than the mosquitoes.

Within minutes we were outside our accommodation, a brightly painted, rusty-red and white clapboard cabin overlooking the terminal moraine of the Kennicott glacier. There were four of these cabins strung out in a line. Only ours, and Mike's next to it, were in a habitable condition. They were originally the homes of the mine managers and administrators and in their day had been real upmarket, privileged homes. Mike helped us unload our gear and gave me a quick rundown of the place while his partner, Laura, helped Audrey with the kids.

In 1900, a couple of prospectors named Jack Smith and Clarence Warner spotted a large green spot on the ridge between the Kennicott glacier and McCarthy Creek which proved to be mineral staining from a fantastically rich copper deposit. The copper discovery sparked the construction of the two-hundred-mile-long Copper River & Northwestern Railroad, which connected the mining camp to the south-coast town of Cordova. By the time the mine closed in 1938 it had produced over four and a half million tons of ore worth a reported $200 million, which in those Depression years was an astronomical sum of money. It was easy from this perspective to see how Alaska had translated itself into a fantastical dream place where paradise and untold riches could be dug out of the earth. This was the other lure of the wilderness—earthly reward, not spiritual salvation.

At its peak, six hundred people lived in Kennicott. The main settlement included all that was needed to mine the ore as well as houses, offices and stores, a school, hospital, post office, dairy and recreation hall. Just down the road, a second community eventually named McCarthy sprang up around 1908. A perfect complement to staid, regimented Kennicott, McCarthy played the role of sin city: among its most successful businesses were several saloons, pool halls, gambling rooms and back-alley brothels.

In its heyday, some 150 people lived in McCarthy. But when the mine shut down only a few people stayed on.

The mine at Kennicott closed overnight, and within a matter of weeks the mining town was stripped clean of anything that was portable. Only ghosts and the red and white leftovers of the mine's architecture of bunkhouses, train depots, workers' cottages and the magnificent power plant, towering up hundreds of feet and looming over the Kennicott glacier, remain. Such places fascinate me. The emptiness echoes with stories and lives that more than a half a century of freezing mountain winters cannot eradicate. It is as if it holds them in cold storage for those who choose to find them. I could feel it already after only a few hours. Mike's brief résumé and the manner in which he told it suggested that he too had found something more than a ghost town here. I was beginning to understand why such places sometimes serve as a quintessential haven. You would never be truly lonely for the ghosts would befriend you.

We settled in for our first night in the mountains and already I was beginning to feel the same kind of snug comfort I had felt in our cabin in the hills above Fairbanks. Only one thing threatened to spoil it—the mosquitoes. Our flight into the mountains had not rid us of these perfidious insects, and over the next few days I was to learn just how many millions of them had come to welcome us.

It wasn't the constant light that awoke us in the morning but the silence, in which the slightest sound is amplified. One's sensual awareness of the surroundings becomes heightened. In the early morning, before anyone was awake (even the mosquitoes), I was up and out.

I looked out toward the Chugach and Wrangell mountains, telling myself that the flight had not been so bad after all. Then another thought set in: those same mountains that looked so scenic and serene were also the impenetrable walls that held us here. But that was the old me already translating newness and undiscovered things into insignificant insecurities. I consoled myself that the ghosts would protect me as I walked out of the enclosure of our mining encampment. I found the skeletal remnants of human occupation intensely comforting in the roaring mountainscape that confronted me.

I was standing in a landscape that was fifty million years in the making. In a bygone age a series of warm interglacial periods had interacted with colder periods, thrusting massive rivers of ice through these mountains. Like teeth on a rake they gouged out the land, depositing millions of tons of rock and silt in glacial basins. I was looking out on the results of this ancient cataclysm as the first strident notes of birdsong echoed around me like Chinese wind chimes. The Kennicott glacier was a hideous moonscape of rubble, rock, earth and the fossilized trunks of prehistoric trees that looked like so many broken matchsticks littered around the ashes of a burned-out city. And if it wasn't the moon, it could have been Dresden or Coventry after wartime bombing; it could have been the decimated outskirts of Hiroshima or Nagasaki. It was huge and ugly and repulsive, but contemplation of the power and persistence of it made those catastrophes seem pathetic. No human hand was at work here and that huge, cratered surface stretching out in front of me was living still, moving and melting and changing everything.

I remembered that Mike had explained how on one occasion the road from the airport had completely washed away in one night, and that thousands of tons of earth and broken timber had been deposited. It was useless to attempt to clear it and the residents of the two townships had worked for months to clear a dirt road around it. I admired their community spirit and laughed when I thought of the man in Talkeetna who had complained about having shoveled more snow in twenty-five years than was on the top of Mount McKinley. Here was evidence, if I needed it, that the wilderness bends to no one's will. Yet another passing thought made me laugh again: if I was the set designer for the Pandemonium conclave of Satan's disciples from Milton's *Par-*

adise Lost, I would set the scene right here on the grisly surface of this glacier, with the blood-red altar of the towering Kennicott mine as a perfect backdrop.

Mike's crowing rooster back at our cabin recalled me to my senses. I was deep in the biggest national park and reserve in the world, contiguous with the national park reserves of Tetlin, Kluane in Canada, Tongass, Glacier Bay and Admiralty Island, all of which constitute a world heritage site of some thirty million acres. And here I was standing on a hill, dizzy with contemplation of it all and imagining *Paradise Lost* being staged on a glacier! Well, if my imagination was running riot, so be it, for the inconceivable immensity of the wilderness in which I had dropped myself demands you abandon all preconceived notions of space and size.

Back at our cabin, everyone was making ready for the day. Mike and Laura had arrived with a wonderful breakfast of fresh eggs, homemade bread, biscuits and rich, dark coffee. Mike had arrived in McCarthy several years earlier after drifting around doing several jobs that offered themselves to him. He had spent almost twenty-five years as a commercial fisherman working out of several ports in the Gulf of Alaska, but mainly Homer. He was originally from Wisconsin and had drifted up to Alaska in search of some kind of adventure that Wisconsin could not offer. Laura had been born and had lived in Alaska all her life and had worked as a law librarian. I suggested it was a big change from surviving off the sea to surviving in a mining ghost town.

"The ocean is not so far away," he said, pointing out that in a light plane he could be in Cordova or Valdez on the gulf coast in a few hours, and probably less, depending on the weather. Anyway, he continued, he enjoyed the pace of life here and preferred looking after his chickens to gutting halibut all day long.

"He doesn't just prefer his chickens, he adores the creatures," Laura put in. "I wonder he has any time for me at all!"

But a few egg-laying chickens and a couple of dogs are hardly a good reason to retire into the hills, I ventured.

"Well, he does have me as well, you know," Laura countered with a chuckle, "and we have three boys between us."

The words "between us" seemed a little odd and I didn't know how to receive them. Mike relieved my curiosity: he and Laura had previously been married to different partners; he had one fourteen-year-old son and Laura had two boys. Mike was quietly candid about the breakup of his marriage, and his love for his son was evident as he spoke. It became obvious that his decision to settle in McCarthy had had a lot to do with his son. The boy had chosen to live with his father, and Laura's children also spent the summer and most of the year with them.

"What about school?" Audrey asked.

"All the kids here are home-schooled," Laura explained. "The state education system supplies everything we need—books, work manuals, stationery, teaching guides, computers and anything we request."

I looked at Mike. I had already decided I liked the man because of his ease and openness, and the air of gentleness about him. Jack had also taken to him immediately, and Cal, who was now beginning to walk, trotted into his outstretched arms without hesitation.

"A fisherman, a backwoodsman, a pilot and a teacher?" I said to him with unconcealed admiration and no small amount of hidden jealousy.

He smiled and answered quietly, "Things happen as much by chance as necessity."

For a split second I thought about asking him which had played the greater part in bringing him here, but decided against it. I was sure he wouldn't know, or if he did he wouldn't want to analyze it. Mike half answered my question anyway as he and Laura left us to our breakfast. "The kids will really love it here," he said. "It's a pity you can't stay longer. We'd love your kids to meet ours." I followed them out onto the porch and called after them that we would meet up later.

I'd entertained confusions about the dual nature of wilder-

ness that Grimm's fairy tales had taught me and how I felt places
to be a perfect haven for recluses, but Mike and Laura were making me think again. He had no such confusion about the remote
area he had come to live in, and his affable nature was not what
one associates with being reclusive. But I was equally sure he
had found some sort of sanctuary in this derelict ghost town.

Breakfast was finished with gusto, and over coffee Audrey
and I discussed how different our hosts' personalities were from
others we had come across en route here. They were so welcoming and open; they'd even shared quite intimate details of their
lives as if they had known us forever. In comparison, the locals
we had met in the café at Chitina and the roadside teahouse were
frozen, withdrawn and uncommunicative. The impression they
had given was that they were intimidated and annoyed by our
presence. But up here in the mountains, we felt at home.

But comfortable feelings proved short-lived. Whatever plans
we'd had for the day were quickly aborted. We had planned a
short hike through the alder and spruce woods that backtrack
along the course of the McCarthy River. The gradient wasn't too
steep and we hoped to get high into the hills without too much
strain. Audrey had Cal papoosed on her back while Jack and I
led the way. But we didn't lead much further than a few hundred
yards. Mosquitoes were everywhere, and the nearer we got to
the river the more their numbers seemed to multiply. Audrey
had made a point of soaking all of us in the mosquito repellent
Deet; we had been warned not to go anywhere in Alaska without it. Everyone swore by it—it was the only thing that would
protect us. But obviously the mosquitoes of McCarthy were of a
different species, somehow immune to the power of Deet, and
within fifteen minutes we were scurrying back to our cabin for
refuge.

It was not an unpleasant confinement. The cabin had been
tenderly restored with white walls and polished wooden floors
that gleamed in the sunlight. A low shelf skirted the whole dining area displaying a collection of various-shaped bottles, blue,

brown, green, ruby and curious lavender-colored ones that had contained medicines and chemicals from the mine's infirmary. On the window ledge, a small set of child's building blocks spelled out its own intimate welcome. It was obvious that everything in the cabin had been repaired and salvaged from what had remained as the mine fell into disuse. Apart from his many other skills, Mike had a craftsman's hands, and his attention to detail suggested someone who enjoyed what he did and took his time doing it. My envy of the man deepened.

There was neither a TV nor a radio in our cabin. I suspected that as we were holed up in the hollow of a mountain, neither would have worked anyway. Instead, Mike and Laura kept a small library of books mainly about Alaska. The small living room held the real treasure: an old glass cabinet with glass shelves, sitting on a small table. It too was an item looted from the remains of the infirmary. I could imagine it filled with small shiny instruments for looking into throats, ears and noses. It would have housed small bottles of all sorts of evil-smelling things, tins of greasy ointments, a selection of thermometers, a stethoscope and various emergency odds and ends of a medical era long since past. But all these supposed things were not to be found. Instead, the cabinet and the table it sat on were filled with animal skulls, teeth and bones. I was just as fascinated with them.

Later, Mike and Laura called to invite us to supper with them. A friend had delivered some fresh salmon and there was more than enough for us all. They also brought over an old incense burner with a handful of anti-mosquito tablets to burn out on the porch. Mike noticed my interest in his collection and he named each of the skeletons for me—brown bear, black bear, wolverine, wolf, lynx, a collection of goose skulls too numerous to name. Outside, as we set up the burner, Mike pointed at several racks of antlers piled inside his chicken coop. "We're allowed to take four moose a year, though I've never shot that many in a season. Ain't got a big enough freezer, and people here generally share their surplus from a kill." He further confessed that his bone collection was only partly related to his hunting skills. The wolverine and the lynx had been given to him, and he was adamant that he would not have shot either of them even if they had been staring him in the eye. Having already got to know the man, I didn't need to ask why, but by way of explanation he remarked that they could be more trouble than they were worth, and anyway, there were some creatures you just left to themselves.

"A hunter as well as your other attributes, Mike!" I said.

"Well," he replied, "it saves a lot of money to hunt your own food, and the hides and the horn supplement your income."

I was curious about the horn, and asked him about it. He informed me that many people in Alaska like to keep a personal hunting knife or a fancy skinning knife, hunters especially, so Mike would collect moose antlers and sell them by the pound to the knife manufacturers. "You go into these places, pick out a piece of antler or bone, make a drawing of the knife you want and they make it for you. They can make them as fancy as you want. But you generally find that genuine hunters don't go in for fancy. There are some people who like to have them hanging from their belt." I remembered the men at Talkeetna. I had admired their bowie knives and had priced several when we were buying our gear in Fairbanks. Boy, was I now glad I hadn't given in to the temptation. As I was thinking this, Mike added that he didn't do much hunting now. Winter was the best time, but he was finding the winters more difficult to endure, and when he could he cleared out during the worst of the weather.

I was curious about the hunting economy and pursued Mike about it. Most people in the area hunted for food. It was a low-income area and its remoteness made the cost of living excessive. Hunting was not a pastime, it was essential to survival. Twenty-five percent of people lived below the poverty level, so harvesting natural resources was as much a matter of your personal economy as it was for the big timber and fish processors. Mike and Laura still picked berries in the lard pail, with a can full of rocks—one for the berries and the other to keep the bears away!

I pointed up at the huge mill building, then waved my hand toward the derelict outbuilding. "Is this what happens when we get too greedy?" I asked.

Mike's answer was ambiguous. "Sure, some people got very, very rich and still are from this operation, but the others who worked here, well, they had a job, a home, an income, they had a school and even a hospital. Whole families were born and raised here. The only thing that didn't work too well here was the church." Mike laughed. "Anybody who was walking down Silk Stocking Road after a hard day at the mine wasn't thinking of his soul."

By this stage it was blizzarding mosquitoes and we both dived inside the cabin. Mike's dislike of mosquitoes was matched only by Audrey's. He complained bitterly that for the past three years Kennicott had been relatively free of mosquitoes, but now it was like a biblical plague. "We came hoping to stay ahead of them," Audrey volunteered, "and now look what you've done. You've brought them with you!" Laura ribbed us, making a mock expression of desperation and anger on her face. All of us laughed together while looking out of the window at the clouds of mosquitoes swirling frantically in the warm afternoon air. It could have been a scene from a Hitchcock film, only this time the waiting predators were insects, not birds, our nervous laughter confirming how helplessly trapped we were. "Mosquitoes have got to be worse than the snow," confessed Mike. "At least you can work in the snow, but these things bring everything to a halt . . . except insatiable itching!"

Mike's distress made me ask what happened in the towns of McCarthy and Kennicott if someone was seriously hurt. "In a medical emergency people can be medevaced out by air very quickly," he explained, but when I asked about crime and policing both he and Laura laughed. "There isn't any crime. It's a very small community and nobody has much to steal, and even if they did, where are you going to go with it? As for the police, it's a known fact that they refuse absolutely to come here unless there has been a murder and the assailant is in custody, chained to a tree with a handwritten confession as evidence." Audrey and I expressed our disbelief, but Mike reemphasized the matter, assuring us that the police would not come unless there were bodies and someone was being held for the crime. "The moral dictates of the Church stop more than fifty miles across the mountains, and they don't seem in any hurry to come here."

"You've got it made here," I said. "You can do pretty much as you wish."

It was Mike and Laura's turn to laugh. "Except for the snow and the cold and the dark and storms that seal up this place so tight that nothing can get in or out. And then there's always this." Mike pointed out at the mosquito storm blowing up a gale outside our window.

Over the next five days I realized just how naïve my utopian dream was and how persistent the plague of mosquitoes was. Visions of Utopia always solve the big questions of existence, maybe because they ignore the incidentals. Had Alfred Hitchcock replaced his birds with these insects in his famous film, he would have been doing no injustice to his work. Our windows misted over with their buzzing blackness. But maybe the mosquitoes were an excuse. I was measuring myself against Mike McCarthy and found myself sorely wanting! Though we still managed some early-morning and late-night hikes, we were more or less under strict curfew during the daytime. I didn't mind much, though. I was enjoying my strolls through the deserted township. With Mike as a guide I discovered the remains of the hospital, the school, the grocery and the post office. There had been a library which I was sure must have supplied the older, mildew-stained editions in Mike's own. There was even a room for a visiting dentist, and a functioning operating theater for the hospital. But there was no bank and no jailhouse, for, as Mike explained, "company script" had bought everything and miscreants were run out of town with exacting swiftness. Those who remained from the past were buried in a desolate graveyard behind the dairy barn. But it had been company policy that whenever possible the dead were sent "outside" to relatives or stored in boxes over the winter until the ground was soft enough to bury them.

Maybe it was the emptiness, maybe it was the stillness and the silence fueled by my reading through Mike's library, but I felt a real sense of the thriving community that had lived here. It was as if you could see and hear the ghosts of babies crying in their mothers' arms as they waited to collect milk from the dairy; nurses damping laudanum over a man's nose and mouth as the doctor cranked some broken bones into place; a small floral bowl by the dentist's chair rattling as the still bloody stumps of tobacco-stained teeth were dropped into it; children's rhyming voices in the square of the schoolroom, now overgrown with alder saplings and forget-me-nots.

While picking through Mike's books I had come across a memoir by someone called Sissy Lommel Kluh, who had moved up to Alaska with her family from Idaho. Sissy wrote with child-like wonder about her first sight of the glacier, reflecting blues and grays and shimmering silver. How different it was now as I looked out on it. But it made me think of my own children and how Jack seemed happy and full of questions about what appeared to him as one huge adventure playground. So Sissy Lommel Kluh became my confederate, and I told some of her story to my own boy, hoping it might make his stay here more magical. For me its magic was real because Sissy was very near.

I chose to believe that our cabin was her own. I could smell the cinnamon sugar bread and game stew her mother cooked. I could see her looking at the pictures in the big catalogue book her mother kept. Sometimes her mother made copies of the clothes in the pictures. But mostly Sissy loved the paper dolls her mother made from the pages of the book. She had names for them all and used to pretend she was the teacher.

One day Sissy lost her favorite doll, the one that Grandma in

Idaho had sent her. Grandma had made it especially with her favorite colors. She called it Sissy too. She lost it in the snow and cried for days, complaining that Sissy would die from the cold. After a few weeks, as the snow was melting, someone found her doll and gave it to her. So she placed it in the oven of the range Mummy cooked on. It was warm there and Sissy would soon be better. Mummy sewed and repaired the doll and she was as good as new until one day she got very sick and worms came out of her mouth and Daddy had to bury her in the cemetery. Years after this incident, when Sissy watched the flat cars being loaded with heavy burlap gunny sacks full of ore for shipment, she thought of her doll.

Sometimes Sissy's mother helped in the hospital. Sissy remembered taking some soup to her one afternoon. As she was leaving they brought in a man whose clothes were soaked in blood and his head swathed in bloody bandages. He died after a few hours. Later her father explained that the cold was so intense that it turned icicles into steel spears. Unfortunately the poor man had been passing underneath when several sheared off. He had too many injuries and had lost so much blood that the hospital could do nothing for him. But the mine would look after him until the summer. She often thought of the bloody man when her father packed glacier ice around the carcasses of dall sheep, ptarmigan and rabbit to preserve them.

Sissy accompanied me on my morning walks, her memories blowing through the clapboard ruins. But now it was summer and half a century had passed. The people of the mine had gone; only fireweed, Johnny jump-ups, forget-me-nots, lady slippers and columbine populated the place. Sissy used to watch transfixed as the men rode the ore buckets to four thousand feet above the camp, believing that up there she would see God through the rays of the sun, like the picture in her catechism book. One day she rode on the bucket, innocently telling the men that she was going up to see God. They all smiled kindly, and one man stroked her hair, telling her there was no God up there, "just sweating, angry, thirsty, love-hungry men!" Sissy didn't really understand them at the time, but when she was older she understood every word . . . and she had only to go down Silk Stocking Road to find it!

*

CHAPTER ELEVEN

A MOOSE MOMENT

I n its heyday in the 1920s and the Depression, when the rest of America was on its knees, McCarthy was the kind of place where just about everything was available at the right price. Fresh oysters and Roquefort cheese could be had even in the dead of winter. One miner of the day complained that beer was served in whiskey glasses and diluted whiskey cost a dollar a shot, "and if we ever got any change from a dollar bill it was because they thought we were sober." But he wasn't the only inhabitant who complained. Margaret Harris, a teacher in the town, wrote, "If I keep my chin elevated at 120 degrees I find everything beautiful and inspiring. It is a place where every prospect pleases and only man is vile. There are 1,600 men employed in five big mines and everything that is outlawed on their private grounds thrives here in McCarthy to the shame of government. The big company insists that they must have a playground for their men! And 300 million dollars does not have to shout, it only needs to whisper." Demanding an increase in salary, she stated that the cost of living was higher than anywhere else in Alaska, and she continued her condemnation of the people of McCarthy with the words, "As to the character of the population, it is 90% bootleggers, prostitutes and gamblers, living as parasites on the Kennicott payroll. They toil not, neither do they spin."

Margaret Harris might well have had cause to complain about her modest income in comparison with another resident, Rose Silberg, a Jewish prostitute murdered by her lover. She was found to have $20,000 locked in a safe in her cabin, and rumor had it that "the Jewish Rosie" had a lot more stashed away in out-of-state properties and investments. Rose was only one of the inhabitants of "the Row," a string of fourteen cabins along McCarthy Creek. Blanche Smith was a black woman and the first non-native to ply her trade in the Row. That Tin Can Annie could reputedly play music on anything makes the mind boggle (there must have been many music enthusiasts among the miners). "Beef Trust," as her name might suggest, was a lady of well over three hundred pounds. The word was that anyone of whom she was enamored and who could withstand more than a few hours of her passion need never be afraid again of wrestling with a giant Kodiak bear! Sweet Marie, Blue Lips, the Snake Charmer and the Tramway Queen were some of the other occupants of the Row, and it was understood by everyone who spent more than half a day in the town that five dollars would open their door and everything was negotiable after that. In payroll days you had to get to the Row early, for the queue there was longer and noisier than the queue at the pay clerk's desk in Kennicott.

Kate Kennedy, a madam whose whorehouse wasn't far from the Row, also ensured her trade was brisk and her girls and her customers were kept well satisfied. Kate regularly shipped high heels, cosmetics and other "fancy ware" from the lower 48, the curious name Alaskans gave to the rest of the United States. But Kate was not a parasite, as Ms. Harris would have described her: she was in fact more civic-minded than her detractor and was a supporter of several charities; she also ensured that the families of those men who were unable to work due to illness or accident never went hungry and always had clothes on their back. Even in *Paradise Lost* there were angels.

McCarthy was a law unto itself. When other American towns and cities were collapsing under the strain of economic depression, McCarthy residents were throwing money around like confetti at a wedding. It was awash with alcohol and snubbed its nose at prohibition. Nine hundred gallons of water, fifty pounds of sugar, ten pounds of corn and the color from dried peaches could make a fine whiskey in a few days. And it wasn't only the bootleggers who were undermining the law—the whole town was behind it. Brewing was endemic, and everyone made money from it. Engineers on the trains blew a special code to declare that revenue agents were on board; even the telephones and telegraphs were monitored to ensure agents could not operate. Any arrested moonshiner was bailed out of jail by the mine-workers. "Old Slippery," brewed in the woods, "aged 3 days, bottled thin, tastes like sin," continued to be sold. Law enforcement was a minor irritation but "Old Slippery," as its name implies, had many ways of evading it.

But that was then. McCarthy today is the well-preserved ghost town I've already described, comprising a dozen or so dilapidated cafés spread along a couple of dirt-track roads. The remains of old mule-drawn wagons and a few vintage trucks lie rotting in the streets, and the Row and Kate Kennedy's whorehouse have long since been washed away by the constantly flooding McCarthy River. Yet something of the old town's spirit remains hanging in the air. McCarthy's bawdy libertinism has mellowed, but Old Slippery, bottled thin and tasting like sin, has finally come of age. The place is friendly and upbeat, still an end-of-the-road community where people mostly do just what they want. The fact that a few days after our arrival the bridge across the river washed away, stranding the whole community, bothered no one.

That evening we went for pizza with Mike and Laura. The girl serving us repeatedly answered "ain't got none, hasn't arrived yet" as we selected several items from the sparse menu. The place was the worst-constructed building I have ever sat in. It looked as if it was thrown together each summer from whatever spare piece of timber and debris had been left over from the winter. No one seemed bothered, though, and Mike laughed at my fears about our safety. He explained that there wasn't much point in building anything more permanent. There weren't enough people for such a venture, and with winds that could get up to 150 miles an hour there wasn't much point in putting up something that may not be there in six months' time. To illustrate his point he explained how the Copper River railway, which used to service the town, had a heavy ball and chain hanging out from the side of the engine; if the chain stuck straight out in the wind, no trains would leave the depot. Sometimes they had to take sledgehammers to the horizontally frozen chain to make the laws of gravity work again! He pointed to several beaten-up trucks parked near the café. They were in an unbelievable state of disrepair. Dust storms could strip the paintwork in a season, and any movable parts such as doors and bonnets were likely to last only another season before the winds yanked them off and tossed them a few blocks away (if you were lucky). So we made do. The homemade pizzas were delicious, and the homemade lemonade, laced with something that could have been Old Slippery, added to the ambience of the place.

Intending to go for a stroll down to the river, Audrey began oiling the boys with the famous Deet repellent. It was Mike and Laura's turn to laugh and issue a warning: the insect oil was apparently so strong that if you drove with it on the palms of your hands the shiny surface of the steering wheel would be corroded in the morning. What it took the wind to do in a season to your car's paintwork, Deet could apparently do overnight. It wasn't advisable for young skins, and most adults only sprayed the stuff on their clothes. "Covering up is better than rubbing up," Mike recommended as we walked to the river.

There was no sign of the bridge and the river was in full swell, sucking huge boulders out of position and rolling them like marbles into its roaring current. Jack was in his element, tossing stones and sticks into the water's edge. Mike was ever watchful. He explained that several people over the last few years had been lost or had almost died trying to cross. The waters were so cold you went numb in minutes; even if you could fight off the iciness, the silt in the water seeped into your clothing, multiplying your body weight until it was impossible to swim and the river just dragged you away, breaking your bones in the process.

What with the life-threatening river, the winds and the ice that cut you like a butcher's blade, it seemed as if the winters in these mountains were fit only for the animals that inhabited them. I was even more deeply drawn to the whores and the hard men who had survived here. If they broke all the rules of civilized society, fine, for beyond here you were outside civilization. The wilderness required you to make new rules and to survive with whatever comfort came your way.

Back at our cabin, when the evening sun had submerged everything in its clear, soft light, I thought about Mike and Laura, the only inhabitants, apart from ourselves, of this mining town. At this time of the day it all seemed perfect. They lived a subsistence lifestyle, surviving as best they could from what the wilderness offered them. They hadn't much in material terms, but the wilderness striking out for hundreds upon hundreds of miles around them was theirs. It was priceless, even awe-inspiring, and they could take possession of its riches whenever they wished. Their snow machine and their four-wheel motorcycle gave them access to an almost limitless landscape. Above where I was sitting on our porch, eagles circled and scanned the ground for prey. It was all too perfect. I was convinced there had to be something more to it than this. But what it was eluded me, and it was beginning to make me edgy and uncomfortable.

I thought of the jigsaw Audrey and I had been doing with the boys to occupy them while the Stygian infestation of mosquitoes imprisoned us. There was one piece missing, but still Jack was delighted. The missing piece was irrelevant to him, though it silently irritated me, and I didn't understand why. It was only a children's jigsaw after all. My own child could not have got any more joy out of completing it even had the lost piece been there. Maybe the greater jigsaw I was trying to piece together about this wild landscape and its power to enrich your spirit and up-lift your soul had a missing piece too, and I was more concerned with what wasn't there. But surely you can imagine the missing piece once you've put all the others in place? I remembered Freya Stark and her sense that whatever she encountered, whether it was an exquisite moment just before sunrise in the mountains, the sensuous wonder of the desert's silence, the noise and color of a souk or the innocent conversation of a shepherd's wife and child, each of these moments was sufficient recompense for her travels, for in each of them there was a small pearl of enrichment to be found. Maybe that's what it was all about—simply accept-ing the revelation and insight of each moment as it happens, and at the end of one's journey placing these moments together and taking from the collective experience what you choose.

Mike and Laura's contentment impressed me more than I'd first thought. They were happy with what they had, even though it was a constant struggle and in the depth of winter they had to leave the place for a few months. I looked again at the map of Alaska spread on my lap and laughed. It too looked like a piece in a jigsaw. Maybe that was it. Alaska was the missing piece, but not simply a piece in a child's jigsaw that you can simply imag-ine into place. Alaska was what it gave to you, like the simple quality of life Mike and Laura had. Suddenly I was thinking again of Jack London's words: "It was in the Klondike I found myself. There nobody talks, everybody thinks. You get your per-spective. I got mine." Yes, I thought, heading for sleep, Alaska sure makes you think—and very, very tired! At the cabin door before entering I took a last look. We would be leaving soon, and sadness was mixing into my weariness.

The day before we left, Mike called on us in the early morning. A moose and her cub were feeding in an alder thicket just a fifteen-minute hike from the cabin. Did we want to go and have a look? While we were preparing, Mike warned us about the dangers of viewing moose. They are extremely unpredictable animals, especially when with their young, and could charge through the bush faster than his quad motorcycle could race up Silk Stocking Road. He told me he would bring a sheathed gun so as not to frighten Jack but to scare off the animal in the event of a charge. I said nothing, but felt uneasy as we set off.

After what were easily fifteen minutes Mike's silent gestures, first to his mouth, then to our feet, then pointing out in front of him, informed us we were near. The willows and alders shot up like leafy fencing foils over our heads. In low, dramatic whispers I stressed to Jack that he must be very, very quiet; thankfully he was at an age where he listened and obeyed without question. Audrey emphasized the need for absolute silence. "The mummy moose is with her little baby, and if she sees us she might think we have come to steal it and she would be very angry with us and try to chase us away." Audrey's calm explanation instilled just the right note of caution. But as we waited for Mike to call us forward, I thought, "How could I protect us if a huge moose charged?" Mike's hidden gun gave me little comfort. In fact, it served only to make me more aware of my vulnerability.

Mike waved us forward, the slow-motion movement of his hands signaling us to be deadly quiet. In Alaska, the wilderness is always only a few yards from any door. When you are as consciously near to a creature as we were, the relationship between you and it changes. Your senses heighten with the same kind of nervous energy that is part of any wild creature's survival mechanism. In animals, it triggers aggression or flight; I could only feel fear crawling slowly up my spine.

Mike gestured us to stand and pointed to a clearing in the alders below us. At first I could see nothing. The comic conformation of the creature made it difficult to discern in the undergrowth. Then the cow lifted her head, and I saw the unmistakably floppy face and jaw. She turned her head toward us and stared enigmatically, her ears twitching with what I imagined was static electricity passing between us. Then she hoisted herself up, first onto her front legs and then her haunches, the flowing movement belying her ungainly shape. It was as if invisible strings were attached to her body, for she unfolded like a marionette being gently lifted to life by a well-experienced puppeteer. But her looming bulk displaced such fanciful associations. She stared at us imperiously. Then the calf stood, its spindly legs shaking as it nudged into the mother's underbelly. Dappled as they were by the sunlight and camouflaged among the bark browns and early greens, it would have been so easy to have walked right past this intimate tableau.

The cow chewed her cud loudly and nuzzled the infant nearer to her body. I had seen a few moose before, but never this close. Until now I had thought of it as a big brown beast of a creature and little more. But now I could see the dark, shiny coarseness of its mane and the tininess of its ears on that great big head. Its hide was a collage of browns; it was like looking at a big bowl of all the various kinds of nuts that festoon a Halloween or Christmas table, hazel, walnut and almond shades flowing down into the soil-dark underbelly where the infant nudged and pumped.

She turned and began to move. Her rear was the color of dry grass at the end of summer when the lightness has been bleached out of it and it turns the color of old pinewood. Then it was gone, and the small blur of quivering chestnut that was her calf was gone too.

Among indigenous peoples, there is a belief that animals give themselves to the hunter, and I liked to think that these moose had given themselves to us for that brief moment. While watching them I'd felt my whole demeanor change from dread caution to a profound sense of calm. I seemed to remember it from before, that time when I ventured out alone into the bush at Denali. There was a serene quiet when the land and everything in it seemed to open itself up to me, and I was flooded with the premonition of the wolf's death.

We returned to our cabin excited by our close encounter and dismayed at the need to pack. We had a last supper with our hosts and talked about moose and the mountains and our different plans for the future. As Mike was leaving I asked if he would have shot had it been necessary. His answer was simple and immediate: "It's never necessary if you obey the rules."

In that moment when our worlds had intermeshed, something had been shared between the moose family and my own. Such was the intensity of the shared moment that part of me felt that the fact she chose to fade before our very eyes into her own dark world was not because she had judged us and found us wanting, but quite the reverse. She had willingly revealed herself and her world to us. At least I chose to think so.

Mongrelized like some animal Frankenstein monster out of the body parts of an African zebu cow, an Asian camel and an American mule, the moose appears to be a Disney cartoon creature animated into life in this Alaskan wilderness where it must endure the most extreme hardships. But in that moment this mother and calf had become a dreamlike, numinous apparition that I felt humbled by and grateful to.

On our last morning I rose early and hiked up into the hills, alone, like the moose. Ptarmigan clucked and shuffled noisily in the alder as I passed. But that all-pervasive sense of being watched which always accompanied me when I took myself into the bush seemed to have left me, temporarily at least. This was the best time to be in the wild, along with late evening, when the midnight sun spreads a quilt of monolithic quiet so intense you are afraid to breathe in it. It's also a time when the lenses of your eyes seem to triple their focal capacity. Everything you see, you see with hypnotic amplification. I stood looking out past the groves of alder and willow, hazy with that pale green of early-summer growth; past the copper greens and the forests of spruce and fir as they spread up to the mountains, only a shade darker than the sky above them, the blushed snow line separating them. Then your eye is sucked into much smaller spaces where real color bristles like burning sparklers. Blue forget-me-nots squat close to the ground and the other lilac blues of lupin and Jacob's ladder start upward, purple monkshood and white mountain avens, and everywhere the tall fireweed burning to its tip. On that morning, as with others I spent there, eagles were wheeling so high they looked like specks in the colossal skyscape. They were not hunting at such a height, but they were watching all the same, like guardians watching over me.

I looked back at the red and white livery of the mammoth mill. It had climbed up the mountain like a caterpillar. Sixty years of Alaskan winters had not destroyed it, nor had the stormy winds blown away its ghosts. It looked like one of those fairy-tale monasteries you find in Syria or Greece, built high on a cliff. Time, age and memory had sanctified the mine too, as it clung to the wilderness serenely.

The last note in the diary of my stay in the St. Elias mountains is a quotation from an artist, Juan Varela Simó:

> The light, this is my remembrance of Alaska. In Alaska every moment is the right time to paint, and the constant light of summer, every hour of the day and night, softly bathing the landscape and revealing the tiniest details of every leaf and every piece of stone. Secondly, the silence; the forests were a true description of the word silence. Just like entering a European cathedral, one feels overwhelmed by the high commanding tree trunks, like the columns of a church . . . the light comes from the treetops as if sifted by the polychrome windows of the cathedral.
>
> And into the middle of all, the sound. The splash of an eagle catching a salmon in the creek, the thunder of another piece of glacier ending its way along the ice tongue. The sudden chat of a jay! Trying to catch the sense of wilderness, this is the task for a lifetime . . .

CHAPTER TWELVE

CHURCHERS, BIRCHERS
AND SEARCHERS

I had convinced myself that I had conquered my fear of flying in a small aircraft until the arrival of our Australian pilot to fly us back to Chitina. She was a diminutive lady, so small in fact that having instructed us how best to stow our baggage, she packed two cushions onto the pilot's seat to enable her more easily to work the steerage pedals and reach the instruments.

I was already sweating nervously as the small Piper Cherokee blasted down the runway, but the amount of crosswind buffeting we took before we leveled out must have pumped blood beads onto my forehead. Our pilot had spent some years flying supplies to outback farmers back home and had come to Alaska for a change of terrain, and to improve her flying skills. I wished she had stayed in her own outback, or at least improved her abilities with someone else on board. Flying into the wind forced the engine to scream with effort, and I was exerting huge efforts on my own part not to scream back at it. But for everyone else's sake, and my own ego, I acted cool and unperturbed. Fortunately I had a camera hanging round my neck, and when I felt panic rising I lifted it to my face and pointed it out through the cockpit glass as if I were taking a photo. It allowed me to shut my eyes on the whole affair and quietly deep-breathe myself out of terror. The pilot was oblivious to my ruse and wanted to facilitate my photography. She would bank the plane steeply and drop several hundred feet. Every time she effected this maneuver I was sure I would roll out from the cockpit and freefall to oblivion. I quickly decided to dispense with the camera trick. In any case, there was no film in the machine and sooner or later the Biggles lady would become wise to the fact that the camera's motor was not winding. From then on I had to endure the fright, with Audrey reassuringly patting me on the shoulder as if she were comforting a child.

From Chitina, our destination was Valdez, and thence by ferry to Whittier through Prince William Sound. In Whittier we would rejoin the main highway system and head for Anchorage, where I was going to leave Audrey and the kids. I intended to fly back to Fairbanks, then make my way onward to spend some time with a tribe of Athabascan Indians in the Arctic Circle. I had remembered Pat's advice to get to any ferry port at least twenty-four hours before we were due to sail and to ensure we had our place confirmed and booked. Because of this imperative there was no time for dallying or sightseeing. We had to backtrack along the road we had taken to reach Chitina, then hook a hairpin left and follow another secondary road which paralleled the oil pipeline into Valdez. We made only three stops, and each of them confirmed our original impression about this area. There was almost an air of repulsion about the place, a preternatural sense that not only were you a stranger here but you were not wanted. It seemed to ooze up out of the ground, and every scenic view out of the *Pequod* seemed to hide something malign, something threatening, something nasty in the air, palpable yet intangible. It actually revealed itself on a few occasions during our hurried drive to the coast.

Somewhere along the road we came upon an emporium displaying the most glorious collection of bric-a-brac, junk and the oddest curiosities imaginable. The ground outside was littered with the rusting chassis of ancient cars and flatbed trucks, what I now know from my experience with Dan were old wooden freight sleds, old tin bathtubs, parts of machinery of whose purpose I had no idea, cast-iron pots and pans, and caribou and moose antlers. Hides and the broken remains of stuffed animals festooned the porch. I couldn't wait to get inside. Audrey warned me we had neither the time nor the space for anything I might choose to buy. She knew that such places were second heaven to me. I was addicted to them. She was all too aware that once I enter them I disappear for ages only to emerge with some hideous, obsolescent piece, my eyes glassed over with rapture.

Inside, I poked through box after box of all kinds of everything. The place was piled to the roof with debris. Broken banjos and busted accordions littered the place; boots and snowshoes hung on the walls with hunting guns and pistols; trays of buttons and broken spectacles with full sets of dentures; the carcasses of old ham radio sets, wirelesses and old Victorian-style telephones. The list was endless and I was left to explore undisturbed. After fifteen minutes or so I began to wonder where the owner was. Just for the hell of it I wanted to know what some of the things were and what price they might be. I shouted several times, but no one responded. I rattled and banged around the place to call attention to myself, but no one appeared. By now Audrey was pumping the horn for me to hurry, and I was about to depart when a voice croaked behind me. I couldn't make out what the old man had said. His voice box had obviously been corroded by more than half a century of tobacco and cheap booze. He had not bothered to wash himself or his clothes for a similar period of time. I doubted he had even removed them in days.

His eyes were jaundiced and watery. He stood and looked at me as if he was sizing me up to be hung on the walls with the rest of his paraphernalia.

"Just browsing," I said, and moved away.

He stood and watched me for some minutes as I slowly edged myself toward the door. I didn't want him to get the impression that I was scared, so I dawdled and fingered a few things with my back to him. I heard him shuffling up behind me. I pretended not to notice, but then, smelling him close to me, deadly silent except for his throaty breathing, I turned slowly toward him. His face was close to mine.

"You want a hand?" he asked, grinning widely and revealing the rotten stumps of his yellow teeth.

Before I could answer his arm flashed up as if about to strike, and my eyes swung up to the hand raised above his head. Momentarily I was breathless with fear. He was holding a big jar, inside it a bluish-gray human hand floating in some clear liquid. I was too stunned to react, and pretending to be unfazed asked where in the hell he'd got it. He tilted his head sharply toward the jar, then, without moving it but darting his eyes across to me, he demanded, "What hand do you use?"

"My right," I answered automatically. Then, feigning a real macho persona, I smiled at him and added with a wink, "But both if I have to."

The grisly shopkeeper shook his head and tutted aloud. "Pity," he said, then walked off into the cluttered gloom without, I was sure, any intention of returning.

After a few moments I concluded that the old man had indeed crawled back into his shell. I returned to the *Pequod*, laughing to myself that the creepy old bastard was probably looking for another limb to make a matching pair.

As we drove off, Audrey asked me if I had seen anything interesting.

"Sure," I told her. "An old man tried to sell me a human hand in a glass jar."

She raised her eyebrows in wary disbelief.

"Honestly," I pleaded. "I told him I had two pretty good ones of my own and didn't need a spare."

Audrey turned away, sighing. "You're so full of it, Brian Keenan."

I shrugged my shoulders and said no more, and Audrey got up and went back to the kids to make sure they had something to drink.

"But I was right, wasn't I?" I asked.

"About what?"

"About me having good hands!"

Audrey yawned, and I put my good hands to use, driving as fast as the *Pequod* would travel.

I could only conclude that the hand in the jar had once belonged to an injured miner from Kennicott and that it had ended up in the old man's possession along with other things looted from the infirmary when that mine suddenly ceased to operate and the town cleared out overnight.

Our second incident was less dramatic but most unusual. We called at a gas station to fill up and purchase some bottles of water. The man who was sitting in the box-shaped office beside the pumps watched me approach but made no movement himself. I thought it only a little strange. On the back road we were on he would have little enough trade. I approached the window and had only asked "Can I . . ." when the attendant told me to go away. It wasn't a case of "Sorry, sir, we have no gas today." It was as plain as the surly look on the man's face that we were not welcome.

I was not pleased. The idea of being stuck in the arsehole of nowhere with a wife and two young children and a ferry to catch was not something I wanted to think about. But I could tell from the man's expression that sympathy was not one of his finer points; neither did I think he was open to any kind of persuasion. A rifle propped against the door dissuaded me from letting the perverse bugger know what I thought of him, his seedy gas station and his cowboy toy. I had not forgotten Mike's warning about the police and murder in these parts. I climbed back into the cab and roared off.

"What's the problem?" Audrey asked.

"God knows," I answered. "The crabby bastard has obviously been sucking too many lemons all day." It was pointless to try to explain as there was no explanation. I drove on.

Then there was the discovery of a burned-out encampment, replete with teepees and log shelters. It had been some kind of community spread over two and a half acres, but not one of the pyramid tents or the log cabins had burned down, though there were buildings that had been razed to the ground, or pretty close to it. No natural fire spreads through any structures that are sited so far apart. The fact that they remained blackened shells, the tents still hung with hide covers and the log buildings upright, were evidence to me that no natural catastrophe had occurred here. The fact that no one had returned to rebuild it puzzled me, but only for a moment. The whole place just stood there in a state of semi-dereliction, begging too many questions. I would have loved to explore, but time was more pressing than my curiosity. Anyway, the sight contributed to the growing feeling that there was something unreal and uncomfortable about the place.

We were now getting near the sea and our jump-off point in Valdez. The sky was filling up with gulls and my ornithological studies at Denali helped me to identify the occasional arctic tern halfway through their twenty-three-thousand-mile annual migration. As we neared the ocean more and more birds presented themselves. I recognized harlequin ducks and the occasional low-flying V of some species of goose or swan that reminded me of Pat and Mary's debate on the Chena. Trumpeter swan or Canada or snow goose—it made no difference to me. But they did serve to remind me that where I was heading I would be alone, without the comfort of my own birds-of-a-feather.

I was beginning again to sense the omnipotence of water in the landscape we were driving through. As the fish started to move upstream to spawn they triggered havoc in the skies, screaming birds intoxicated with the fish feast below them. Sea and river vegetation also exploded, larval life and plankton multiplied and matured at incredible speed, and fish life with it. The sockeye and king salmon were already shaking off their sea lice and making a move; sea otters, seals and sea lions would be waiting for them out in Prince William Sound. If they made it upstream, shore birds and birds of prey such as those circling above us would be waiting to take them. And every single fish that avoided these hazards had yet to face the bear and the wolf.

I knew now why Juan Varela Simó had worshipped the light the way he did. I did too, but I was still troubled by the sense of rejection I was feeling. I couldn't explain it. I just had this horrible feeling that the *Pequod* and her crew were being chased out of the place. Something unnatural existed out there which was somehow out of sync with the light and the urgency of life. I wanted to be away from it, and I stood hard on the pedal of the *Pequod*.

Valdez is located at the end of the Valdez Arm, a long, narrow, curving fjord that reaches in from Prince William Sound. It reputedly has the most beautiful natural setting of any town in Alaska, mountains curving round it on three sides as if they had just shot up out of the sea. It is affectionately known to some as "the Switzerland of Alaska."

In 1964 a huge earthquake seriously damaged the city of Anchorage over one hundred miles away. The result of this event in Valdez had been more drastic, for the quake was followed by a huge tidal wave that destroyed the town, claiming more than forty lives. It was subsequently rebuilt three miles from its former location. The job had obviously been done in a hurry without any thought for the magnificent scenery in which it sat, for the new Valdez was an unpretty mishmash of prefab homes, acres of trailer parks and the remnants of barracks-style housing erected by the oil-line contractors to house their workers and their families.

Apart from being the terminal port of the oil from Prudhoe Bay, eight hundred miles away on the Beaufort Sea in the extreme north of arctic Alaska, Valdez's other claim to fame is that in 1889 it was the site of the first hanging ever to take place in Alaska. A prospector named "Doc" Tanner, who murdered his two partners in a drunken brawl, was reported to have declared, with the noose already around his neck, "Gentlemen, you are hanging the best man with a six-shooter that ever came to Alaska." While driving through the small town in search of the terminal booking office I thought that the planners who designed new Valdez should have suffered the same fate as "Doc" Tanner, for their crime was just as heinous.

There were plenty of fishing boats in the harbor and their multicolored hulls and superstructures made a picturesque contrast to the backdrop of snow-capped mountains and steely-blue sky. The salmon had not quite started to run yet so, like the town itself, they bobbed idly on the water.

The evening before our ferry departed I called in to some of the bars. They had a smart seventies look about them and had the appearance of a downtown bar in Manhattan. Obviously they were a hangover from the days when Valdez was full of construction and oil executives. But now that the pipeline was complete and the oil flowed into waiting tankers at the rate of a thousand barrels a day, the executives with their need for familiar comforts rarely came here. The bars were mostly empty, a few customers glaring at the three or four TVs that blared out, each of them tuned to a different channel. The noise drove me back out. Kennicott and McCarthy had been empty too, but even though Valdez had a hundred times more people living in it, those ghost towns had more sense of life about them than this sterile terminal town.

The last bar I called in to was a bit outside the center of the town. It was more like a trucker's café than a bar, and it had a lot more customers. They were all men, and none of them had the appearance or spoke the language of the boardroom. It was easy to start up a conversation. I was an early tourist, and coming from Ireland made me something of a rare bird. When I explained to a few men drinking shots of whiskey with occasional beer chasers that I intended to travel through the state for three or four months, they were even more impressed. When I introduced a few more details about my travel plans I found myself amazed at just how little experience they had had of anywhere off the state highway system. Some of them had worked seasonally at Prudhoe Bay; some had been drivers on the five-hundred-mile "haul road" from Fairbanks to Deadhorse in the far north, the supply town to the oilfield at Prudhoe; but the oil industry was no longer the huge employer it had been. With the completion of the pipeline the demand for labor had been vastly reduced. The men were picking up work where they could, mostly in fish processing or timber felling, but such industries were vulnerable to seasonal conditions and a variable economy. There was little indigenous industry to keep any of them employed permanently from year to year. As one of them jokingly remarked, "This is the take-out state. Everything Alaska produces is shipped out in its raw state and processors down the line make the big bucks. Oil, gold, fish, copper, timber—it's all shipped out." The man wasn't angry, he was simply stating the obvious. When I asked him why he didn't move to the lower 48 for work, he answered in the same tone that life was different here and that there were plenty of compensations. In any case, he had no intention of working 365 days a year somewhere he neither liked nor could afford just to keep the IRS (Internal Revenue Service) in business. All of his friends were of the same opinion, and, I had to admit, so was I.

I told them I had just arrived in town after spending some time up in the mountains at Kennicott. They showed some surprise, but when I informed them that I was leaving my family in Anchorage to travel into the Arctic regions to live with the Athabascans for a week or so, they said I was both very wise and very foolish. It was wise to leave my family as my wife would most certainly have left me after a few days in an Indian village, and foolish because anyone who chose to go and live out in the Arctic wilderness was plainly insane and would probably not return. I laughed along with my newfound friends, hiding some unresolved anxieties about my intentions.

At least these men were open and friendly and there was no sign of any of the hostility I had felt en route to Valdez. I asked one of them who seemed genuinely interested about where I was traveling, and more importantly why, about the burned-out encampment and the unprovoked hostility from the gas station attendant. At first he was dismissive, then evasive; he said he had heard something about the camp and that it was probably a forest fire. But I explained that the teepees were erected well away from the tree line and, significantly, they were only partially destroyed. A forest fire would have razed everything to the ground. There had been several items left untouched as well, as if the occupants had left in a hurry and chosen not to return to collect them. He shrugged his shoulders and said, "It's bad country out there, and they just don't like strangers."

"Come on," I said, letting him know I wasn't satisfied, "they have to not like strangers for a reason."

One of the other drinkers cut across before his friend could answer. "Some people out there just don't need a reason. They have their own ways of doing things." He finished abruptly, and I could see he was serious and was already looking for a way of explaining what he meant.

The man I had first been talking to saved him the effort. "A lot of weird people go to live in settlements back off the road. Some of them are the families of homesteaders who might be too poor to be sociable. But there's a lot of others who come up from the States to make a new life for themselves. The trouble is, most of them have a strange set of beliefs. Have you heard of the expression 'the Churchers, the Birchers and the Searchers'?"

I shook my head.

"There are a lot of cults that arrive in Alaska to set themselves up away from the kind of attention they would get in their own home states. Some of them are religious groups who call themselves Christian but who hold pretty extreme opinions and don't want any involvement with the world of sinners like you and me. Then there are the Birchers. You ever heard of the John Birch Society?"

I had, and answered, "Some kind of extreme-right-wing white supremacist anticommunist organization that wants to create a new republic of America. Something like the lost tribe of Israel, the Nazi Party, the Ku Klux Klan and the Archangel Gabriel all rolled into one." My exaggeration silenced a few of the company. Obviously they weren't members of the secret society, but I got the feeling that I might just be standing ever so slightly on someone's holy cows.

But my friend continued. "Then of course you have the freaks and hippies and long-haired weirdos who just want to do their own thing their own way." He stopped to think for a moment. "If you think about it, that is the strangest bunch of believers to be let loose in the wilderness. Basically, they can't stand each other. The longer they have been out there the worse their fanaticism gets. There's real bad blood out there, and some very ugly and very nasty things have happened to some people. The police are never invited in to investigate, and like your friend in McCarthy told you, they don't much want to go anyway." He turned to me, as if something had just struck him. "You know, you were pretty damn lucky at that gas station. There was a time when a black family traveling in an RV like yourselves was refused service. The guy made a bit of a fuss about the matter and the whole thing got so out of hand that state troops had to be brought in. The man should have said nothing and driven on. He was lucky he and his family got away alive. There are more than a few stories of babies being burned in their beds and dead John Does turning up that no one out there knows anything about—or so they say."

Had I not driven through that place and seen and experienced the things I did, I would have put the story down to tall tales for the tourist. But I had no cause to disbelieve my companion and lots of circumstantial evidence to back up what he had told me. I took a long sip of my beer, then turned to my informant and remarked, "And you think I'm insane for going to live with the Arctic Indians!"

*

CHAPTER THIRTEEN

THE HAUL ROAD

E n route to the Arctic I stayed over in Fairbanks for a few days. I was beginning to think of the place as home. People lived here in this bush town not because it was the last city from here to Siberia but because they chose to. To me it was still a place of choice, whereas Anchorage was a city of settlement. Anchorage functioned in response to everything else and was there because of what happened beyond its precincts; Fairbanks had no precincts, but millions and millions of square acres of unimaginable emptiness, and people chose to live there because of that, regardless of the reasons that had brought them there.

But history in Fairbanks was yesterday, far too recent to bother about. Everyone here was more interested in today and getting ready for tomorrow, and that became my own preoccupation. A couple of days were spent rummaging through car-trunk sales. There seemed to be several of them every day in the town. At one of these I procured a small two-man tent for the same amount of dollars. "Why spend serious money on expensive equipment that I might use for only a few weeks?" I thought to myself. A few visits to the army surplus stores yielded ground cloths, mosquito netting and a lightweight rucksack; at the Meyers supermarket I purchased quantum supplies of insect repellent. I borrowed a sleeping bag, water boots, flashlights and batteries, and I quickly realized the necessity of having friends here. Pat's statement weeks ago that you needed lots of stuff in Alaska was proving true. I carefully ticked things off the list as I acquired them, wondering where I was going to keep it all after returning from my trip. I now had enough baggage for the four of us, and being the inveterate archivist of exotic but utterly useless ephemera that I am, my travels were already threatening to burden me beyond Audrey's endurance. I could hear her voice even now: "The reason, Brian, why you can't find anything in this RV is because it is so full of the rubbish you insist on collecting!" I could only agree with her, but little did she or I know what was to come.

Anyone learns within hours of arriving in Fairbanks that there are only two ways to head north: either take the "haul road" (the Dalton highway) some four hundred miles to the Prudhoe Bay or fly into any accessible destination in the bush. Driving the haul road in some great behemoth of a multiton truck appealed to me the way flying in a tiny two-seater aircraft, exposed to any and every elemental outrage, didn't. But it was impossible to hire any kind of vehicle to make the journey on the Dalton highway. No company, big or small, would permit any of their vehicles to drive on this road, for the term "highway" is an exaggeration of gigantic proportions. The surface of the road is guaranteed to strip the tires of any unsuitable vehicle in less than half an hour; if the razor-sharp shale and rock doesn't get you, then sudden hurricane winds, temperatures ten degrees below freezing or even an oncoming truck out of control because of any of the above will. The journey is more hazardous than anything the *Starship*

Enterprise ever saw. The haul road is not a digitally remastered adventure for the imagination, it's for real. Its death toll and the loss and destruction of million-dollar trucks and million-dollar cargoes confirm it. It is unquestionably the world's most extreme highway. One trucker described it as being like "riding on a tiger's back, only the tiger ain't got no muzzle on and he doesn't want you there." I thought such comments were good-natured bravado, but I was to learn otherwise. Superlatives in Alaska are not just colorful talk; they are colorfully expressive because sometimes it's the only way to accommodate the truth.

I took to hanging around the haulage depots and truckers' cafés and managed to contact a driver named "Tex" O'Neill who agreed to take me along with him so I could get a taste of the Arctic wilderness before disappearing into it. Tex's Irish ancestry was a big bonus in convincing him to accommodate me. I had been told that most truckers didn't like carrying passengers, especially strangers. Some drivers are even superstitious about them, regarding them as a "Jonah." The fact that I was researching a book on Alaska also intrigued Tex. He told me he liked books and enjoyed reading, as it made his work a lot easier. I wasn't quite sure how reading and driving a sixty-foot truck and fifty-ton trailer on the most hazardous road in the world were compatible, but I was yet to learn just how widely read Tex was.

He was approaching his "three score years without the extra ten," as he put it, had been driving the Dalton for almost thirty years and was still enjoying it. But Tex was not the clichéd caricature of a hard-living, hard-driving, hard-drinking, womanizing trucker that so many movies give us. He was a tall, stocky man. The white hair on his temples contrasted with his black baseball cap. He wore the mandatory checked shirt and blue denims with his feet encased in stout working men's boots, which he obviously took some pleasure in polishing. That feature alone marked him out from every other Alaskan male I had seen. He had an air of avuncular quiet about him that matched the slow grace of his movements as he walked or drank coffee. The man exuded deliberation and calmness, which the soft blue of his eyes seemed to emphasize.

He had moved from a small town in Texas with his parents and retinue of half a dozen brothers and sisters more than half a century ago, and though he had spent his early childhood and whole adult life in Alaska, he still spoke with a marked southern drawl. He had left school early, like some of his brothers and sisters, and begun working with his father on the railroad. Even then, with the rail system still under construction, he felt there was little future for the railways. They were never going to open up Alaska the way they had done in the lower 48. "Even if the tracks were made of vulcanized rubber you still couldn't bend them across this place," Tex observed. Like many Alaskans of his age Tex spent his early working life in a series of jobs and seasonal work for the federal government, or on heavy construction sites. He was construction foreman on the road he now drives on. "I figured if I built it, I should be able to drive on it better than some of the rig operators who were moving in to snatch up the big bucks the oil boom was paying." Tex wasn't being boastful or dismissive, he was simply stating a fact, and after almost thirty years of making the thousand-mile round trip from his home to Deadhorse and back, few would argue about his guru-like knowledge of this semimystical motorway. When Tex wasn't working he supplemented his income and larder by hunting and trapping. The two or three runs a week he made on the road still allowed him time to set traps a few miles from the road in the remotest bush.

We set off from Fairbanks at six p.m. with about sixty thousand pounds of cargo inside a heated fifty-three-foot trailer. There was everything in there from mail, food and drink to tools, spare parts and drums of transmission oil. It made for bulk, but not the kind of weight Tex preferred. "It's just fine for this time of year," he explained, "but in the winter, with cross gales and treacherous ice slicks, you need weight to hold you to the road like a

bluebottle on flypaper." When I asked him if he had any preference, he matter-of-factly explained that every load was different
and the weather conditions could change dramatically, especially in winter. "There are winds that blow through the Atigun
Pass that can load a slope with snow in under an hour, and the
next thing you know you're driving through a snowstorm like
blind Bartimeus, and then bang, you're nailed in your tracks by
an avalanche."

"What do you do?" I asked, fascinated and excited.

"Keep the motor running and the heat pumping, light up the
cab like it was the fourth of July, boil up some coffee or soup, get
out a book and hope some inexperienced young driver doesn't
come ploughing into you, panicked by the weather."

"Does it happen a lot?"

"Not much now," he conceded. "Truckers keep in constant
communication by CB radio, informing each other of hazards or
stalled rigs. But twenty-five years ago, when the boom was at its
height and when anyone with two hands and two feet and not
much between their ears was trying to strike it rich on the road,
the danger of rollover or collision was always present. Even in
the best of times the road is a creature you come to understand
but never really know. You can never let your guard down or become lackadaisical. The road has its own moods, and you come
to know and accept them. You can't fight against them or you'll
end up off the road, maybe for good. You've got to be patient."
Even as he said that, with his easy southern drawl and gentle
mannerisms, I knew Tex was the absolute epitome of patience.
"New drivers push too hard at the wrong times," he continued.
"They cut corners on their gear and food. They drive off the
shoulders or take the grades too slow or too fast. That impatience thing is what makes some guys drive into areas where the
wind has come up, or leave the safety of Coldfoot when they
should stay put. This road ain't Daytona. I may have a five-
hundred-horsepower Detroit engine under my hood but that
counts for diddly shit when the weather gets on a growler. The

wind at Atigun could whip a bobtail off the road as easy as if it was a spinning top."

"What's a bobtail?" I asked.

Tex smiled benignly at my ignorance. "A bobtail is this truck cab without its trailer. Most other people in the trucking business might call them simply semis."

I tried to make up for my tenderfoot innocence by cracking a joke: "I suppose you have to be semi-crazy to do this job!" I thought the subtlety of the remark might have been lost on him and was about to say something banal to cover up the silence between us when I noticed a slow smile spreading across Tex's face as he negotiated the traffic out of the city.

"Semi-crazy! You're downright committable!"

By 6:30 there was little traffic in Fairbanks, and soon we were clear of the city. But just beyond the small community of Fox, Tex pulled in to fill his plastic water container from a spring. He had been doing it every day since he'd started trapping in the hills. After another half an hour we pulled in at a gas station, which would be our last before reaching Coldfoot, a truck stop just under halfway to Deadhorse.

"How much will this beast take!" I queried.

"A hundred and fifty gallons should take you to Coldfoot, then we'll top up again for the rest of the trip."

Tex was obviously a familiar face, and soon he and his friends were huddled together, exchanging conversation. They were momentarily curious about the stranger in his cab, and once he'd explained who I was they were keen to say hello. One of them joked, "Best be careful with this man. He's not called Killer O'Neill for nothing you know, and it's not just because of the wildcats he snares up in the Brooks Range." Tex climbed into the cab and made some remark back, which was totally lost on me but had the group of men smiling and laughing.

"I told the guys what an Irish writer had said about being semi-crazy to do this job," Tex said. "They all said you were very perceptive and wanted a copy of your book so's they could read just how crazy I was!"

The inside of Tex's cab was as comfortable as it was confined. The driver's seat was state-of-the-art design in armchair comfort, and the double passenger seat was more like a living-room couch. For trucks that rarely carried passengers, this was luxury. But Tex was quick to let me know that the combined passenger and driver seat doubled up as a kind of daybed. The windows all had roller blinds and blackout curtains—a must during the summer months with round-the-clock daylight.

Driving the Dalton was as demanding psychologically as it was physically. The constant attention to road and weather conditions and the ever-changing calculations about breaking speeds up and down the steepest inclines in the world balanced against weight distribution, which would change as materials were unloaded en route, created a fatigue that could creep up on the inexperienced driver suddenly and with devastating results. As Tex put it, "Twenty minutes' shut-eye every two or three hours could save you and your cargo or someone else out there traveling in the other direction." In my own mind I could see why having a stranger "riding shotgun" was not encouraged. After all, I was sitting on his bed, in his private quarters. I recalled him explaining how the road had moods and you had to become familiar with them and fit in accordingly. What relationship he had established with the road, his responses to it and the demands of his body all had to be revised to accommodate me. For a moment I thought Tex would be more comfortable if I was back in the trailer, just another piece of cargo.

There was something reassuring about the man and his machine. It smelled of old leather, strong black coffee and Old Spice cologne. Behind us were the sleeping quarters, with an immaculately made-up bed, cooking facilities including a microwave oven and coffee percolator, a small color TV and sophisticated mini hi-fi equipment. A double bookshelf above the headboard complete with reading lamp disclosed an assortment of books and magazines. The former were American masterpieces by authors ranging from Nathaniel Hawthorne and Mark Twain to Saul Bellow and John Updike; the latter were principally about hunting and fishing.

"I thought you might have been a Hemingway man," I suggested.

"Yeah, I got some of that guy as well. Pull out that small compartment under the bed," he instructed.

I did as I was told and discovered another neatly kept library of books on tape. Histories, mysteries and westerns were there, as well as heavyweight stuff such as *The Rise and Fall of the Third Reich*, presidential biographies and some classics of English literature. Some years ago he had joined an audio books club and had become an enthusiastic customer.

When Tex was a younger man he used to pick up songbooks with sheet music and lyrics, attempt to learn them, then belt them out as he hurtled or crawled along the highway. I asked if he was a good singer, to which he replied, "Hell no, can't sing a note to save myself, but there ain't an audience out here to be bothered one way or another. So I just tell myself move over there Pavarotti, Elvis or whoever it is and let rip." He paused for a moment and I was about to laugh when he explained that not only was it good for the soul but it eased accumulating stress levels when you were fighting the elements to get to a safe resting place. Though their modes of transport were a million miles apart, Dan the dog musher and Tex the long-haul driver had a lot in common.

So engaged was I in the cockpit of our cab that I had missed the straight run up to the Elliot highway. We were now on the haul road proper and making our first uphill climb. Within seconds the speed of the huge tractor-trailer plunged and the engine began grumbling under the load. Flicking a switch on the console to the right of him, Tex locked the drive axles and differentials to increase traction. His progression down through eighteen forward gears syncopated the droning rhythm. It was like a move up the music scale by a colicky bass soloist. Do, re, mi, fa, so, la, ti, do—each note followed by hesitation then acceleration as the rig rumbled upward. Whatever throaty crescendo the big five-hundred-horsepower engine was giving off, Tex's finger moved through the gearbox with all the grace of a concert pianist until we crawled over the crest of the hill, at which point he immediately released the locked axles and the undercarriage began hissing and exploding like small-arms fire. As the truck gathered speed on our descent, Tex shifted the gears up through their sequence with the same dexterity as before. This time the engine hummed like a svelte baritone.

Sitting some ten feet off the road you get a false impression of distance in front of you. The endless monotony of the road soon corrects your perspective. From my crow's-nest position I watched giant cow parsley, wild rhubarb and goat's beard waving their white heads. They were far below me, but had I been standing beside them they would have been up to my shoulder. The tree line was becoming sparse, and those that remained were stunted, with girths not much bigger than garden bamboos. The further north we motored the more the land in front of us turned to shrub and grassland, patches of bent grass, sweetgrass and hair grass mixed with sedges and red fescues. The panorama spreading out around us was like a watercolor wash of silvery green impregnated with a purply-red cast. And when we rumbled across the Yukon River Bridge, 2,300 feet of wooden planking, I really felt we had somehow crossed the edge and were bulldozing into the beyond.

"What happens if you break down or get snowed up somewhere?" I asked as the weight of the emptiness pressed in on our truck.

Tex explained that no one is ever stranded for very long. "It may be a bitch of a road at the best of times but twenty or thirty trucks use it every day. With your CB, a backup generator and enough food for at least three days you can survive easily."

"But," I insisted, "what if all that fails?"

"Well, that's where patience comes in. You've got to have patience, and one of those." Tex jerked his thumb over his shoulder at the bed. "See that sleeping bag? I don't go anywhere in this truck without it. It cost me near on a thousand dollars, and worth every cent. It'll keep the cold away from you long enough for someone to come find you. And this makes sure," he added, pointing at a piece of equipment on the truck's elaborate dashboard, which looked more like the flight deck of an aircraft. "Most trucks are fitted with a recorder box that stores data about every stop, start, gearshift, brake and acceleration, like the black box in an aircraft. It's also tuned to a global positioning satellite that allows a computer in Fairbanks to display the exact location of any truck at any given time."

"A bit like Big Brother," I suggested.

"A bit," he replied. "But only a bit. There are still lots of blank spaces out there, and when real mean weather sets in it snows up the airwaves so bad it's like looking for a tiny needle in the proverbial haystack—only the haystack is half the size of the state of Texas!"

I looked out of the window, not wanting to admit to myself that I was becoming bored with the incomprehensible and unending vacuousness of the landscape. Perhaps that was why every fifty miles or so there were turnoffs with display maps and information about the particular area we were traveling through. When we crossed the line that marked the Arctic Circle there was a huge display unit with a brightly colored circumpolar map illustrating the imaginary demarcation line and loaded with information about extremes of seasonal change and how they affect the flora and fauna. It was interesting, but I thought that Tex, like Hemingway's "Old Man," was a more interesting, living testimony to the experience of this blasted wilderness.

The road line toward Coldfoot crossed several rivers and streams and bypassed small lakes. Tex informed me that if his load was light and he was making good time he stopped to fish here. "Best grayling fishing in Alaska," he commented. He always carried a big icebox to keep his catch fresh until he got home, although on more occasions than he could count he shared his fish with other truckers at Coldfoot. Being an old hand on the road, he often had the fish cooked for him at the truckers' restaurant, but only if he had enough left to sell on to hungry drivers.

He spoke in a matter-of-fact way about his experience over thirty years. That time had given him a mastery of his gigantic truck that allowed him to work through all the technical nuances as if they were simply second nature to him. Like some ancient sage he could feel the density or danger of the shoulder's soft edge through the throttle and the response of the steering wheel. He could navigate ground blizzards without anxiety and "feather" through his triple braking system as easy as sliding a full wineglass across a polished table—no mean feat when you have to brake down a twelve-in-one ice-encrusted incline while maintaining enough speed and forward thrust to pull you out of the dip and up the next hill. But such acquired skill is never enough in itself. Though his truck was modified for extreme conditions— diesel heated and circulated in the tank, alcohol in the pressurized air brakes, special filters and equally specialized heavy-duty tires the cost of which would put a family saloon on the road— he still carried a rigorously maintained spares box of tools, hoses, fuel lines and filters. "There ain't no repair shop out here. Once you hit the haul road, you're on your own!" It could take another nine hours to reach Coldfoot at this time of the year, and in the winter you could possibly double that. Understanding this kind of time schedule, I began to realize why preparation and patience were essential to travel in the Arctic wilderness.

I questioned Tex about how he dealt with the monotony I was already experiencing. Tex seemed startled by the request, as if he had not really thought about it before. Sometimes he counted the number of white winter hares that shot across his headlamp track, he said, comparing it with the number he counted on the return journey. On one outbound trip he stopped counting after 570. Alternatively he listened to a selection of his twelve-hour book tapes, wryly commenting that you could acquire a doctorate from the gravel under his wheels. But best of all he liked to sit and check his trap lines with the powerful spotlights mounted on his cab. However, he reminded me that whatever else he looked out at, he had always to be mindful of the condition of the road in front of him. Sometimes the surface was streaked with shiny stripes where inexperienced drivers had ridden too hard on the brakes, especially on steep descents. These froze over in an instant and created ultraslick patches that were a curse for other drivers. To emphasize this he pointed out several almost perfectly rectangular gaps in the tree and bush cover that clearly denoted where a previous rig had left the road. It only takes a momentary lack of attention or slight miscalculation to "spill your coffee"—the trucker term when your rig runs off the road.

I was beginning to feel incredibly tired and put it down to slow-motion fatigue and the now-comforting growl of the engine. I excused myself, saying I needed some shut-eye. Tex was unbothered. "Sure," he said. I leaned my head back and with my eyes already closed murmured to Tex to be careful not to "spill the coffee." He drawled laconically, "Don't worry, you'll be the first to feel the splash." I fell asleep, thinking about how the landscape wearies you by its sheer volume. You keep making unconscious calculations to attempt to put dimensions on it, but you can't. It's that old Sisyphean task that saps you into sleep.

Coldfoot lies about 180 miles from Fairbanks, but in a sixty-thousand-pound truck and trailer traveling on a road whose surface is little more than compacted rock and full of more holes than a chef's colander, it seems longer. Moreover, with gradients that make you believe you'll either never make it to the top or that the engine's going to explode before you reach the bottom, you begin to understand why it took us some seven hours to reach this curiously named truck stop. Originally named Slate

Creek, it inherited its pseudonym in 1898 after a group of miners got "cold feet" at the idea of having to spend winter in the place. They left and headed south, but the name stuck.

There wasn't much to the place—a visitors' center dispensing information for real hardy outback types, a services center selling gasoline, tires, oil and spares, a repair shop, a launderette with showers and a saloon cum restaurant built by the truckers themselves with the lumber they hauled, sometimes at their own expense. It proudly boasted the legend "the furthest north saloon in North America, open 24 hrs." A meal here was expensive in surroundings that can only be described as "basic with a table cloth"; anything else would be a travesty. As the hotel in Talkeetna, the walls were lined with framed photos of overturned trucks and pictures of drivers who had lost their lives, but not many. "It's usually the rookies that don't make it, and they haven't been driving the road long enough for anyone to get to know them real well," Tex explained. "But the coffee is good and the pie is the best you'll get anywhere." There obviously wasn't much point in dwelling on the dead, then. He was right about the food and drink, though, and the pie serving was appropriately large for men who drove gigantic vehicles.

Coldfoot didn't really have to provide much to make itself welcoming. The atmosphere everywhere in the tiny settlement was one of easy camaraderie, full of sly innuendo and banter. I expected it to be boisterous and noisy, full of truckers letting off steam and boozing too much, but that wasn't the case. The atmosphere was more akin to a church social, and when the drivers weren't bantering, conversations tended to be quiet and thoughtful. Tex unloaded some mail and supplies he had to deliver and went off to get some sleep in his cab before the long haul north. I remained behind to catch up on some reading and note-taking. Tex nodded, but suggested that if I changed my mind I could "slide over onto the shotgun seat until we were ready to roll." I didn't take him up on the offer and over the next few hours I scanned my map and read up on the forward journey.

Tex seemed hardly to have gone when I heard his southern accent softly declaring that it was time to "get the big girl back on the road and earn us a few more dollars." As we drove out of Coldfoot I thought that the truck stop offered little to encourage you to remain. I reckoned I would have had cold feet too at the thought of having to remain there all winter in freezing temperatures. But to Tex, the "fall" along this stretch of the road from Coldfoot up into the Brooks Range was incomparable to anywhere on earth. "The rivers are as good as McKay's apple and blueberry pie for canoeing and fishing," he said. "There are more species of bird life than there are leaves on the trees, and if you like to hunt there's more bear, moose, caribou, ducks and geese than you could fill the trailer with."

"What about in wintertime?" I asked.

Tex rolled his eyes as if the question didn't really need answering. "Most creatures out there find it hard to survive winter out on the Brooks. Most of them don't even attempt to. They hibernate, migrate or move as far south as they can get. For human beings to consider spending the winter out there they need to do two things before anything else: one, make sure they have arranged for someone to come and rescue them, because no one else will; and two, post your suicide note before you leave!" Tex's tone of voice, soft but deliberate and unhurried, struck me. He wasn't being smart or even trying to make an impression. Instantly I thought of Chris McCandless and his last words, desperately scribbled before he died.

Tex had spent his early years hunting and trapping in the wilderness a few hundred miles from here and had been driving through this particularly impressive stretch of remote landscape for thirty years, so I was a little embarrassed by my next question. I stared straight out of the window and asked, "Are you afraid of it out there?"

The answer was an excruciatingly long time coming, and I could hardly bear the silence. I turned around to crack a joke and relieve the atmosphere, but something stopped me. I felt that some throwaway remark would have been offensive, no matter how unintentional. Tex was unmoved, and I was sure he was not simply contemplating the question and framing a reply; I was convinced that he was scanning his memory and locating specific experiences for an answer rather than reasoning one out. Finally, he spoke.

"It's very, very frightening out here. Too many things are waiting to happen. You can't really prepare for the unexpected. If you could, nothing would really be unexpected. The unexpected wouldn't exist. You're a writer, you should know that!"

This time it was my turn to roll my eyes, secretly admitting to myself that at this moment I was a little frightened of the unexpected myself.

"I have been frightened a few times," he continued, "so frightened that I can still feel it at times. You know, like soldiers who still feel the pain of a sudden wound thirty or forty years after the event. Ghost bullets coming back at them." Then his mood lightened as if the memory had passed. "I would be less frightened if the Lord God Almighty came out of the forest with a flaming sword and threatened me with perdition itself! Jesus, you've got to be afraid out there or you won't last five minutes."

Whatever influence the apocalyptic imagery had on his concluding declaration, his opening statement about being very, very afraid spoke to me more. I felt it would be ignorant and indulgent to pursue the matter, so I sat back in the droning hum of the cab and let myself soak up the vista through my window.

The road in front of us stretched itself out to point zero on our horizon as if a giant plowshare had turned up this strip of rubble and rock, then poisoned it for eternity. Everywhere along its surface were the carcasses of blown tractor tires and the bony remains of caribou swarming with flies and being picked over by huge black ravens that looked at you as you passed without budging from their carrion supper. Their great black eyes glinted with dismissal and warning. Once we had passed them I imagined them craning their necks to watch us, their eyes blinking with amused contempt. Maybe it was the manner in which Tex had spoken to me but I believed that a cohort of ravens like ghastly black amoebas were trailing in the sky above us chorusing a dread warning. "I will show you something different from either your shadow in the morning striding to meet you, or your shadow at evening rising to meet you; I will show you fear in a handful of dust."

As well as tires and carrion, the road was forever throwing up shards of metal and broken glass, number plates and castaway cans of oil and Coca-Cola and other detritus that clung to the edge of the road. "Damn litter louts!" exclaimed Tex as he watched me making notes. "They should never have opened this road to day-trippers and sightseers!" It was the first time I had heard or seen him angry, but I could understand it. He was an initiate who knew from long experience that the Arctic demanded more respect.

The hours passed, the big diesel groaning and panting up and down impossible gradients like some giant creature giving birth. The view from my seat above the road left me breathless. I was suffocating in superlatives—my very own labor pains, trying to squeeze out the right words. But it was hopeless, or at least I was hopelessly inadequate at describing what I was seeing. Tex was aware of my fascination and smiled at my gasps of wonder and disbelief. "Who would want a better job, driving through pretty country like this twice a week!" I envied Tex his understatement and familiarity. He was so completely at ease with something that I found majestic yet frightening, inspiring and beatific yet repelling. The road was dragging us into this inexplicable landscape, and with every mile we descended more parts of myself were being ripped off me and cast along with the rest of the debris behind us—for the birds to peck at!

After some time I complained to Tex about just how difficult and physically exhausting it was to try to find the words to convey what I was witnessing. Tex spoke like a holy man from the hills, which in his own way he probably was. "I guess writing books is a bit like driving this road," he observed. "You have to have patience and only try to do what the conditions allow you to do. It took more millions of years than you or I could count to create this wilderness, so you can't expect to write it down after a few hours. Anyway, wilderness is a feeling you get more than what you see, and looking out of this tin can of mine gives you one set of pictures but altogether a different feeling. You have to be in it to experience it. I'd rather read a book about what I thought and felt about something rather than what I saw."

When he'd finished, I thought about how he had confessed his feelings of fear. I looked out again, comforted but still feeling defeated. There were undiscovered places out there where no human foot had trod. There was animal and bird life out there that had neither seen nor smelled humans. Out there was another world that perhaps required another language. One writer attempted to describe the country we were moving through as a "fine dream, unattainable as the end of a bright double rainbow," but I discarded the image as being too clouded with the soft focus of wish fulfillment. There was nothing soft and wistful out there. Even sitting inside the protective skin of our truck cab I could feel it seeping in under the door, like an odor of rejection and dismissal, as if the land itself was whispering a warning and a command. It seemed to be saying, "Venture no further, stranger. Get yourself gone from here."

But if I was experiencing difficulties trying to bring alive the world outside our snug cab, Tex had none. The road, for him, was a book of stories. Here's a hill where a rookie driver lost control of his truck and went screaming past O'Neill with his brakes burning red-hot flames and his tires billowing black smoke for nearly five miles. Further along the road, we passed more caribou skeletons. Tex declared that the creatures are "plumb dumb" and haven't learned any road sense in half a century. "One minute there's a bunch of them way off in the bush and the next the whole lot of them will run straight toward you. It's like a bowling alley sometimes, and it leaves a big mess and big problems if anyone is coming up close behind. The only thing you can do is keep flashing your lights and blowing your horn and hope they move away from you." Later he pointed out some of the spots where he laid his traps. Last year he had caught several dozen lynx and some wolverine. The hides fetched good money, although he admitted he had no need of it. He wouldn't know what to do with himself without trapping. Besides, it took some of the monotony out of the driving and gave him something to look forward to.

I thought I might revisit the subject of fear with him and asked if he had ever been worried about bears. A dead animal might attract some of the huge grizzlies the Brooks Range was famous for. I reminded him that both the wolverine and the lynx were predators with great spiritual power; to mistreat or dishonor them in any way could bring a lot of bad luck, or worse, to the offender. His answer was not dismissive, but it was hard to argue with. According to Tex, the fact that he caught so many of these creatures showed that he hadn't broken any rules; and as for the bears, "Well," he explained, "every bear out there needs something like a hundred square miles to sustain itself . . . I didn't go anywhere near that deep into the forest. In any case, I always carry a .395 Magnum to dispatch live animals in the trap. But it ain't much to deter a bear—unless I can ram it right down the back of its throat before pulling the trigger!" Tex had answered my question without telling me what I really wanted to know. His way of speaking wasn't evasion, it was as if he had learned long ago to live with this world and his place in it. I turned once more to my window, and stopped attempting detailed pencil sketches of the view beyond the glass.

For the next few hours we hauled deeper into the Brooks Range. We stopped only a few times, to stretch our legs or just to sleep off fatigue. A miniature excursion into the bush was impossible. The mosquitoes here had the tenacity of piranhas and were as big as bluebottles. I gave up after a few attempts. Even Tex, who was well used to them, remained in his cab during the periodic sleep stops. I tried again to make notes, but soon chose to read instead. I had brought with me several books and was currently immersed in Joe McGinnis's collection of essays about his travels in Alaska. I marked the part that described how natives in the villages rubbed motor oil into the noses and ears of their dogs to keep the mosquitoes from eating into their heads. I could not imagine which was worse, motor oil or mosquitoes.

Before long I was reading about his experience with some friends while hiking in the Brooks. A character called Ray Bane, their guide and wilderness expert, had been complaining bitterly about people's lack of understanding of wilderness, or worse still their confusing of wilderness with beauty and then trying to take possession of this beauty by building cabins in it. His argument was that when humans inhabit wilderness they destructively change the relationship of everything else in a delicately balanced ecosystem. His views were uncompromising: "Wilderness is to visit, not to live in. People see a lake and say, oh, what a beautiful place to build a cabin in. I say, what a beautiful place not to build a cabin." I could understand the reasoning behind the guide's zealously held beliefs. But the history of human civilization is marked by mankind's quest for beauty and his compulsive desire to possess it, to make it part of himself, and thus to reflect something about himself. Reading the book helped me sharpen my thinking. Perhaps Alaska, as the last frontier, is merely a metaphor, meaning last chance. Lose it and we lose part of ourselves.

When reflecting in the nineteenth century on the emergent America and its democratic idealism, Alexis de Tocqueville stated, "Democratic Nations will habitually prefer the useful to the beautiful and they will require that the beautiful be useful." Nearly 120 years later, in 1950, the Atomic Energy Commission scientist Edward Teller proposed to create a deepwater harbor near Point Hope, on the coast of the Chukchi Sea, with an atomic blast. The detonation would have been incalculably more powerful than those which destroyed Hiroshima and Nagasaki, but it would also have allowed the scientist and his team to test the effects of atomic fallout on a remote population. Undoubtedly Cold War politics had much to do with this insane project. It was de Tocqueville's views taken to extremes. Eventually sanity prevailed, but not before the Eskimo people, conservationists and other scientists and religious leaders with more moral and ethical backbone protested publicly.

There are still Alaskans and many other Americans, George W. Bush among them, who believe that hard work is a virtue in itself and that the world is but a blank canvas on which they are destined to write their superior legacy. Their thinking is old and tired, like an ancient circus elephant that has no memory of where it belongs nor of what manner of creature it is. They huddle in their air-conditioned offices and plan a new world order, while out there a unique life system more intricate, fragile and magnificent than the great basilicas of human civilization thrives and looks back at us with curious disdain.

I envied Ray Bane and his ability to communicate that quality of transcendence the wild world embodies in itself. Bane's writing was close to my own feelings about the wilderness experience as being like some kind of rite of passage. When we enter into this other world it's both an exorcism and a revelation. It exposes dread and enriches faith. When I encounter mountains like those that bind the landmass of Alaska together, I understand why primitive people believed that God was there.

Tex, beside me, could not have been aware of the nature of my reflections, or perhaps he was, for he remarked to me that even after thirty years the place never failed to amaze him, nor did he ever tire of it. Every time he considered doing some other job he was always lured back to the road. I was grateful for his words, for just before he had spoken them I was seriously beginning to question my sanity. Engaging in semimystical contemplations by way of a book, a sixty-foot-long haul truck and a dirt-track road into the Arctic Circle was a heady concoction indeed.

I decided to give up on the long drive across the coastal plain to Deadhorse, for it had not been recommended for its scenic beauty. I intended to sleep through most of it then catch a flight back to Fairbanks. From the Atigun Pass, the highest in Alaska at some 4,800 feet, the road descends and sweeps its way through approximately eighty miles of treeless, windblown oblivion. Whether I was too exhausted after the drive through the Brooks Range, or whether my mental energies had been used up trying to find words to convey the terrifying majesty of the place, I couldn't be sure. One thing I could be sure of was that this endless emptiness now inspired no response but a depressed yawn.

However Deadhorse got its name, it well suited it. It was a hideous boneyard of a place, a huge industrial garbage dump where the oil industry had dumped all manner of things—pipeline equipment, building materials, prefabricated homes and Nissen huts, the rusting remnants of vehicles and acre upon acre of huge spare parts and cast-off machinery. This was abandonment of incredible proportions. No one cared as few people lived here all year round and those who did were blind to it. Though thousands of people worked here on rotating shifts, there were no church buildings, schools, movie theaters or any of the trappings of bona fide human community. You would have to leave the human part of yourself behind in Anchorage, Fairbanks, Fort Worth or Dallas to come here.

I thought again of Tex's reference to perdition. No wonder he was unafraid of it. He had been in and out of it more times than he could count, and now he too was blind to the immense ugliness. For only a brief moment I considered that my reactions were conditioned by the majestic magic of the mountains, but I quickly erased that thought from my head.

"Jesus, Tex, how do you keep coming to this place week after week for years?" I asked.

"I just don't see it anymore," he replied, "and I never stay long enough to look at it."

I could completely understand. I have never before experienced such an instinctive need to be gone from anywhere. "The sooner I am out of here the better," I said, gaping in disgust and disbelief.

My good-byes to Tex were brief. He had a cargo to unload, and then he had to get himself "a shower, a shave, supper and some sleep," as he put it. I would have welcomed the same, but the option of an early flight was a godsend. Tex had been a great guide and a good companion. I had enjoyed riding shotgun and felt like I was deserting him when he dropped me off at the airfield.

"Good luck, Tex. We'll have a beer back in Fairbanks soon, I hope."

He hardly heard, answering only with his soft smile. Then, in a cacophony of hissing explosions and deep-throated hums, he rumbled off.

Before boarding my fifteen-seater aircraft, I wrote, "Leaving Deadhorse, Transit Camp of the Damned. 'Look on my work ye mighty and despair.' " In the men's washroom I scribbled on the cubicle door "Ozymandias was here and got the f*** out as fast as he could!"

*

CHAPTER FOURTEEN

INTO THE ARCTIC

There are different maps to describe a country. I had been poring over the geographical variety, but I was now at the edge of understanding another map for Alaska's Northland territory, a cultural map that recognized ownership long before the purchase of the region by the American government in 1876—the famous $7.2 million, equal to two cents an acre, which was originally howled down in Congress and the Senate and is now equally howled over with scavenging proprietorship. The land I was now intending to travel into was culturally richer than their commercial measure. This was the country of the Athabascans, the original native peoples of interior Alaska and western Canada. Ranged around it were the Inuit, the Yupik and, in the far southwest, the Aleuts.

Arctic Village, where I intended to stay, was located a few hundred miles inside the Arctic Circle and was one of the traditional villages of the Gwich'in people, part of the greater Athabascan nation. I would overnight in Fairbanks, shopping for last-minute supplies, then fly to the village, which was hosting a "Gathering" of all Athabascan peoples and their friends. Its purpose was to celebrate tribal and ethnic identity, and also, more pertinently, to discuss issues of human rights, the development interests of the oil industry, and the future of the Arctic refuge and the Porcupine caribou herd (named after the Porcupine River) with its annual migration of 150,000 beasts. There were also to be talks on nuclear energy, global warming and alternative energies. Between these heavyweight discussions, the program informed me, "We will celebrate by singing, praying, dancing and feasting, gift giving, laughing and visiting with our families and friends."

With my shopping completed and bags packed I headed in search of a plane and pilot to get me to the village. At the far end of Fairbanks airport, well away from the main terminal for the commercial carriers, there are several small businesses running air-taxi operations. Each of them has up to half a dozen small aircraft with a maximum carrying capacity of ten passengers. Every major airport has them, and without them there would be little point in going to Alaska. The state is the biggest in the USA with the smallest ratio of people per hundreds of square miles, making it one of the least inhabited landmasses on the globe. But there are very few places you can't get to. All you require are a map to show the pilot where you are going and where you want to be picked up, enough food to maintain you, a tent and sleeping gear, appropriate clothing and sufficient survival knowledge to make sure you make it to the predetermined pickup spot.

It all seemed routine enough, even mundane, as the assistant at the air-taxi offices weighed my bags, then asked me to get up onto the scales. Having noted these details, she checked my return date and informed me quite deliberately that I must ensure I was at the pickup point at least twenty-four hours before my plane was due; furthermore, I should not leave this point for any reason, bar life-threatening danger, until my plane touched down. The manner in which the young woman addressed these instructions to me left me just a little bit uneasy. She explained that weather reports, no matter how authoritative, can never be relied on 100 percent. Conditions were always subject to sudden, dramatic changes. "The pilot will always endeavor to get to you," she said, "but there might be a few hours' or a few days' delay if you are really unlucky. But the thing to do is always stay put, keep your eyes on the skies and listen for the motor." She must have noticed the anxiety immediately apparent on my face, for she smiled and her voice softened to a reassuring tone. "Don't worry, at this time of the year there are rarely any real emergency situations." She paused for a moment, then cheekily concluded, "As long as you don't allow yourself to become bear bait." I tried to return her joke, remarking that I was really more worried about mosquitoes. "Oh yes," she said, her voice becoming quite serious again, "there's going to be lots and lots of them where you're going!" I nodded knowingly. I knew all the advice about bears and how to avoid them, but mosquitoes were a problem that refused to go away, nor could they be avoided. I checked my bags again. Almost a quarter of their bulk was taken up with various repellent sprays, antiseptic creams, sunblocks, after-sun lotions, salt tablets and water purification drops. "At least I came prepared," I thought to myself, not believing a word of it.

There was only one other passenger traveling with me to Arctic Village, and the pilot asked us to spread our baggage over the remaining seats of the six-seater Piper Cessna aircraft. By now I knew the reason for this and was steeling myself against the buffeting we were about to endure. "We don't want to be blown halfway across Canada!" the pilot joked. I smiled nervously at the woman passenger, who informed me that she had come from Canada. She asked if I was going to the Gathering and I confirmed that I was, adding that I had traveled from Ireland. She told me that I was a long way from home and that I would find the Arctic very different. "But," she continued, "the Gwich'in are very friendly and hospitable, just like the Irish, so you might not find it so very different."

We were about to carry on with our conversation when the pilot called out to us. He would need a copilot up front with him. My companion signaled with her eyes for me to go up to join him. I was too confused by the request to question it.

As I buckled myself into the copilot's seat the pilot handed me a set of headphones. "If it's blowing hard this is the only way we'll hear each other speak," he said. I blurted out that I was not a pilot and that I knew as much about flying airplanes as earthworms did about the solar system. He was unmoved by my obvious anxiety and explained that it was better for weight distribution to have two people behind the engine and that he needed someone up front just in case anything went wrong. At this point I was about to eject myself from the cockpit before he had even started the engine. "It's just a safety precaution," he added, "in case I become unable to operate the bird." He looked at me and smiled. I was not reassured. He proceeded to give me a five-minute breakdown on the manual operations, and which instruments were what and how I should read them. "I'll go over it quickly again once we're airborne," he concluded. His words were going into my ears but were being engulfed amid paroxysms of panic. "I've just got to check on a few things in the office, then we'll be off."

As he climbed out of the cockpit I turned to the woman behind and asked, "Is this guy serious?" Like a good mother hen she quietly confirmed that it was merely a safety precaution and that it was a ten-million-to-one chance that he should become so ill that he would have to instruct me how to fly and land. "These pilots are very rigorously tested and have regular six-monthly health checks. If there was even the remotest chance that he was unfit he would be grounded until he was cleared again." I was relieved to hear this and thought the pilot should have told me instead. In any case, I would make a hopeless copilot. If anything were to go wrong and I was required to fly, everyone on board might just as well sprout wings then and there. I didn't confide this to my companion.

After a few minutes the pilot returned. He told us we would have to make one stop to unload supplies, then buckled himself in and checked his instruments, ticking off items on a checklist fastened to his knee; underneath this was a map with our proposed flight path. The pilot pointed to the village of Fort Yukon, where he said we would have to deliver some food supplies. Weather reports from the village were warning of extreme winds, so we would fly at about fifteen thousand feet, under the cloud cover. If the winds are bad it is imperative to remain under the clouds or you can get blown so far off course that it can take hours to get a visual bearing and regain your flight path.

Our pilot was from somewhere in upstate New York and had only been flying in Alaska for a few weeks. He was still unfamiliar with the landscape and needed to keep referring to his map. I didn't know which was more reassuring, the presence of the map or the young pilot's honesty about his inexperience. The lady passenger behind us said that she had made this trip lots of times, and if we kept visual contact with land she would ensure we didn't get too lost. And with that the pilot fired up the twin engines, blasted down the runway and leapt into the Alaskan airstream. Copilot Keenan clamped down on his back teeth and silently speculated about just what not getting "too lost" really meant.

Once we'd cleared Fairbanks the panorama was one of monotonous green and brown—the northern tundra; straight ahead loomed the steely-gray clouds, looking like big Brillo pads. I remembered how Jack had described the tundra during our flight to McCarthy as looking like broccoli. I was making a mental note of the broccoli/Brillo pad imagery when the pilot's squeaky voice came through the headphones. "It's going to get bumpy as we approach the Brooks Range. Winds blowing over the Arctic North Slope can be lethal to light aircraft. We might have to detour up a few valleys to avoid the storm that's brewing up behind those clouds." That was all I needed to know from this rookie pilot! I nodded my head nervously, already redefining the meaning of "too lost" as the first blasts of wind banged into the aircraft and flung us like a stone from a slingshot up into the first wisps of cloud. "Sooner than expected," crackled the pilot. I nodded again, while swearing to myself.

As the clouds began to establish an icy mist on our windows, I was wondering just when we were going to make a move to get out of them. The pilot was obviously telepathic, for with a descending leftward maneuver he cleared the cloud. For the next thirty minutes I watched him as he studied the ground below us, then the map a few feet from his face. I didn't know how lost we were, but it was obvious that our pilot was opening up new routes to Fort Yukon and our final destination, Arctic Village.

"It's okay, I can see a way in," the pilot declared. "We'll be a bit late but we'll make it before night." Those last two words illustrated just how new the pilot was to Alaska. "What night?" I thought to myself. Night doesn't happen here at this time of the year. And then it struck me, like one of those gusts of wind that kept hammering us down lower and lower to the ground: what would he have done had we been flying through a winter night? He could not have cross-referenced from the ground and his flight map, and that lady behind could not have prevented us from becoming "too lost."

Before I myself became too lost in my morbid speculations, I heard the words "Fort Yukon" followed by "ten minutes to landing, maybe another fifteen minutes to unload, then we're off again." I nodded and began removing the headphones, then felt a tap on my shoulder. I turned to face the woman, who had moved up a few seats to say to me, "You could get all of Ireland into the Yukon plains maybe a couple of times!"

I looked out on the landscape below. Nothing but an infinity of emptiness, the green serge of tundra as inviting as a bowl of cold, greasy soup, the murky Yukon River sullenly making its way toward the horizon before us and out of the horizon behind us.

At 2,300 miles in length, this was one of the world's great

rivers. It ranked with the Amazon and the Ganges. It had spawned fabulous stories, not least from my mentor Jack London. It had been here before men could write, before they even arrived here. But to me it looked utterly desolate, coming out of nowhere and going into nowhere.

The runway at Fort Yukon was nothing more than a narrow gravel strip. I could still see nothing but emptiness. Where was the habitation? Who were the food supplies for? Then, out of nowhere, trails of dust blew up and maybe eight to ten quad motorcycles and their riders descended on us. The young men helped unload the several boxes of foodstuffs, distributed them among the motorbikes, and then they were off again, waving and smiling. It was obvious they had come for more than the few boxes; they wanted to see if any new faces had arrived, and to pick up on any news. That we were two strangers going to the Gathering met with their approval, and they wished us well.

Forty minutes later we touched down at Arctic Village, the most northerly native settlement in the Arctic. I clambered back from my copilot's seat and heaved my luggage onto the stony runway. I had come prepared for the wilderness, but as the Cessna turned and disappeared I began to feel a lot less prepared than I thought I was. I had been literally dropped here, a bewildered outsider. I stood in the middle of nowhere feeling the burden of my strangeness. I had decided to come here, but my desire to participate in the Gathering had had to be approved in advance. Courtesy was paramount with these people, and my stay with the Gwich'in was to teach me anew about the meaning of courtesy and respect, and about how the life of a community built around such values can function.

An old broken-down Mazda half truck took me and my companion from the airfield to the village. I sat bundled up on the back among baggage, food cartons and sealed cardboard boxes with family names etched on them in heavy felt-tip. I was just another piece of cargo being carried into the wilderness, into the heartland of the Gwich'in. I tried to get my bearings. Here I was

somewhere between 145° longitude and 68° latitude, south of
the Brooks Range and east of the Romanzof mountains. I was at
a midpoint several hundred miles east of the haul road and west
of the demarcation line that separates Arctic Canada and Arctic
Alaska. But all that did was place me in the middle of nowhere
with immense wilderness surrounding me.

After some fifteen minutes, the truck trundled into the village.
It was little more than a few dozen wood cabins in various states
of disrepair scattered across several acres of bush. My Indian
driver and his son put me down near the center of the encampment. I unloaded my rucksack and then some of the tribe helped
unload the supplies. A few of them smiled, and some even welcomed me to their village. But there was much to be done in
preparation for the Gathering and I was left to my own devices.

I had wanted to experience the wilderness, and here I was
right in the heart of it. Yet I had never felt so alien in any place
before. Everywhere, the tiny settlement busied itself while I stood
undecided as to what to do until something inside me commanded me to move, and I walked off in search of a site to pitch
my "boot sale" tent. Having found somewhere close to a large
pile of caribou antlers, I flung my pack to the ground and began
unpacking.

Inside a separate bag I kept my notebook, camera and reading
material, and if Ray Bane's contention was correct, then I should
be writing down this first experience of the Arctic wilderness. I
looked at the books I had brought with me. Young Chris McCandless had brought books, but he had also brought imaginary
friends, the same people I had admired and befriended in my
youth—authors, poets and philosophers. I wrote in my notebook, "Why did Chris not listen when his friends told him to go
home? Had Chris coveted more than he could carry psychologically and spiritually? He was only another young man who was
overwhelmed by romantic imagining and who had the courage
to pursue it. But the wilderness had closed in on him. Like
Icarus, his fall to earth must have been the most excruciatingly

terrifying ordeal. In his last moments, did the wilderness receive him benignly? Did Chris refuse to go because he was already home? Home is where you return to, not where you go to." I re-read the last desperate query in my notebook. I knew immediately I didn't want to know the answer. I looked at the village people hovering about the building I'd learned was the community hall. A few yards from it tables were being set out, and beside them a rough field kitchen was in operation. It was time to set up my own accommodation. For better or for worse, this was my home too.

With my tent erected, I had declared my intention to stay. As I knocked in the last peg a voice behind me called, "Come, you must eat with us." I turned to see a family wave to me as they passed on their way to the "potluck," an informal gathering and sharing of food and gifts, and my heart lifted. Sometimes we really don't know what we are hungry for! Far out in this isolated wasteland, company was more important to me than the grumbling of my stomach.

At the communal supper of moose, caribou meat, chicken, beans, corn and salad, I realized I was not the only stranger here. Some photographers on assignment for *National Geographic* introduced themselves, along with some people from an Australian TV crew who wanted to get some shots of the Gathering before moving on to film the caribou migration. I immediately took advantage of the situation and stated that I would love to tag along, if that was okay with them. "No problems, mate. As long as you can get yourself back it's okay with us. You might even be able to give us a line or two for the commentary."

That evening as I was walking through the spread-out hamlet I found it hard to work up the energy or the enthusiasm for the days ahead. The village comprised approximately two dozen chipboard cabins strung out over a few acres. They were shoddy and unkempt and had little in the way of personal adornment. They looked more like shelters than homes. I kept reminding myself that I was living in a subsistence community and that was precisely what these structures were. A shelter in which one lived might translate in the developed world as home, but to these people "home" was the shared community in which they lived. The home place was primarily the experience of tribal belonging. The honor and shared experience of being a tribal member was deep-rooted, psychologically and spiritually, with these people. And this belief in shared belonging was not exclusive to the tribe: it expanded itself out into the natural world. Every rock, plant, animal, fish and bird was a respected part of this shared home world. A part of me was deeply attracted to this philosophy. It was not romantic attraction, it had more to do with the inherent sense of well-being and harmony that such a life experience must impart.

But these people were on the very edge of survival. The issues were enormous. How could fewer than one hundred people in the Arctic outback take on the global problems of human rights, climate change and alternative energy proposals, and at the same time take on an oil industry which would create wars to have its way. It was a David and Goliath standoff, and the Gwich'in had hardly a shot in their sling. Even if they were morally, ethically, culturally and spiritually superior to the enemy, that enemy could still crush them out of existence under the weight of its powerful lobby.

But who were these people who stood like the Spartans at the pass of Thermopylae attempting to hold back the voracious forces of global capitalism?

I resolved that as I was here among the Gwich'in I should let them speak for themselves.

*

CHAPTER FIFTEEN

GOING NATIVE

My second day in the Arctic Village began after a most uncomfortable night. It had rained heavily and my two-dollar tent was obviously not made for Arctic extremes. Although I had picked the highest piece of ground it was still tundra, and tundra is synonymous with boggy conditions. The unevenness of the earth and the accumulating wetness underneath me had made my first night in the wilderness seem more like a night on the ocean. By morning my ground cloth had several puddles in it and my sleeping bag felt as if it had just been washed in from the Beaufort Sea. I was tired and soaked to the skin, and I resolved to get myself dried out before another downpour washed me out completely.

My efforts to dry my equipment revealed me as a complete greenhorn. First I dried out my tent and left the entrance flaps wide open to allow the bright morning sun to complete the task. Then I draped my saturated sleeping bag on the pile of caribou horns behind me, and changed out of my wet clothes and hung them over the dwarf alder and birch bushes around me. For the first time I noticed a few other tents pitched some thirty or forty yards from mine on much lower ground. They were well-made tents suited to the harsh conditions, but I was puzzled as to why their occupants had chosen to shun the area of high ground I was camped on.

There was no possibility of my coping with another rough night in my tent. The walls at each side had collapsed under the force of the rain. In any case, I had not sufficient metal pins to stretch the canvas enough to hold the walls taut and ensure the water kept running off instead of through the material. The waterproofing had long since vanished from the material. The tent was really a children's backyard plaything, and here was Grizzly Adams Keenan trying to fend off the forces of the Arctic in it. As I struggled with my predicament I noticed some people pointing at my ridiculous efforts and making whispered remarks. I thought they might be laughing at my antics, but their faces were not laughing. They displayed something between sympathy and scorn.

I remembered from my walk around the village having seen some unwanted heavy blue plastic sheeting. I assumed that the prefabricated plywood boards the cabins were constructed from had been delivered encased in this material. I asked myself why the villagers had not used it as additional waterproofing for their homes. Whatever the reason, I was happy they had no use for it. I certainly did. Also, not far from the community hall I had discovered the shell of what had been an old caravan, *circa* 1950. The interior fittings had been gutted and the rear wall was hanging from it, but the inside was full of polystyrene sheeting. I suspected it was left over from some building project and had been lying exposed for some considerable time. My needs were great and urgent. I was living among a community that existed by and upheld the tradition of subsistence, so I was convinced they would not mind me taking one of the sheets.

Within less than an hour the breeze and increasing heat had

dried my tent and I spread the plastic sheeting across it. I cut the polystyrene to the exact length and height of the tent walls and inserted the strips alongside the inner walls. The rest of the sheet I cut into a large triangle which I propped against the rear section of the tent. With the plastic outer skin weighted down with boulders, I stood back and admired my inventive handiwork. I was sure I had redeemed myself, in some measure, in the eyes of my hosts. But the response to my efforts by some of the villagers was not what I was expecting. Some simply stared at my improvised home, others whispered in their native tongue, but no one showed any signs of admiration or approval. Anyway, it was finished and it would be dry for the remainder of my stay, so I walked off and headed for the long community hall where the events of the Gathering were to take place.

The building was approximately sixty-five feet by thirty and was constructed of pine logs, which I suppose had been barged in on the Yukon River. Inside, the walls were lined with villagers of all ages. Their rounded features and skin color were an ethnic mixture of pale Siberian Asian and the deep copper and aquiline features of the Plains Indian. But there were other faces that were neither Asian nor Indian. I looked briefly at the leaflet outlining the day's speakers. Names such as Shawn Martinez, Mabeleen Christian, Princess Peter-Raboff and Kimberly Carlo hinted at bloodlines other than Athabascan. Even the young chief, Evon Peter, sported looks that were more Mediterranean than native Alaskan, and his name sounded as if it might have Scandinavian roots.

I casually read over my program again, learning first that "Arctic Village" was the white man's name for the place; at all times the village was addressed by its Athabascan name, Vashraii K'oo. The principal part of the day was to be taken up by ceremonial dances and song. After songs of prayer and dedication there were to be four welcome dances celebrating the caribou and the raven, and at the end of these there would be an invitation dance in which everyone was expected to join to become one with the herd. The dances were given Athabascan names which I could neither spell nor repeat. Above the names of the dances, printed in bold capital letters, was the warning, NO CAMERA OR VIDEO OR RECORDING PERMITTED. Obviously the Gwich'in were determined that their culture was not to become a sideshow.

The ceremonies were not to begin until everyone had arrived, so I walked outside to mingle. A group of young men were chatting and smoking near me, gathered around a large ghettoblaster radio, listening to rock music. They were dressed in baseball caps, T-shirts and training shoes and they spoke American English with the slow, pronounced rhythm of the native. But their talk was not about tribal politics, it was about cars and TV programs, or about some action movie and who had what video to exchange. Young girls moved in and out of the group with ease, and with equal ease roared about the village on quad motorbikes.

Gradually their numbers depleted, and I was sure the festivities were about to begin. A few of the Australian crew arrived and introduced me to some members of a TV crew from Washington, French photographers and some people from Germany and Sweden. If this kept up, the international contingent would out-number the natives. Most of the non-natives were media people, so I remained outside while they went in. All of them intended to observe the prohibition about cameras, but I didn't want to be seen as another TV person.

After a few minutes I made my way inside. Not much had changed. The tribe were ranged out around the room on plastic chairs or benches. It could have been a village get-together anywhere. The village elders were already making speeches of welcome, reiterating tribal values and giving personal testimony of their own life in the village. The speeches were innocent, and perhaps because of this were irresistibly moving.

One particular white man stood out among the rest. He was obviously not a media person. Underneath a shabby corduroy

coat with leather elbow patches he wore a purple shirt and clerical collar. He had a heavy beard and wore his hair in a long
ponytail. Across his chest he wore several rows of beads. His
well-worn jeans were filthy and tucked into a pair of plain cowboy boots. Beside him stood the local Indian priest, who had
been speaking as I entered. There was nothing remotely clerical
about him. He had at one time been a Gwich'in chief and was
still the local fiddle player, but somewhere along the line he had
become ordained as an Episcopal priest. The man standing beside him, I learned later, was the Bishop of Alaska.

Soon the speechmaking came to an end. Evon Peter, the hand-
some young chief, walked to the head of the room and informed
us all that the dances were about to begin. He reminded us that
these dances were sacred to his people and asked those who had
come to "share" with the Gwich'in to respect this and refrain
from taking photos. "Any of these dances you take home with
you should be taken home in your heart, that you may remember us and the caribou from which we first came. There will be
other dances during the time we spend together that you may
photograph."

Even as he was explaining, dozens of tribespeople poured in
through the doors. Men and women young and old, children
and babies, all wearing yellow and brown buckskins decorated
with the most elaborate beadwork. It was as if someone had
opened a great chest full of giant butterflies. The atmosphere in
the room instantly changed from one of serious intent to intense
excitement as the dancers milled about in disarray. Then, from
somewhere, a slow, rhythmic drumbeat began, and from different parts of the room a native chant started up. I was sure this
was not by any prearranged design; the villagers were engaging
in spontaneous prayer and worship. It was, I suppose, the equivalent of Christian plainsong, but this was much older and more
primitive. It didn't move me in the heart as a plainsong did. It
unleashed itself and resonated into the pit of my stomach.

Soon, again with unorganized spontaneity, the dancers began

to wheel about the center of the hall. There was no distinction between sexes or ages. The dancers became one amorphous whole,
wheeling slowly and releasing instinctive guttural chants. The
hypnotic drumbeat tightened about them as native rattles set up
an eerie free-form accompaniment. As the circle of bodies moved,
their shuffling feet added a kind of *basso profundo* note to the
primitive tempo. The chanting cries of the dancers had the effect
of coming not from individual voices but from the lumbering
ruck of the caribou people. As the movement became more intense it produced an unnerving trancelike effect in the onlookers.
Everyone stood in awed silence as the four ritual dances moved
one into the other. Then, as if the pull of the circle was too much
to resist, the people sitting and watching outside the circle were
pulled into it. They became one with the dancers, one with the
animal energy of the herd.

I, too, felt the irresistible pull of it. Only the fact that this was
a sacred moment and that I was an outsider kept me from falling
into the vortex. The colored beadwork set against the soft browns
and yellows of the hide costumes was like looking down a kalei-
doscope. The unending patterns, endlessly fascinating, had their
own kind of power. It was like some wondrous flower raptur-
ously opening.

This was the invitational dance, and I noticed some white faces
swaying in the ring. This was the secret of the caribou dance. The
sacred dances had honored the spirit of the beast and it had
come among us. It invited us into its world, where we were all
one with it and its wilderness spirit. This is what bound the
Gwich'in to one another and to the land they inhabited. This is
the power they drew on to exist in this extreme place and to
overcome against all the odds. This is what made them the few
Spartan warriors holding back the incredible might of the forces
of Persia. Every instinct in me felt the lure of what was happening in front of me. I wanted to be part of its incredible embrace,
but something held me back; something told me I wasn't ready
to lose myself. My rational self was putting a harness on my de-

sire. I didn't know it yet, but my power creature was yet to come to me in another place where only the invisible eyes of the outback would witness it.

In a rising crescendo, with drum, rattle and chant rending the air, the dancing stopped and within seconds the dancers fell away to the margins of the room. Like a scattering of caribou, they were gone. Chief Evon stood on a chair and announced that all had now been welcomed, and he invited us to share in the discussions that we might better understand the Gwich'in and their plight. But first we should all take time to reflect and make our hearts ready to listen. Then, as an afterthought, he added that we would have to wait until the dancers had changed and put away their costumes. "It takes many hours and much hard work to make a costume," he stated, "and because these dances are important to us we must treat the costumes with respect."

During the break, many of the villagers and some of the visitors went to partake of the communal lunch. I joined them. I asked one of the camera-crew men, whom I had noticed in the final dance, about the roast chicken and the loaves of sliced bread. It did not seem to be native fare to me. The chicken, he explained, was probably ptarmigan or wild duck, and as for the bread, he explained that home-baked bread had been introduced by Russian traders and missionaries, but as money was scarce in these villages, very little was spent on shipping in flour. He had been working sporadically in Alaska for many years and had witnessed many changes. "Modernism is making it harder and harder to maintain the old subsistence ways of living. The kids here are like kids anywhere, they are conditioned by TV, and as they get older they expect the things they see on TV. When they're older, some of them go off to university or to learn 'white men's work.' They train as electricians, pipeline workers and house builders. They earn regular money and spend it on consumer goods. TVs, radios and videos are always a preference. Years ago, I remember working on a program about the Eskimo people up near Bettles. At one of the village's councils the debate was about which TV programs should be allowed and which should be banned, and it went on for some hours. It was a real toss-up between *Starsky and Hutch, Charlie's Angels, The Six Million Dollar Man, Sesame Street* and some Disney cartoons. The village elder, who had never been to school and who only had some pretty basic English, argued as hotly as the younger people. It was like an addiction. They were all high on TV, even if the older people could not have understood the language and speech rhythms of *Starsky and Hutch!*"

I could imagine the impact of TV and radio after centuries enduring the wilderness. I could imagine sitting in one of the village homes through the long, bleak months of winter when everything was dark and nothing moved but the snow and the wind blowing it. To flick a switch and instantaneously have your landscape transformed by a million hallucinatory images must have been electrifying. I looked at the piles of food and the growing number of people. I could imagine that many of the rituals about killing and preparing such food had also been abandoned. It is important to understand that for these people subsistence is more than a matter of "living off the land" and specific protein intake. As a way of life it is close to the concept of "kosher" in Jewish belief or halal observances in Muslim society. The Alaskan natives had traditional ways of treating their fish and meat and preparing it for consumption or utilizing it for clothing and tools. As in other orthodox societies, there are certain rules and rituals that must be followed to ensure a future harvest and the well-being of the people. I asked my new acquaintance about this. He felt that many of the native villages were attempting to recover their lost traditions and restore them in a modern way. Their way of life was under tremendous pressure. The young people especially were torn between two worlds. I remembered the compelling rhythms of the dance and how so many of the young people had given themselves to it with genuine abandon. The spirit world of the caribou dance was certainly one they entered into with unembarrassed ease.

Perhaps the ancient stories were no longer told long into the night. But even if modernism had thrown up the opportunity for these young people to live better than at any time in their history, and even if some of them were lost to their tribal traditions, they had still come back here from Anchorage, Fairbanks, Washington, Seattle and Canada. The pantheon of the new gods of Paramount Pictures and HBO, Schwarzenegger, Stallone and the retinue of action heroes, had not yet erased the power of the old gods. The raven, the bear and the caribou still moved across this land, and their spirits could still be felt.

I asked my new friend about the lavishly colored beadwork on the caribou costumes. He smiled. "That's the Russian concept of fair exchange. Before the Americans bought Alaska from Russia they used to exchange colored beads for animal pelts, which they sold to the Chinese. Apparently, Russian merchants were fascinated by exotic goods from China. I suppose the natives were equally fascinated by the rich color of the beads. Native people here, like many other indigenous peoples elsewhere, believed that the hole in a stone or shell, for example, was a portal for a spirit power. The blue and red beads were highly valued, and the Russian hunters and traders got very rich." I didn't know if he believed in the "power" of the beads, but I did, and I understood immediately why the costumes were special and the beadwork so meticulous. The circling caribou dance was another portal, like the concentric holes in the beads. I was glad I had resisted the desire to join in. I felt sure I would have been swept away.

I finished eating, told my friend I might catch up with him later, and moved off among the villagers. I engaged in easy conversation with a few of the camera crews and was assured that I could travel with them after the Gathering, but I found the villagers hard work. They were polite and answered any question I asked them, but they hardly got beyond formalities. There was a reticence about them I could not fathom. At first I put it down to shyness or embarrassment, on both our parts, but the more it happened the more convinced I became that it was more than just social awkwardness. I was the only stranger here who was not part of a TV team, so I was different. But that was hardly sufficient reason to justify the kind of distance I was being held at. Maybe another day, once my face had become more familiar, I assured myself as I walked away from the crowd toward the communal building.

Evon Peter, the young chief, was introducing the old chief, or what some people called the traditional chief, to a few outsiders. Moses Sam was in his nineties and hardly able to walk. Evon and a few other younger villagers led him about the hall with an obvious display of tenderness and ceremony. Moses Sam seemed happy to meet the strangers, though I was certain he could neither hear much nor understand what they were saying. Because of my own anxiety about how I was being received, I inched away from the presentation and stood near the door.

"Well, are you enjoying our gathering so far?" a woman's voice behind me asked.

I turned round to see the Canadian woman who had flown from Fairbanks with me. I smiled in deep gratitude. She was the only native person who had approached me so far. I told her how much I had enjoyed the dancing and explained how after being washed out during the night it had greatly lifted my spirits. "An Irishman shouldn't be afraid of a little rain," she joked. "Have you met many of the Gwich'in yet?" I admitted that I hadn't, and tried to sidestep my feeling of displacement by asking her if this was her original home village. She said that her mother had come from another village on the Yukon flats but she had moved to Canada with her mother and father, who was a Canadian Athabascan, when she was young. She made several trips home to visit her cousins and other relatives. "The family is important to us," she stated, then questioned me about my own family and why I was in Vashraii K'oo. I told her I was researching a book. Curiously, she then proclaimed how kind it was of me to come to the Gathering. "We need lots of friends now," she said.

At those words, and because of the way she had befriended me, I made my confession that I was finding it difficult to get into conversation with the villagers. She looked at me puzzled. I told her how the villagers had walked past my camp whispering and pointing, and how one of them had just stood and looked, then walked away in silence.

"Oh," she said, "you are the man who has hung his sleeping bag on the caribou antlers, the one with the tent covered in a big blue plastic sheet?"

"Yes," I said sheepishly.

Suddenly she started laughing and gave me a big hug as if I really was some innocent abroad. Then she called over Chief Evon and explained who I was, identifying me by my tent. He too laughed loudly, and shook my hand. "I wondered who it was," he said. "Some of the villagers had been asking."

Now I really was perplexed.

My traveling companion, whom I now knew as Margaret, continued, "I thought, Evon, that you should explain. It would be kinder, and would help our friend feel less lonely."

The chief smiled softly again. I must have been twice his age and his solicitation and sympathy were increasing my discomfort. But as he spoke the penny dropped very fast.

"We are the people of the Porcupine caribou herd," he began. "They are, to us, like brothers, like our own family. As a mark of respect for what they give to us we keep the antlers of these creatures we have hunted. Where you are camped is like what you would call a graveyard. It is a sacred place."

My look of absolute horror struck him immediately.

"Please," he reassured me, "you are welcome here, and we are honored that you have chosen to come to be with us. My people did not know how to say this to you for fear of offending. But I know now that you have come a great distance and would not be expected to know many things." I attempted to make a profound apology, but the chief only squeezed my shoulder. "It is not a great problem that you should worry about." He turned to Margaret. "I should tell him also about the plastic covering on his tent?" Both of them laughed again. "The plastic sheet you have on your tent is a product of the oil industry. Our village has decided against using this material as a protest, and also because it is unnatural. It will remain uselessly cluttering up our tribal lands for many generations. You may have seen the trailer full of polystyrene that has been abandoned near here; this too is manufactured, a by-product of oil, so we forbid its use in the village."

Had I had one wish at that moment, it would have been that I should immediately turn into a mosquito and fly off into oblivion. I hesitated for a moment, then confessed that I had used some of it to prop up the side of my tent.

"I know!" said Evon, and laughed again. "Your tent and sleeping bag are not made for this kind of country, and in any case there was no dishonor in what you did. I can arrange for you to stay with one of the families, or perhaps you would like to stay with my family?"

I was too embarrassed and too overcome by my own bungling stupidity to accept. "No," I replied, thanking him. "I will move to somewhere else immediately."

"There is no need, my friend," he said. "We are happy for you to stay here if you wish. Anyway, I think maybe the caribou wanted you to stay close to them also. I must go now. We must start again soon. We will talk again, I hope." Then he got up and left, and I watched him speak with some others at the far end of the room from where we had been sitting. They smiled and nodded as he undoubtedly filled them in on my predicament.

For want of something better to do or say I took some of the insect spray from my pocket and said, "Well, Margaret, I've brought the wrong kind of tent and an inadequate sleeping bag, I've slept on holy ground and broken all the tribal taboos, and this spray is about as useless against mosquitoes as I am feeling right now."

Margaret was determined I should not feel sorry for myself. "It's not really holy," she said. "That is a Christian way of thinking. But it reminds us who we are and our debt to the caribou, and I think your camping there with your plastic sheet and wet sleeping bag hanging from the antlers may have helped us focus our mind a little more."

"So I'm not totally useless then!" I exclaimed.

"Oh no. No one is ever totally useless." Then she fumbled in her bag and pulled out some incense sticks. "You left the flaps of your tent open. By now it will be full of mosquitoes, so you should burn these for a while to clear them out. I think you will learn much from the Gwich'in before you go."

✴

CHAPTER SIXTEEN

ATHABASCAN ANGLICANS

Margaret was right. My tent was humming like a hornets' nest when I returned. Had I tried to enter it without first fumigating it with her incense sticks, it would have been like jumping into a tank of piranhas. They could have piled me in with the rest of the caribou remains beside my tent.

I looked out beyond the camp while the incense purged the mosquitoes. These Arctic wetlands remain wet because of permafrost, but with temperatures rising every summer the whole area becomes a breeding ground for black storms of mosquito against which there is no defense. But it is also the home of the caribou, the arctic fox and squirrel. The rivers and lakes teem with sockeye salmon. Far out beyond the village bear, musk ox, hawk, ptarmigan, penguin and short-eared owl scavenge the vast tundra desert. It is famously known as the "Arctic Serengeti."

Alaska's landscape is in flux, and one needs to know the confusing language of the geologist to begin to grasp a timescale that defies imagination. Billions of years are not conceivable to our brief tenancy. Geological time is a gigantic jigsaw and earth science has given a name to defining ages we cannot fathom; we learn them by rote in an attempt to comprehend this incomprehensible corner of the earth. "Well," I thought to myself, "if that took aeons and aeons of evolution and the Athabascans had only been here maybe a few centuries before the white man, then I'm entitled to my few cultural blunders after only a few days." And with that closing thought I made my way back to the village to listen to the elders and the tribespeople as they addressed their concerns about cultural extinction, just as catastrophic as any of the ice ages.

When I arrived it seemed that everyone was in the community hall. At a long table at the head of the room the various speakers were seated. Chief Evon stood and thanked everyone for attending. In his right hand he held a short staff, richly decorated and hung with what I took to be eagle's feathers. This instrument was called a "Tok," and as each speaker arose it was handed over. This act invested the speaker with a kind of authority that declared to everyone that they alone, at that precise moment, had the sole right to speak.

Chief Evon stressed that this gathering was crucial to the Gwich'in. Over the last few years they had found themselves pushed to the very edge of extinction, so he particularly asked the "strangers among us" to listen with an open heart and carry the message of the Gwich'in predicament with them into the wider world. "What is happening here is of global significance," he said, "and whatever happens in the future will have significance for the greater human family." I thought Chief Evon was pitching his points very high, but I had only been here a few days; the Gwich'in had existed here for generations, acting as guardians and stewards of this tundra desert.

The argument was simple, even though the Arctic National Wildlife Refuge (ANWR) means different things to different people. Environmentalists see the nineteen-million-acre tract of land in northeastern Alaska as a last remnant of wilderness, home to wolves, wolverines, polar bears and snowy owls; oil developers see it as the last best hope for the US; and the Gwich'in people see it as a critical birthing area for caribou, and for a way of life. The 150,000 caribou of the Porcupine herd annually migrate hundreds of miles to the ANWR coastal plain to give birth to their young. The seven thousand Gwich'in people living in fifteen villages along interior Alaska and Canada have always been dependent on the Porcupine herd. The caribou are not just another animal to the Gwich'in, they are part of them.

I had heard and read much about these differing views since my arrival in Alaska. I naturally had my own views and sympathies, but now that I was experiencing the subsistence lifestyle first hand these views were being put to the test. And as each of the speakers took the Tok, I was made more aware of the poignancy of their plight. This was not only a question of cultural survival, it was also about spiritual solidarity between the Gwich'in and the creatures they shared this land with. Furthermore, it was about respect for life itself, and the sacredness of life. As I listened, I realized that these people were talking from the heart about profoundly moral and spiritual matters.

"We have always lived like this," said one woman speaker. "We even have a creation story that we came from the caribou." According to her, the Gwich'in and the animals struck a deal. "The Gwich'in would retain a piece of the caribou heart, and the caribou would retain a piece of the Gwich'in heart. So whatever happens to the caribou happens to us, and whatever happens to us happens to them," she continued. "We're dependent on the caribou. If drilling were allowed, slowly we would lose aspects of our culture. We just want to pass along what we have to our future generations. I want to pass it on to my daughter, and she's only two now." She then explained how "the caribou comprises as much as eighty percent of the Gwich'in diet. The hides are used for clothing, the bones for tools. Caribou have inspired traditional songs and dances. In summer, it's everything—spiritually,

culturally and socially. Like when we're on the mountain hunting. It is very important for us to have the time up there with the
caribou. During the hunt young boys are taught the role of being
the provider, hunting and giving thanks. Young women are taught
to prepare the meal, and other traditional roles. We live in modern communities, we have TVs, we have telephones, but we need
that time of year with the caribou." I thought about what she had
said, particularly about "giving thanks" and "needing that time
of year with the caribou." This was the language of worship and
religion, and it was moving in its openness.

Sarah James, another Gwich'in villager and the organiza-
tional matriarch of the Gathering, agreed about the importance
of the hunt in teaching the youth "survival, patience, sharing.
The hunt also provides specific sustenance to the Gwich'in. We
need fresh meat for our bodies; we survive year to year by hunting or fishing. If that's missing from our bodies, we feel different.
Going out [hunting] like that, that's the way I grew up." I found
myself wholly caught up in what Sarah was saying. I had, for a
second as I entered the hall, stood looking at the speakers' table
thinking that the scene could have passed for a marvelous ethnic
tableau of the Last Supper; now, here was Sarah James speaking
at a very simple and unsymbolic level about everything the Last
Supper is meant to represent. Without eating the blood and flesh
of the caribou, she felt herself somehow different and incom-
plete, no longer at one with the landscape she had been brought
up in.

After Sarah, the Bishop of Alaska, a man I had earlier thought
was some eccentric backwoodsman, took the Tok. It was still only
the purple vest and clerical collar that distinguished him from a
fur trapper or a logger. By way of introducing him, one of the
Gwich'in elders explained that most Gwich'in are Episcopalian.
"We have been Episcopals in Alaska for about a hundred years,"
he said. "My great-grandfather was one of the first Episcopal
ministers; he helped translate the Bible into our language. We
say the Lord's Prayer in our language, sing traditional hymns in

our language." A female elder saw no real distinction between traditional Gwich'in spirituality and Christianity. "It's the same," she said. "We have our traditional songs, our traditional dances."

When the bishop folded his arms across his ample girth, cradling both the Tok and his own golden staff of high office, his presence seemed both incongruous and iconoclastic, and appropriate to these subsistence people. Before he began to speak he asked everyone to join him in prayer. Almost at once every head bowed in silence. After the short prayer, he spoke. "Gwich'in Christianity has become a way to affirm and embrace the old ways and the new ways, without losing cultural cohesiveness and solidarity. The Gwich'in are brilliant theologians. Gwich'in traditional culture is much closer to Christianity and Jesus than the dominating culture—Christian or not.

"The Church has found ANWR a compelling issue since the General Convention in 1991. This is because it involves both an environmental concern, in the protection of ANWR, and a human rights concern, in the protection of the Gwich'in way of life. The Gwich'in people, arguably the most Anglican group of people in the world, are directly dependent upon the Porcupine caribou herd for survival. A threat to the herd is a threat to the Gwich'in cultural and physical survival. The house of Bishops of the Episcopal Church last spring renewed its support of permanent protection of ANWR in spiritual solidarity with the Gwich'in people."

The bishop then elaborated on this spiritual solidarity, explaining how the culture of the Gwich'in is almost a manifestation in the twenty-first century of the early Christian Church of the first and second centuries. I wasn't too sure where he was going with this comparison, but when he hinted that modern man had much to learn emotionally and spiritually, even in the sense of being more fully human, from the Gwich'in people, I understood him. In his closing remarks, he described the Arctic Refuge as a kind of paradise. For a place so far north it features a huge diversity of species—over 160 birds, 36 land mammals, 36 fish and nine marine mammals according to the US Fish and Wildlife Service, which manages it. "The Arctic Refuge is among the most complete, pristine and undisturbed ecosystems on earth. In fact, it may be among the most complete, pristine and undisturbed truly Christian communities on earth!"

As I listened to the man talking from behind the Indian Tok and the golden eagle staff of office, I sensed that he meant what he was saying but was convinced that the oil industry cared as little for the censure of the Church as it did about a few thousand Indians stretched across Arctic Alaska and Canada.

At this point, another speaker from one of the environmental lobbies stood up. He was obviously committed and well informed, but his delivery did not have the same sense of composure and profoundness with which the native women spoke. "There have been constant efforts to open ANWR to oil development ever since the Trans-Alaskan pipeline started delivering oil from Prudhoe Bay in 1977," he began. "A federal study released in 1987 recommended full-scale oil development. But the *Exxon Valdez* oil spill scuttled the momentum. Images of dead sea otters, killer whales and shorebirds on the TV every night really changed all of that."

At the end of this speech Chief Evon decided to call a break so that people could absorb the points made thus far. I took the opportunity to talk with some of the speakers.

ANWR may seem remote, but choices being made by distant industrial economies are now affecting the Gwich'in, most notably in the case of global warming brought on by fossil fuel combustion. The Gwich'in see many alarming changes related to global warming, including transformations in plant life. But warming is just a symptom of a bigger problem. People are depleting the earth's resources too fast. "The earth won't be able to sustain life," said one native woman. "Many native people, not just the Gwich'in, are saying stop, give the earth time to heal." I also chatted briefly with the bishop over a large mug of steaming coffee. It was obvious he considered the situation of the

Gwich'in one of great urgency. He believed this was more than an isolated skirmish over preserving the environment or protecting human rights; there was a bigger issue at stake. "Many of the arguments the Church has found compelling in supporting the Gwich'in and other indigenous groups are based on similar views of the spiritual and cultural authority of a 'people' and a nation," he said. "These arguments are at the center of our basic moral spiritual teaching. This is the first major skirmish in what may prove to be one of the decisive moral battles of this century. A quarter of the world's usable land is in the hands of indigenous peoples. Their human survival depends on it. They are the thin line holding back the insatiable greed and total destruction of our moral, spiritual and physical environments." The bishop was preaching salvation at me, but I knew he felt it was for real.

I returned to the hall to listen to more speeches, but they were reiterating things I'd already heard and after some hours I left to return to my tent. Two thoughts remained with me. One of the native speakers had declared, "One of our main cultural values is respect of the land and the animals. One of our spiritual beliefs is that any birthplace, any spawning area, is sacred." The young man was in his mid-twenties, but his voice was filled with passion and anger. A part of me felt that he was already on the warpath, and I sympathized with him: sacred places should be preserved, as they had preserved these people for generations. What could the god of Mammon offer in exchange? But it was Sarah James who summed it up. "I don't see many places where the natural ecosystems still work," she said. "We're talking about caribou that are still wild and healthy. It's a small place they've gone to for thousands of years. It's a safe place for them. It's a special place, a healthy place tucked away in that corner of the world, and it needs to be protected." One and a half million acres of wilderness on the freezing Arctic coast amounted to a small area on the map of Alaska, but the 150,000 caribou that migrate there to give birth and rear their young are an annual miracle, and part of me believes that miracles are what hold our world together, ensuring that it will endure when all the oil and gas fields have dried up and left nothing but a wasteland indicative of man's ingenuous vanity and greed.

Back in my tent, as that last phrase about man's ingenuous vanity and greed spilled onto the page, I recalled some young children blissfully playing with a small puppy. They were filthy and seemed oblivious to the mosquitoes spinning dizzily about them. The older children raced four-wheel motorcycles along the dirt track that made up the main street. They too were covered in a film of dust and grime. It was impossible to keep oneself or one's clothes clean for more than a few hours when you lived this close to the earth. I suddenly understood why the Bishop of Alaska looked more like a hobo than a hierarch of the Church. For the first day or so this accumulation of dirt hadn't bothered me, but now it was becoming irksome. Still, the next day the tribe was hosting a ceremony of dedication for alternative energy. A new village washeteria complete with banks of washing machines, driers and several shower units, all powered by a mixed system of solar and wind power, would be made available to all. I, for one, was glad of it. It was a classic example of what the bishop meant by the imaginative capacity of the Gwich'in to marry the old ways with the new and still maintain their subsistence lifestyle.

However, tomorrow was many hours of daylight away. That evening there were to be more traditional dances, songs and prayers, and all were welcome to participate, no matter what form their spiritual beliefs or practices took. Obviously, no matter how Episcopalian the Gwich'in were, they still maintained a sense of the spirit world that many Christians would shun. Such is their respect for this spirit realm that they would never decry another human being's beliefs, no matter how remote they might seem from their own. After supper there was to be the first of several fiddle dances to take place during the Gathering. The final note on the day's rota of events, which was pinned on the wall in the hall, read, "No dancing after 4 a.m."

Back in the hall, it was about nine o'clock. The place had an excited yet congenial atmosphere. It was a time to celebrate. The visitors and the villagers had got to know one another during the interval after the speaking. The dancers were back in costume and talked happily about them. Many of them had been made by the great-grandmother, grandmother, mother and daughter of one family. They were regarded with great respect and represented several generations of tribal life. I thought of them as a unique kind of family album, made before cameras were invented. Their costumes were made for dancing, and the exuberance and shining eyes of the young people seemed in absolute harmony with the riot of color and pattern in the beadwork.

Soon all the dancers and many others were circling and chanting to the primitive rhythm of the skin drum. I watched with more composure than before and tried hopelessly to catch some of the action on my camera. But I was less concerned now with the costumes than with the faces of the dancers. I wanted to see if I could witness that moment when the spirit of the dancer is overwhelmed by something more than the music; indeed, when that moment took a collective hold.

I watched and listened, taking sheepish photos I knew would not do justice to the embracing atmosphere of the place. But my attention kept returning to one young man. His costume had not the lavish adornment of the others and the finish of the hide was less fine than some. Also he was taller and leaner than the average Gwich'in. Neither did he have the marked ethnic features of his brothers: he had no epicanthic folds around the eyes, his head and face were not rounded like his supposed Siberian ancestors, nor had he the long aquiline features and beaten copper coloring of his Plains Indian relatives. His hair was curly and fair, and I was sure it would be golden by the end of the summer. But there are many different bloodlines in the Alaskan native, and while studying the young man's face I recalled something I had heard before during preparations for my visit: "With the Athabascan people, it doesn't matter what or who you are, Eskimo or English, Irish or Finn, Russian or French, you have family wherever you go." And I had to admit that this evening was the first time I was beginning to feel at home. I was even feeling that if I should feel the pull of the dance, I would not hesitate to join in.

But this young man continued to distract me. When he moved in the dancing spiral he moaned with more concentrated abandon, and his guttural chants, which were the first to emerge before being swallowed up in an echoing chorus, seemed to me to have their source in something less human than the circle of bodies in front of me. I looked closely at him every time he passed me, but I never saw any discernible moment of "possession" in him. His face only became animated at those moments when he threw his head back to chant to the sky. There was something quite unearthly yet beautifully moving in the noise that came from him. It was, in every imaginable way, the call of the wild. None of the other dancers seemed driven in the way he was. There had to be something more than spiritual ecstasy there, some powerful driving force not triggered externally by the dance. I did not know what it was, only that the whole dance centered and moved around his fierce energy. These were not the sacred dances we had earlier witnessed, they were invitational and celebratory. They were meant to be enjoyed, and to enrich the sense of community and sharing which were essentials in the Gwich'in culture.

I was thrilling to the euphoria of it all when Chief Evon approached, asked if I was enjoying myself and began introducing me to a few other villagers. We exchanged cordial words, and the chief even joked about my special relationship with the caribou. I laughed too, feeling less bothered now by my transgression. I did, however, remark that I was really looking forward to a shower and would be attending the dedication ceremony at the washeteria the next day. Chief Evon was happy, said he wanted me to meet one of the younger generation of Gwich'in and called over some of the young dancers. Among them was the young man I had been studying. Instead of introducing them to me, he stated that I was a visitor from Ireland who was traveling through Alaska to write a book and that after the ceremony tomorrow they might like to speak with me. They all nodded obligingly before moving off. I asked the chief about the young man. "It is no surprise you should be interested," he replied. "His mother was Irish. Tomorrow you should speak with him. We are very proud of these young Gwich'in. But I must leave you now—and remember, my Irish friend, there is no dancing after four a.m." Then he smiled and was gone before I could assure him that I would be fast asleep long before that curfew.

Before midnight, the platform at the top of the room was cleared and a drum set appeared along with some PA equipment and a few well-worn amplifiers. Dancers quickly removed their buckskin costumes and hovered eagerly around the room. After a brief spell a guitar player took the stage with the drummer and two young fiddle players, and after a few minutes' tuning they began to play some country and western tunes that everyone seemed to enjoy. It was obvious the young fiddlers were merely a warm-up act, as after about half an hour three older men, though still in their mid-twenties, took over and really turned up the tempo.

At first I was completely thrown by this event. Some moments ago I had been watching native people perform sacred caribou dances, now here I was watching the same Indians playing country and western music! It took some time to recover from the initial shock. I watched the older couples dance intricate two-foot shuffles while others waltzed with unexpected finesse. And as I listened, the incongruity of what I was witnessing diminished. Athabascan ballroom dancing inside the Arctic Circle seemed less absurd and more unique. I should have realized that with so many mixed bloodlines in the Athabascan gene pool— Russian, Irish, Spanish, Scandinavian and French-Canadian—it would have been impossible to hold back cross-cultural influence in their music.

Fiddle music, I learned from Margaret and her friend, was a long-standing tradition in Alaskan villages. Irish, Orkney Island and French-Canadian fiddle music had arrived with the Hudson Bay Company in the mid-1800s, and a second wave of fiddle music arrived in the 1900s from Appalachia via the Californian gold fields as the miners migrated with their get-rich-quick dreams inspired by the Klondike. Finally, country and western and Cajun music cassettes added their own flavor to this unique fiddle-playing tradition. I was really getting into the swing of this luscious hodgepodge of styles and influences. I considered it would have taken several generations for this grafted music to bury itself so deeply in the native culture. Margaret explained that many native people have a well-honed ear for sound and melody. I knew what she meant. I had experienced the quality of quiet in the bush, and how the slightest sound carries. Natives, too, she insisted, have a great sense of meticulous application, and most players are self-taught.

As she was explaining these things, I was thinking how the idea of subsistence living was not only about shelter and survival. If it was about creating something useful out of whatever came your way, then obviously that meant music too. When Margaret told me that many of the early instruments, like many things in Alaska, had been ordered through Sears Roebuck catalogs, and then added that at one time the Sears Roebuck business empire had accepted pelts as payment, I had to laugh. An image came into my head of an advertisement in a Sears Roebuck catalog, *circa* 1950: "One G-string banjo, $75, or ten quality beaver skins. Fiddle and bow in case, $120, or three wolf hides. Both items on special offer as presentation set—$165, or two brown bearskins."

That night I lay in my tent going over the events of the day while mongrel fiddle music reeled out over the expanding tundra to the accompaniment of youthful laughter and applause.

*

CHAPTER SEVENTEEN.

PATRICK AND THE CARIBOU

lcohol is absolutely forbidden in native settlements, but the following morning the village had a distinctly hungover air about it. Although the music did stop around four o'clock, people were too excited to sleep; I could still hear talking and laughter after six. I eventually struggled down to the field kitchen at about half past nine, and relished the steaming coffee that was available. There were a few dozen young villagers there plus members of the various camera crews. Everyone looked dog tired after the previous night's exertions, though the cameramen were particularly pleased with the shots they had got and an Australian soundman spoke in raptures about the fiddle playing. I walked among them exchanging hellos and chatting about plans. Most were staying in the village for another day, then heading north to get some footage of the caribou migration. I was again assured they had room for me if I was still keen to go. There was little doubt about that.

As I passed among the growing breakfast crowd I became

aware that I was being watched. The young man I had witnessed dancing with such intensity was hovering about, occasionally speaking to his peers but more often on his own. At first I thought it was my imagination—another hangover from my fascination with the aggressive, trancelike quality of his dancing. So for a few minutes I dissuaded myself that this young man was really watching me. But as I moved from one acquaintance to another, and when I walked over to the community hall and back, there he was, either sitting not far off from where I was speaking or watching me from a distance. I decided to forget the matter entirely, and after warming myself at the great log fire I headed back to my tent for a change of clothes to take to the washeteria.

I must have been twenty minutes or so sorting things in my tent, checking to see that my sleeping bag was still dry and lighting some incense before emerging and setting off through the village. My young stalker was waiting for me behind the pile of caribou antlers. He said nothing when I looked in his direction, turning his face from me as if he had other concerns to deal with. But during the few minutes' walk to the shower he was never far behind, and when I emerged in my fresh attire, there he was again. I had to admit I was now becoming a little disturbed by this. After all, I had no idea what was on his mind. Had he noticed me watching him with such interest? Had this somehow offended him? I could hardly go off to Chief Evon or one of the elders with this problem.

Instinctively I took the bull by the horns and walked directly over to him. I stopped in front of him and smiled. "Did you enjoy the music last night?" I asked nonchalantly, drying my hair.

He was startled neither by my action nor by the question. "Yes," he replied, "I liked the music." There was not the slightest hint of animation or interest in his face.

"It was much too late for me—an old man needs his sleep," I continued, trying to extend the atmosphere of ease between us. "Are you going back to the village?" I added invitingly before moving off. Without answering, he walked alongside me. "Chief

Evon introduced me to so many people last night, but I remember that you're Patrick." (Patrick is the pseudonym I have given the young man, as I am quite sure he would not be happy to have his real name used. The native mind has a thing about names. A name tells of who you are. It locates you in your family, in your tribe. Usually it is chosen in compliance with certain codes and spiritual beliefs. Respect a man's name and you respect the man. So I have chosen out of deep respect to call him Patrick.)

For a few minutes we walked in silence with me busily pretending to dry my hair while hoping that Patrick would open up rather than simply answer the innocuous questions I was putting to him. It was not to be. When I queried him about his costume, he told me that it had been his father's; when I asked him if his mother had sewn the beadwork, he abruptly answered, "No." But it was the way the answer came that struck me—as if he was trying to choke back something. The word was almost inaudible, and it fell out of his mouth like a stone. I needed to change the subject quickly or else the silence between us would crush us.

"How old are you?"

"Nineteen, almost twenty," he replied, then put the question back to me.

"Oh, much, much older than that," I told him, smiling openly at his inquiry.

"Yes, that is what I thought," he commented.

I laughed. "But not old enough to be an elder, I hope, Patrick?"

"Maybe," he answered enigmatically, but this time I was sure there was some devilment and a vague hint of a smile behind the word.

We were by now almost back in the center of the village and more people were thronging around the food tables.

"What part of Ireland was your mother from?" I asked, assuming from the earlier reference to her that she had died.

"I do not know," he said coldly, and then, with some passion that I knew veiled other emotions, he announced, "She has gone," and abruptly walked off.

I was totally confused by Patrick's mercurial behavior. Obviously he had sought me out for whatever reason, yet now he had stormed off for no reason I could understand. I wondered if there was any point trying with him.

Later, I made my way back to the washeteria for the dedication of alternative energy, a ceremony that had been organized by the young Gwich'in adults as a statement of how they saw the future of the wilderness. To a community that lived by subsisting, alternative energy produced by solar and wind power was an obvious extension of their normal way of life. As one villager explained, "Nature will give you what you require, but you have to work with it. We do not need to gouge open the earth and tear it apart for a few barrels of oil. Look out there, what do you see?" Before I could answer he continued, "Silence and beauty, a world at peace with itself. Now close your eyes and look again." I did as he asked and held my eyes shut as he spoke. "Now you see roads and trucks, airfields and oil platforms, storage depots and processing plants, turbines and engines, and people everywhere. And what do you hear? Noise, noise everywhere. It is the earth screaming, and it is my people dying in their hearts. If we stand by and allow this thing to happen, we will be killing our own souls."

I had opened my eyes as the man was speaking. He wasn't looking at me as the words spilled from him, he was looking out across the land. There was a quite stoic composure on his face, though to me his despair was Job-like. All of us need these wilderness places in order to reharmonize the soul, cleanse the spirit and detox all the clutter and contagion we take into ourselves without knowing. As I stood beside this man and felt his prayer pass out over the land, I knew his words were not romantic rhetoric or sentimental indulgence, they were a war cry and a warning. And they were coming at me off the land itself.

I could only pat my friend on the shoulder in an act of sympathy and solidarity. He turned to me with the same stoic stillness in his face and nodded. Then we both walked quietly to where the dedication ceremony was to take place.

It was warm and bright, and most of the village was in attendance. The old chief was there, having been helped into a chair, and Evon Peter gave a short speech about the importance of alternative energy as a way forward for the Gwich'in. This was why he particularly wanted the young adults of the tribe to dedicate the installation. I looked at the dozen or so young people gathered in front of the building. All of them stood behind a large red banner with a yellow motif outlining the silhouette of a male caribou, which formed the backdrop to a raised, clenched fist. I was stunned by the militancy of it but could perfectly understand the sentiment behind it.

Chief Evon introduced the group by name, adding personal details about each of them, but he reserved special praise for my friend Patrick, whom he described as a true Gwich'in who honored the ideals and lived the life better and more fully than anyone in the village. Such was his standing that Evon good-humoredly hinted that Patrick might one day be chief. True to form, Patrick stood motionless and unmoved, but I was convinced he was intimidated, not so much by the praise heaped upon him as by the announcement that some of the Gwich'in youth would give short speeches about their lives and why being Gwich'in was important to them. There would not be enough time to hear them all speak at this ceremony, but Evon promised that the rest would continue back at the village—except Patrick, whom he required for some other duties.

Only the first few of these family honor speeches had been delivered when thunder rolled over us and a sudden downpour forced us back into the hall sooner than expected. The impromptu nature of the storm and the consequent rescheduling of the event allowed me a little time with Chief Evon. I casually asked him what had happened to Patrick's Irish mother. He informed me that he understood she had lived in Arctic Village only for a short time and had left when Patrick was a very young baby. His father, with the support of the tribe, brought him up alone. The chief then became confessional as he continued. "To the Gwich'in this was a very sad thing to have happened. The family and the community are of central importance. For a mother to leave her child would be most unusual. She might leave her husband, particularly if he was a poor provider. She might take the child and live somewhere else in or near the village. But to leave and never return like she was dead or is a ghost! This is not the Gwich'in way. Such things do not happen." He looked at me. "What I am saying is that such things do not happen within the villages. But often, when families leave to live in the cities they have many problems and they break up. In the village environment a mother would never desert her young child. She would share her troubles with the tribe and they would do what they could to help. The Gwich'in are one family." He paused again. "I must go now."

I thought this over for some moments and it began to dawn on me why Patrick would not make the honor speech like the others, why he was such a fine hunter, and perhaps why he had chosen to stalk me. I decided there and then to reverse the situation and hunt him down.

I found him outside the community hall. He was wearing a sleeveless jacket over a white T-shirt with the same caribou-and-fist symbol emblazoned on it; the back of the jacket had the word "security" printed in bold letters. A few of the other older teenagers wore similar jackets, though I could not understand why a security team was required. Patrick was gently shooing some of the smaller children off the steps that led up to the hall so as to allow the ceremony to continue indoors.

"I have two small boys about their age," I said, as if our conversation that morning had not happened.

"You left them in Ireland?" he asked, accepting my casual remark.

I explained that I had brought them to Alaska with me but that I had left them in Anchorage with their mother. He nodded at this, then immediately changed the subject, asking me lots of questions about Ireland—what it looked like, how many people lived there and what type of animals we hunted. I answered him as best I could without going into too many complicated details, although he did seem really surprised when I said it was a large island though smaller than the Yukon flats. I had no proper answer for Ireland's shortage of wild animals, which perplexed him.

"What will you teach your sons to become?" he asked.

This, I thought, was going to be difficult to answer. The Gwich'in learned everything in a family context; school was a separate kind of learning for them. I tried to explain that my children would choose their own course in life when they were old enough. But it did not convince him. He sat silently thinking about this.

"Have you ever been to Anchorage or Fairbanks?" I asked.

"No," he replied. "Only to Venetie a few times." He explained that his father had been to the city and to America, but that he would never go to these places. He would stay here always! Then he asked me how long I would stay and why I had come. He hardly seemed to take in the answers before asking me more questions about Ireland, then about my wife, and about my own parents and grandparents. I laughed to myself. I had come to hunt him down and here I was answering questions as if he was the author researching a book.

I asked him which season he preferred, the winter or the summer. "The hunting season," he answered. And which animal did he prefer to hunt? He looked at me with genuine puzzlement and shook his head slowly. I realized immediately that hunting to him was not a matter of choice or preferment; hunting was something you did out of necessity, and there was a time for hunting every species. Had his father taught him? "My father taught me everything," he replied. I noticed his tone was getting less dismissive when I brought up family matters. When I asked if he was still alive, he told me he was but that he was out at the airstrip. I assumed he was waiting for a supply plane.

"Chief Evon says that one day you might be chief also," I said, changing the subject.

The statement seemed to pass over him entirely, and he answered flatly, "I will never leave!" I wasn't sure what exactly he meant, but it seemed to bring an end to our conversation.

"We should go in now," I suggested, and we both climbed the steps into the hall.

The rest of the young Gwich'in speakers were already assembled. In turn, they introduced themselves and explained who their parents were and what they did. Then they related stories about growing up in the wilderness, and all of them addressed the importance of the Arctic Refuge as a home. Most of the young women were at college and would invariably end up working in the cities; only one young woman declared her intention of returning to work in the villages. She had studied and was in her final year as a social work student. But her story was not as cozy as the others. She spoke slowly, often looking at the floor or fixing her gaze on an empty space at the back of the hall. She did not display the same outgoing self-confidence as many of the others. Indeed, her demeanor reminded me of Patrick, though she seemed more withdrawn whereas he was sullen but more assured. At first I thought she was just unused to public speaking, but it was more than that.

The young girl didn't just pause to reflect on what she was saying, it seemed that the whole weight of what she was about to say was too much for her. Many of us in the hall shifted about uncomfortably, embarrassed by her discomfort. Then she lifted her eyes from the floor and declared with a faltering voice how she had been raped when she was younger. The embarrassed fidgeting stopped. The whole room sat in suspended silence. Slowly, and with great effort, she explained how she had been assaulted at the university, by another native person, and how she had left her studies for several months and come home to her village. It had taken her a long time to learn to live with what had happened. But even as she spoke it was obvious she was still having great difficulty dealing with it. Yet here she was, perhaps eighteen or twenty, opening up to the community of the village, and as she spoke so haltingly I could understand that she believed her own community could help her and eventually take the pain from her. She concluded by stating that she knew many young Gwich'in would have difficulties going into the world outside and that is why she wanted to return and work with her own people. When she finished and handed the Tok on to the next speaker, it was obvious that the strain of her confession had taken a great toll on her, and I was convinced that this was the first time she had spoken of the trauma to anyone but a few very close friends and immediate family.

The next two speakers were young men who spoke on the different ways in which the Gwich'in had to take control of their future and ensure the future of the Arctic Refuge. There was militancy in their voices, and in its way it inadvertently added to the poignancy of the young woman's tale. As they were speaking, I noticed Patrick take up a chair and seat himself at the speakers' table. The reaction on the face of Chief Evon informed me that this was an unexpected event.

When the last of the speakers returned the Tok to Chief Evon, he simply announced that there was one more person to speak and he introduced Patrick as the finest example of truly living the Gwich'in way of life. A young man, he insisted, who was an example to everyone, young and old. A hunter whose skills and knowledge of the wilderness were without compare, and who used his skill in the service of his whole community. There was never a hungry mouth in the village when Patrick went hunting. But the accolades were lost on Patrick.

He stood and spoke softly but directly, first giving his name, followed by the simple declaration that "I am Gwich'in, from Arctic Village." Then he continued by stating to the assembly what he had told me, that he had lived all his life in the village with his father, who taught him everything he knew—how to track and hunt, how to skin and tan hides, how to read the sky in winter and in summer, how to survive hundreds of miles from the village in the depth of winter. He could sew and fashion clothes from a skin. He could make baskets and he could cook. But as he mentioned cooking I knew he meant that he knew all the rituals associated with preparing animal food. As he continued in his soft, almost self-effacing tone, I had the impression that Patrick was neither speech-making nor self-promoting. He was stating the facts of life in a Gwich'in village, and behind the facts was the rhetorical statement, what more do I need? Also, he was implicitly demonstrating that he had everything he required for himself and his village yet he took nothing from anyone. Unlike the oil industry! I was sure Patrick was unaware of the implications of his speech, and I am sure it took as much effort for him as it did for the young woman. Yet I knew also that Patrick needed to make this honor speech in the same way she did—to locate herself and to give herself an identity the rape had stolen from her; to be part of something that would love her, define her and nourish her. When Patrick ended his short speech by saying "No matter who comes or who goes I will stay, for this is my home!" I sensed he was not so much throwing out a challenge to the oil industry as exorcising the long-buried pain associated with his mother's desertion.

I had to admit that these speeches had more effect on me than all the arguments about the disastrous footprint of the oil industry in the Arctic. They were living testimonies and had the power of living reality over mere facts.

As we exited I picked up a leaflet, just one of many on display at the rear of the hall. It was about the Gwich'in way of life and the ideals and values that every Gwich'in was supposed to develop in themselves, and display in relation to others. The list read as follows: self-sufficiency, hard work, care and provision for the family unit, humor, honesty, fairness, love for family, sharing and cooperation, responsibility to village, respect for elders, respect for knowledge, wisdom from experience, respect for land and national practice of tradition, honor of ancestors and, finally, spirituality.

Patrick passed by as I was mulling over the list. "Good speech!" I said, and was about to continue by saying that I thought his father would have been very proud of him, but part of me thought it would be too patronizing. Patrick, after all, was a man. In any case, it was really his mother's attention and praise that he wanted, though he hardly knew it himself.

Later that evening I lay in my tent listening to the giddy fiddle music lilting out across the tundra. I could tell it was going to be another long night, that the revelers would do their best to burn up the midnight sun. The gaiety and laughter emanating from the community hall seemed at first somewhat at odds with the list of qualities the young Gwich'in were expected to display. But as I read through the leaflet again I thought it extremely demanding. If one was to attempt to work out all these qualities in one's daily life it could make you appear sullen, self-righteous, or just plain dour and boring. So the wild fiddle music, the hedonistic laughter and the dancing were the perfect antidote. Even if it meant I could get little sleep for another night.

I thought about what the bishop had said in his address, about the Gwich'in being fine theologians, and likening them to the early Christian Church. If one could live one's life according to such precepts, then I could see how one could come to terms with the big question of the human condition and the existence of God.

I remembered the conversations I had overheard when I first arrived. The young people were talking of movies, videos and cars. The outside world had already eaten into the fabric of village life. The oil industry would bring the adolescent fantasy world closer. Already I was sure that many of the young people who spoke of village life and who were now at the university or college would not return again permanently, especially the young women. Yet I concluded that whatever their innocence and naïveté, these young people did display a marked degree of integrity, responsibility and respect that was well in advance of their urban contemporaries in the lower 48 or anywhere else.

I thought again of Patrick, with his passion and intensity. I remembered how quickly this young man had been caught up and transported by the spirit dances. I also recalled how the chief had praised him for his true Gwich'in qualities. Then I remembered how he had stalked me, wanting to talk but too shy or too stubborn to ask. I was sure there was a great anger buried in him. His questions about Ireland were really an attempt to fill in some of the blanks about his mother, yet in his own way he had become a mother to the tribe, hunting and providing for the village during the long, dark winters. Yes, I was sure Patrick would remain here. The outside world would draw back the restraint on his hurt and resentment just as the wilderness could contain it. Maybe its vast emptiness mirrored another kind of emptiness inside him. He could live with it and lose it here. The code of the Gwich'in allowed him to live in some kind of peace and harmony. Of all the young people who spoke that afternoon, it was Patrick's speech that was short, direct, even defiant. He had found something that was worthy, and worth protecting. He would not desert it. I envied him.

*

CHAPTER EIGHTEEN

CLOSE TO THE CARIBOU

The bowling-ball surface of the tundra on which I had been sleeping for four nights now was taking its toll on me. This would be the last day of the Gathering and I was looking forward to moving on. I had spent part of the last uncomfortable night thinking about Chris McCandless and Patrick. They were of a similar age and both had taken refuge in the wilderness, though culturally they were poles apart. It seemed to me, though, that they were driven by the same aesthetic. The code the young Gwich'in were expected to adhere to would have been something young McCandless would have admired.

They had both chosen the wilderness as a place where they might find a quality of existence that would nurture them, but it was obvious why Patrick alone would survive. He was part of the wild, and his uncluttered imagination allowed him to live in harmony with the place. Chris, on the other extreme, was an aesthete of the imagination who I felt had brought himself to an intellectual terminus. Perhaps he chose to refine himself out of existence and find some living, revelatory correspondence in the wilderness. Both young men were compelled by different kinds of hunger, one more emotional and the other intellectual. A part of me wanted to believe that it was a love hunger, one human and the other spiritual. Patrick had found the care of his community and the world he inhabited sufficient compensation for his lack of motherly love, and had in his own way become a kind of foster mother to the village. Chris was a doomed Icarus and had flown too near the sun and too deep into the wilderness, and it had taken him into itself.

You can only receive what the wilderness offers, and already I was beginning to feel that I would find living here very difficult. It would be physically and psychologically very demanding. You would need a code of living such as the Gwich'in had in order to steel yourself against the harshness of life in the Arctic. Everything in their way of life was conditioned by respect, responsibility, integrity and sharing. Chris McCandless had had no one to share with, and I was already doubting what I could share with these people.

Eventually I'd had enough of this thinking. I was tired, sore, cold and hungry, and already people were gathering for breakfast. I hurried out of my leaky tent, unashamedly wanting the warmth of coffee and the companionship of people.

Over a mug of coffee and some moose mince gravy and biscuits some of the camera crew informed me that everyone was packing and heading for Caribou Pass, so if I wanted to catch a ride I should get my gear packed and get myself out to the airstrip in the next few hours. Some of the crews had arranged for inflatable rafts to be flown up from Fairbanks so they could navigate down the Kongakut River that winds through the easterly end of the Brooks Range, where they hoped to film the caribou "on the hoof." There was already excited talk about fifty or sixty thousand animals on the move out of their coastal calving grounds from a pilot who had already arrived and was waiting to load the crews. A four-day float down the Kongakut River seemed thrilling, but I had already learned just how ill prepared I was. I could only just about survive in the village, and in any case I had used up all my film and my pocket "idiot-proof" camera would be useless in such a vast landscape with thousands of caribou grunting over it and the majestic mountains looming down on us.

I breakfasted heartily and decamped rapidly, making sure to return the polystyrene boards and plastic sheeting to the caravan. I made as many good-byes as I could, but they were awkward as I was still an outsider. One of the village elders said to me as I tossed my backpack onto the small Mazda truck that I had arrived in, "When you see the caribou you will understand why our brothers, the caribou, need our protection." Then he winked and smiled. "And you must thank them for letting you sleep on their grave." As the truck bumped its way along the dirt road to the airstrip I had an odd feeling that that last statement was more than simply a joke at my expense. Another part of me wondered if this small native village would still be here in five or ten years' time.

When our six-seater Cessna took off I closed my eyes as inconspicuously as I could. This time it wasn't so much my fear of flying as exhaustion. Four almost sleepless nights added to the intellectual energy one spends trying to observe and understand the experience of living in a remote outpost had drained me. We were touching down on the tiny airstrip at Caribou Pass when I was gently nudged awake.

Everyone spilled from the aircraft enthusiastically. There were a few other small aircraft waiting. Their occupants had already disembarked and were scouting the immediate environs for the best vantage point to film the caribou. Our pilot, who had made this trip hundreds of times, suggested we would find good viewing about a few hundred yards from the airstrip on a bluff top that overlooked the vast sweep of the Kongakut River.

The hike to the proposed site was quickly achieved. Everyone was too keen to get a sight of the herd as it moved south to worry too much about having to carry heavy camera equipment. I had no such encumbrances and quickly had my tent erected. Within the hour, everyone was on serious caribou alert.

From our vantage point you could look down on the river as it meandered with effortless indulgence through the valley and disappeared into the distant mountains that filled the horizon no matter where you turned your head. The pattern of sandbars and shingle islands that the river threw up gave it the appearance of a gigantic but magnificently mosaic serpent. The Brooks Range seemed to go on forever, and to take on the blue hue of the Arctic sky. The silence was so absolute that all of us instinctively whispered, afraid to shatter the impressive fragility of it all. We sat watching and waiting, allowing the silence and the magical light to enfold us. I prefer to think that each of us chose not to speak because a part of us was swept away on that magnificent river and another part of us was gliding through the cerulean haze of mountains and sky. It was intoxicating, because it heightened all your senses and lifted them onto another plane.

Occasionally a small group of caribou, no more than half a dozen strong, would drift into our sightline and there would be a few seconds of excitement. But this was not what we came here for and none of us would be content until we saw several thousand or so of these creatures rolling across the landscape, shattering the stillness with their beastly presence.

From another point I could look out over the coastal plain, which has been the battleground of environmentalists and oil magnates for decades. Through a set of borrowed binoculars it looked like a huge empty meadow. This tussock and tundra bog meadow stretched into the famous calving grounds designated "area 1002" by Congress more than a quarter of a century ago. It seemed an ignominious name for one of the most spectacular birthing sites on the planet. But when something is reduced to the blandness of a number, it loses its power to impress, and that I'm sure is why the oil interests that want to rip it asunder prefer a number to any proper description. At the moment it was empty and desolate. Within a day, or less, we hoped it would be submerged in a huge ocean of animal flesh as the migration got underway.

I recalled what the Gwich'in had told me about the caribou. They were extremely sensitive to humans, noise and vehicles. I could understand that any creature born into this silence would be. But I could also imagine looking through my binoculars at a hundred miles of service road, pipelines, oil and air pollution, and a few sickly animals scavenging a living. The Gwich'in also explained that the herd could not simply relocate. This calving ground offered ample nutritious plant growth to enrich the production of milk in the pregnant animals. If that was reduced, then the calves would not have enough winter fat to survive and the females would be unable to produce new calves the following year. Everything was so delicately balanced that even the slightest tampering with nature could have dramatic consequences. One of the villagers had explained that even the wolf and the bear do not come here to hunt, for they too understood that this was a sacred place.

That evening I didn't miss the fiddle music, and I slept better than I had the previous night. At this high level the ground was less uneven, and I had enough sense to make myself a mattress out of handfuls of bearberry bushes.

I woke to the sound of aircraft arriving. It was the cargo of inflatable rafts that some of the crews had ordered in Fairbanks. Our pilot, who had stayed with us, chatted with the newly arrived pilot, who informed him that the herd was making its way out of the calving grounds and moving south. With this announcement the camp exploded into activity. My hopes dropped and I thought we were going to miss the migration, but our pilot told us there was a small strip near the calving grounds where we could get some shots of the herd as it moved off. They might not be as dramatic as the river shots would have been, but at least it wouldn't be a wasted journey. We packed hurriedly and were off in some twenty minutes.

In another fifteen minutes, after scanning the tundra beneath us, we landed near Demarcation Bay on the icy edge of the Beaufort Sea. It was late afternoon, but the sun could not dispel the chill air. As we unloaded, the pilot passed his binoculars around. In the foothills in the distance we could see swathes of animals, but they were miles away. The pilot gestured for us to gather our gear and move away from the aircraft. When we had gone far enough from it so as not to be immediately associated with it, he told us to camp and wait.

I was only too happy to get inside the canvas. The chill here soon bites into you. I hoped we would not have to spend the night. Some of the crew went prowling around taking stills of the eerily empty plain. I lay back and waited, munching on biscuits and dark chocolate, and started updating my diary. This trip to try to catch the caribou migration had not been on my original itinerary. It was a bonus to get this far, but I was sure it wasn't going to be our lucky day. I was feeling a bit deflated and was wondering how I would explain to Audrey and the kids about the close encounter with the caribou that never happened. The numbing cold was making me sleepy. I lay back and closed my eyes, recalling again the events of the last few days. Then I began to hum to myself.

It must have been about one and a half hours later, after eating, writing and dozing, that I looked out of my tent. Unbelievably, we were surrounded by caribou. There were several hundred of them in small groups and in larger bands, some mothers and their young idly munching the tufts of tussock grass. They seemed oblivious to us as they trudged indolently to the south and east. The cameraman and soundman had moved away from the tents to make the best of this opportunity. I was left alone in the middle of this mass movement. Every so often some of the creatures would stop, look momentarily at me, then emit a comical grunt and move on, their spindly legs and feet making sucking noises in the boggy land.

I had to admit I felt very alone and more than a little frightened. Being in the middle of this phenomenon about which I had read and heard so much was disconcerting. I looked around for the crew, needing to keep contact with where they were. Though the creatures avoided me with total indifference, my panic grew. What would I do if something spooked them and they suddenly stampeded? I remembered what I had been told about bears and wolves avoiding the calving grounds, but I reminded myself that we were miles from that special place. These animals were caught up in some kind of primal drive that took no heed of me. Then I also recalled what I had been told as I left the Gwich'in village: "You must thank them for letting you sleep on their grave." The statement had been made in a half-joking manner, but it was the other half of that advice that had to be considered. I remembered the moose mother at McCarthy and slowly turned in a circle, silently thanking the caribou for coming to visit me.

Then I spotted the crew carefully walking in and out of the main group of caribou families. The young creatures seemed giddy and vulnerable, and the older animals, looked at individually, were scraggy and skinny. But the huge herd was moving with one mind and one purpose. They were magnificent. I thought of the dance in the village hall and how all the dancers there had moved as if with one mind. I didn't feel afraid anymore, and I chuckled softly. The caribou grunted in my direction as if they were laughing too.

I watched this shuffling, snorting, grunting procession for another hour. The caribou came in fits and starts, in large and small groups, and then seemed to vanish into the thick sea fog that began to settle on the coastal plain. I thought we had seen the last of them, but they just seemed to keep coming like shadowy forms moving in and out of breaks in the mist. Inside a minute there would be nothing but gray mist against a gray sky, and then the head and antlers of several males would appear and disappear. Then, just for a few seconds, you might see three or four juveniles, less driven by migratory instinct, run and leap into the mist as if they believed it would support them. Then they too were gone and all that was left was a ghostly grunting and snorting. For a moment you believed it was an Arctic illusion or the backwash of a dream the place had instilled in you.

Soon we were all huddled together, confirming excitedly that it was no dream. Then one pilot who had seen it all before and was more earthbound than the rest of us suggested we should leave before the fog became too thick. This was the sort of weather that could delay you for days. If it got any worse, to attempt to take off and navigate through such conditions could be fatal. "You could still be here in the new year with the caribou licking the lichen off your bones," he warned good-humoredly. I remembered what Tex O'Neill had told me about impatience and leaving things to the last minute, so we packed quickly and roared off out of the foggy nothingness.

Our pilot informed us that out of the possible thirty or forty thousand calves born here, only half of them will survive predators and the severe winter, and those that do will return again next year to do it all again. "That's the way it's been here forever," he concluded.

Sometimes we caught a glimpse of them from our vantage point in the heavens—a seething mass of brown flowing over the land, unaffected by every obstacle this sublime ecosystem put in their way. One daunting memory stuck with me, a momentary vision of an adult male charging out of the mist. His antlers seemed bigger than the bony frame of his body. His nostrils glared and steamed against the chill air and his big black eyes looked right through me—then he was gone. Or was he?

The extraordinary act of thousands of animals migrating thousands of miles, year after year, across this primeval landscape of earth and water to give birth and perhaps to die is profound testimony to something living and unseen in the land itself. Neither science nor language has the capacity to explain or reveal it, and the raw experience of it is greater than language or logic. Aldo Leopold, the great proponent of the concept of ecological science, once wrote, "Only when the end of the supply is in sight do we discover that things are valuable." Later, he wrote, "It was here that I first clearly realized that the land is an organism, that all my life I had only seen sick land, whereas here was a biota still in perfect aboriginal health."

I had had my stay in the wilderness, and I had found it warmly enriching. I'd come up close to a unique life experience for which I remain grateful. But I had to acknowledge that I didn't have the resilience to make a life there.

*

CHAPTER NINETEEN

COUNCIL OF THE RAVEN

I arrived in Fairbanks exhausted and weak, less from the physical rigors of the past week than from another kind of exposure the wilderness creates in the heart. It was good to be back in my cabin in the hills above the town. A couple of days here would allow me to think through the whole experience with the Gwich'in and the caribou. Now that I was away from my Arctic encounter I had to admit I wasn't quite sure what I made of it all. But one thing I did know: it was making me ask more questions about the wilderness than I thought I had answers for. I also had to admit that I was glad to be back in a place I knew, with familiar things around me and people I knew nearby.

The place had changed a lot in the few weeks since I had last been there. The road up to the cabin was deeply rutted and muddy with permafrost melt. The *Pequod* would have been useless here and would have had to be abandoned like a landlocked *Marie Celeste*. Also, the place was less quiet: birds and birdsong were everywhere. A big raven stared down at me studiously as I kicked and scraped the muck from my boots. And my old companions, the mosquitoes, were still in abundance.

The drive up to the cabin had shown me just how fast things change. Wildflowers were everywhere, clumps of bluebells contrasting with the blue flowers of Jacob's ladder and the deep pink hue of wild rose bushes. In many places the diamond willow was already laying down its blanket of seed fluff. The cottonwoods were also casting off millions of seeds, creating miniclouds of white fluff with every summer breeze. That evening, as I sat on the porch with a steaming mug of coffee, a plate of digestive biscuits and slices of processed cheese, I also thought I noticed a difference in the clarity of the light from what I had witnessed up in the Arctic. Maybe it was just the burgeoning colors that softened it. It certainly didn't have the austere quality I'd found in Arctic Village, and even more so at Caribou Pass and beyond. It would be summer solstice soon, I thought. The big black raven paraded up and down on his branch cawing impatiently, as if to say, "Everyone knows that, bimbo, now throw me a biscuit!" As I watched him, flotillas of tiger swallowtail butterflies pirouetted past the cabin and alighted on the ground, flapping their wings where they sat. They, at least, were applauding me. I arose, took a bow and headed for bed.

I made a few notes before turning in. I had been thinking how oriental the evenings were. It was a mixture of the omniscient quiet, the curious quality of light that lulls the mind and makes it more receptive to how the wilderness opens itself up to you. When I was here before, at the end of winter with the snow still on the ground highlighting the ghostly black trees, I had thought of haikus and Japanese prints. It had all seemed so pristine and eternal then. Even with summer coloring up the canvas of the landscape, there was something quietly revelatory about it like the best of oriental art.

Kno Hsi, an eleventh-century Chinese painter and philosopher, proposed the idea that man relishes natural landscape because it enriches his own nature. Like me, he was an irredeemable romantic and seeker after things. He writes, ". . . the din of the dusty world and that locked-in-ness of human habitations are what human nature habitually abhors, while on the contrary, haze, mist and the haunting spirits of the mountains are what human nature seeks, and yet can rarely find." The ancient painter philosopher obviously believed profoundly in the restorative and redemptive quality of the wilderness, and a part of me wanted to believe but still needed to be convinced of his thesis.

I skipped through my notebook until I found some references about travel as a search for a spiritual homeland and a heightened sense of authenticity. I tried to apply this to my own recent travels in the Arctic refuge. Had I found beauty or a vision of paradise? No, I had to confess I hadn't. I could not apply these nouns to my stay in the Arctic. I had another list of words to convey what I felt about the place. It was about hardship and endurance. It was brutal and confining. It was a struggle, physically and psychologically. But it did make you think and examine your own values. There were moments when you felt moved, perhaps by something sublime. Maybe that's all it is really about, not the search for beauty in some earthly paradise but rather something more transcendent. Something akin to a beatific experience that flares up like a candle in the wind and is gone again. It may leave you once more in the dark, but it will have lighted your way.

All this thinking brought me back to my Athabascan Anglicans. I had not expected to discover the Gwich'in to be a confessed Christian community who found spiritual consolation in the wilderness. In a way they were like modern-day Essenes, who dwelt in caves near the Dead Sea and lived a life of purity and simplicity while awaiting the Second Coming. And their reverence for nature, and especially their empathy with the spirit of the caribou, was a very Franciscan view of the world. Indeed it could even be Hindu, Jain, Buddhist, Shinto or Taoist. Eastern thought had never made the schizophrenic division between man and nature that the West had. Neither had the Gwich'in, and that was why they were primitive but profound theologians. They knew that everything in life and in nature was sacred and that man was only another sacred creature. When they spoke about their brother the caribou, they meant it.

All this theological speculation was making my head light. I suddenly remembered St. Augustine and his constant admonition that man should not take joy from life but rather should spend more time in contemplation of his salvation. With that kind of advice, no wonder we couldn't see the wood for the trees and no wonder the modern traveler is essentially still a pilgrim in search of a spiritual homeland. St. Augustine and his confederates in classicism had been misdirecting us for centuries.

As if he had been reading my thoughts, the big black raven that squatted on the tree outside my cabin started strutting up and down the branch, cawing and calling out in what seemed like hysterical derision. It was as if he was both mocking my speculations and laughing along with me. Then he would perform clownish leaps from branch to branch and sit for a few moments lecturing me, his throaty voice becoming stern and almost threatening. Then he would suddenly flap away to another tree and march drunkenly along, proclaiming with complete abandon that I was absolutely right about that self-indulgent Salvationist, St. Augustine! Next he would flutter down to a low branch near the house and sit silent for a few moments, staring at me with imperious disdain before barking at me, "Be careful, Keenan, you don't become too saintly yourself!" Another time he flew with such ease and immense grandeur to another high branch, where he fluffed his shiny black feathers like a wise old academic adjusting his gown and announced that he knew stories from the shadowy edge of history that philosophers and theologians had not yet even conceived of. So it went on for what seemed an hour or more. I sat thoroughly enraptured until finally this egotistical and audacious wit of a bird decided he had entertained me enough and was gone. Even in daylight this great black creature could disappear as if by magic.

I thought, as I scanned the sky for him, perhaps he was magic after all, and he had flown off into the invisible world. The rudeness of his disappearance reminded me how the natives believe that to hear the raven call in the dark of night is a sure token of death. I had been listening to this utterly undignified jester for quite some time, and the sun was still shining even though it was late in the night, so I was safe from the raven's malign intentions. Besides, I could not believe my raven had any such designs. In the distant-time stories of the indigenous people, the raven was the creator of the earth; they believed that, like God, he had the power to grant wishes. Part of me wasn't sure I could trust wishes granted by a bird-god who contemplates the world with cynical scrutiny.

I had to admit I liked the complicated nature of this big black raven. He was, for me, the quintessential enigma. Once you thought you had penetrated the spirit of this bird it immediately transformed itself, but that was what made it so intriguing. It stripped you of your self-delusions, just as it had done for me as I sat watching it.

I remembered how the Norse god Odin had kept two ravens, which represented thought and memory. Each day they would circle the world and return to report to their master. I liked to think of my raven like that. In its own clownishly curious way, it had made me question a lot of things about my trip. So I made my wish to the empty sky that the spirit of the raven would visit me again. It was late in the evening and the raven's departure had informed me that it was time to sleep. I had some people to visit before I moved on. A gold miner, a Siberian émigré artist and the most northerly composer in the world. It really was a motley assortment that you could only find living within a few miles of each other at the edge of the wilderness. I went to sleep half believing that the trickster raven had conjured them up especially for me.

CHAPTER TWENTY

MORE MAMMOTHS
AND MUSICIANS

During my first visit years ago I'd tried to meet John Reese, a gold miner, at his mine several miles outside the city. I hadn't found him, but the remnants of the mine remained; the extreme temperatures of Alaska have a way of embalming things. All I'd gleaned from that first attempt to meet the man was that he owned a few more gold mines somewhere further out from the city and that he proposed at some time to develop the gold mine into a quirky holiday venue. It seemed then a feasible if absurd notion. The gigantic earth dredge was still there, a monstrous machine that had created much of the moon landscape in the hills outside Fairbanks. Then there were the miners' bunkhouses, the store, pens and dog shelters, a big parts shed for equipment, communal latrines, and a "doc" shop where injured miners could be quickly attended to, though with what degree of efficiency or care I could not imagine. There was even a small theater at the entrance to the mine that amounted to a stage, rows of stools and an entrance hall where the hard-working miners shelled out their money for some dubious but well-received relief. Although the theater was only just outside the mine complex, at least the workers had a sense of getting away from their eternal labor. Laughingly, Pat Walsh informed me that the theater still operated even though the mine was long deceased. They put on "shows" for tourists, who I supposed wanted to be indulged in the same way the working miners had. It was very Alaskan kitsch, but the locals enjoyed the garish amateur dramatics, Pat explained. But that was then, and now I was going to meet the man himself.

We met in his machine shop, located near the railway lines. It was a clapboard and corrugated-iron structure which from the outside looked abandoned and hopeless. I shuffled through the door, expecting to find the same kind of obsolete clutter that dominated the backyards of every homestead in Fairbanks. Instead, I found myself in a gleaming labyrinth. Here was a machine shop dating back to the 1920s—lathes and machine presses, heavy-duty stamps, a forge and industrial machine cutters, and not a cobweb in sight. The place was a small factory, but everything was spotless. Shiny black contrasted against the burr of dull silver, and everywhere the gorgeous shine of olive-green casing. Everything was in perfect order, and everything was still running. The lamps to light the place clung to long slender lines with cheap cupcake-like shades. They, too, were working. They shone with an ocher-yellow light. I was amazed at my reaction. This place was an art gallery! The muscular curve of wheels, spindles, knobs and machine hoods was everywhere. This was muscle turned into magic, latent power that was pristine in its silence.

When gold mining was at its height, parts of the great Goliath-like earth dredgers had to be manufactured on the spot. Steel was fired and turned here to precise dimensions every day. Huge locking bolts and nuts were manufactured and threads turned on them. Trying to pile iron and steel into the permafrost was a titanic struggle. The earth always won, for Alaska's low temperatures snapped pig iron and machine steel like chicken bones.

John Reese was a giant of a man, not only in stature but also in his thinking and in his heart. "Jesus," I thought as I looked up at him the way a child looks up at an adult. "I've climbed up the beanstalk of the world. If he says "Fee fi fo fum" to me, he can keep his golden eggs. I'm out of here, pronto." My friend Pat had told me that John was rather wealthy, with a few gold mines, some property and even a coffee plantation in Colombia. I was to learn later that this was a gross underestimation. But the man in front of me looked nothing like an Alaskan millionaire. He wore an old battered baseball cap whose peak had collapsed so that it fell over his face instead of jutting out above his eyes. His baggy sports trousers looked as if they hadn't been washed in weeks. They hung off him as though they were two sizes too big, which, given the size of the man, would have been impossible— unless the trousers had been made by a sailmaker. To complete the ensemble he wore a washed-out T-shirt under a very worn fleece jacket, which dragged down in the front due to the amount of junk he had shoved into the pockets.

John's face was as dissolute as his appearance. It was obvious that razor blades were not high on his hygiene agenda. He sported a huge walrus-like mustache that would have made Nietzsche look Chaplinesque. His eyes were hidden behind wraparound sunglasses that reflected a garish greeny blue, which created the illusion of his having the grossly protuberant eyes of a huge insect.

Surprisingly, our conversation was labored. All Mr. Reese's wealth and stature had given him no advantage in conversation. At first he seemed brusque and uninterested, as if I had entered into his world like an annoying mosquito. But as I persisted, asking him about the machine shop's history and his own life in Fairbanks, he slowly began to open up. I soon realized that it was reticence and shyness that had made him seem so dismissive.

As we walked through the workshop I asked why he had acquired such a redundant piece of industrial history. He told me he had bought it as part of the package in the portfolio of an old mining corporation that had long ago ceased operations in Alaska. "Thought I was just buying up property and mining rights," he explained, "but a whole big parcel of other stuff came with it, including this here workshop and a load of warehouses with more machinery in Pennsylvania." I asked him what he intended doing with it all. "Don't know," he said. "When I realized this came with the deal I had a notion to knock it down and maybe sell on the land. But I like it in here. It's peaceful, and even pretty. Keep all the machines clean and in running order, though most of them have never been worked in twenty years or more. It's like having your own private museum." But the way he spoke told me that this shabby, retiring millionaire was no museum caretaker. His manner could not hide the affection he had for the place. It was more like a private chapel than a museum, and I could imagine this giant of a man quietly polishing and tending the sacramental lathes and turning machines with loving adoration.

As we walked around I stared out through a cobweb- and grime-encrusted window. Wrecks of old cars and trucks dating back to the forties and fifties littered the grounds. The colossal bric-a-brac of the gold-rush era sprawled all over the place. It was a graveyard of rusting iron and inert man-made machine parts that in their day had busted open the spleen of this hard country.

Tucked away in one corner of the workshop I discovered real fossils. A pile of oddly shaped bones stood alone, and beside them three huge, arching curves of tusk. Then more tusks appeared as my eyes adjusted to the light. Some of them were wrapped with heavy-duty tape and others had clamped to them what looked like massive chrome jubilee clips. John explained that the bones and tusks were from the remains of a woolly mammoth he had unearthed in one of his mines. The tape and chrome clips served to pull the cracked and ruptured curve together once he had glued and sealed them. Some of them were more than fifteen feet long and impossible to lift. Even John's huge frame had difficulty with them. Why he had a collection of mammoth bones and tusks was beyond me. I couldn't resist asking him. He explained that mammoth remains could make big money in Japan; the larger and more complete the piece, the more they would pay. Apparently, Japanese businessmen like to carry one piece of mammoth ivory carved with their own personal business stamp.

"Is it hard to find?" I queried.

He explained that there was a lot of fossilized bone being dug up. But it was unusual to find whole tusks now. Probably in the past the miners would have discarded these finds without another thought, but today mammoth ivory was worth lots more than gold. He fumbled in his coat pocket and produced a piece of tusk that he had sanded and polished on one of the machines. It glowed with a deep earthy brown and oxblood coloring. It was neither cold nor hot in the hand, but its shiny surface had a deeply sensuous feel. It was curious to think that here I was, holding a piece of a gigantic animal that was millions of years old, and now it had been transformed into the personal talisman of some wealthy business samurai. As I rubbed my fingers on it I felt as if I was rubbing away millions of years of history and touching something elemental that centuries and centuries of evolution had not eroded.

Big John gave me a rough fragment of tusk as a keepsake and we arranged to meet up in a few days' time to drive up into the hills and visit a few of his gold mines and the men who worked them.

"How many mines do you own anyway?" I asked as I was about to drive off.

"Don't rightly know, maybe three dozen or so," he said as he walked back into his magical museum.

Over the next few days I visited a few other citizens who had settled in this town at the edge of nowhere. I had already noticed that Fairbanks had more than its share of creative people. I thought I could understand why. The wilderness made you challenge yourself and your perceptions, and I wondered how others who lived here felt about this.

Vladimir was a Russian emigrant who had lately arrived from Provideniya in Siberia. He lived in a studio above a very nondescript pub in the worst part of downtown. It would take a strong character with lots of determination to live there. My first impression of Vladimir was that he did not seem the type to survive in this dreadful part of town. That was before I learned he had been a prison guard back in Siberia for much of his working adult life before coming to Alaska. I looked at his tight-cropped hair and beard and his lean muscular stature. Only for a brief moment could I see him as a prison officer. There was something very open and uncomplicated about his face, which was the perfect mirror for his personality. He felt more like a young monk to me. He was immediately talkative and friendly. Even though I had been in his home only a few minutes, he spoke to me with the easygoing assurance of someone who had known me for many years.

Vladimir insisted I share his meager lunch of bread, cheese, tinned ham and pickles, which we washed down with raw vodka flavored with horseradish and garlic. This in turn was washed down with refreshingly sweet water, which was made from sugary resin drawn off the silver birch trees that were in abundance.

Though Vladimir lived on the edge of penury, he seemed untroubled and content. He had acquired quite a reputation as an ice sculptor, and I was impressed as he leafed through a photo album of his work. Vladimir was unbothered by the temporary nature of his work. He felt that it was appropriate that these images in ice melted away and were lost forever. It added a dynamic to his art. It prevented complacency. Ice was so fluid; you could do things with ice that you could not with other mediums. You had to work fast, and that kept your thinking sharp. I remembered watching an ice sculptor at work during my visit years ago. The essential tool was like a broad wood chisel attached to a short spade handle. The speed and precision with which an expert can evolve the most fantastical images was truly amazing.

We drank more of the horseradish-flavored vodka, then Vladimir walked me to his studio and displayed his ice-carving implements. They were like a cross between a blacksmith's tool kit and a medieval surgeon's operating instruments. Vladimir poured more vodka as he laughed at my description. "Yes, yes," he said through his guffaws. "Only it is much colder and there is less blood!"

I was about to ask him where he had learned his skill when I noticed a large unfinished painting mounted on an easel near the window. It was of a herd of bull walrus sunning themselves on a rocky outcrop. Now, male walrus are ugly and aggressive creatures, but not my Russian painter's walrus. They lay in sublime repose and looked out of the painting, inviting you to join them. I could see why ancient mariners had mistaken them for mermaids and mermen. Each of Vladimir's walrus looked the same, yet each expressed its own personality.

"It is a fabulous piece, Vlad," I said, suddenly using the familiar diminutive of his name. "Would you sell it?"

"No," he said firmly. Then, in a softer tone, he explained, "I cannot, because it is not finished. I have been working on it four and a half months, but I think it will be maybe a year old before I am finished." I declared that his painting was superior to his sculpture and he looked from me to the painting and back to me again. "You are right, of course, and you know why?"

"No."

"Because they remain with you longer."

I wasn't sure if I was able to take this debate on the arts any further and declined another top-up. Vladimir was not drunk, but he enjoyed stimulating conversation and I was interested in how this ex-gulag guard who had the soul of a saint had found himself in Alaska. His answer was surprising, but exactly what I should have expected. "It is too confusing, and more importantly it is wasteful of time," he began. "People here spend too much time doing things to save time so that they can do the really important things. But they never have any time to do these things. They sleep for eight hours, they spend three hours eating and drinking, then another two hours on insignificant things. Why do they not do what they want to do?" I was listening intently, but the complex mechanics of what he was trying to say were baffling me. He finally got to the point. "The spiritual dimensions of people's lives are hidden from them. Life," he said, pointing his finger toward the heavens and then at his heart, "has little meaning without it."

I left his apartment as he had to go and collect his wife, who was a Russian teacher. I took a last glimpse at the sparsely finished room and the studio packed with half-finished paintings, photos of ice sculpture, brushes, hand-made ice-shaving chisels of every description, and a table full of charcoal sketches and photos of his wife and his family taken somewhere in Siberia. Vladimir hadn't got much, but his room was full to bursting.

My next port of call was with John Luther Adams. The name suggested an eccentric revivalist preacher or an attorney at law from somewhere in New England who could trace his ancestry back to the Puritan founding fathers and whose own father had written a book on religious ethics and the history of religious dissension. John Luther was nothing like this. He described himself as the most northerly composer in the world. Inside his meticulously maintained cabin in the woods, John spoke with single-minded passion about Alaska, and particularly the Arctic region, as an inspirational place. Here was a man who was used to being alone. I supposed that was in the nature of being a composer.

I spoke with him of my book about the blind harpist and men-

tioned my mysterious correspondent and her confiding to me
that the composer I was writing about was a "Dreamwalker"; for
some reason I didn't mention that I had met this woman again.
The word seemed to knock down the awkwardness between us.
I had come to ask this man about what brought artistic and creative people to this extreme land. I never needed to ask the question. My book about the Irish composer Turlough O'Carolan had
done the trick.

John was about my age and had come to Alaska when he was
twenty-two. He was, as he described it, "looking for a home
place," somewhere his creative energies would be liberated. The
minute he arrived he felt that the landscape resonated with
something that commanded him to stay. This was home! I had
already discovered that when I asked people why they came to
this northern extreme, or indeed why they stayed, they spilled
out in front of me a tea chest full of ready-made reasons. Yet all
they seemed to do was obscure the essential answer I was looking for. John Luther Adams, like everyone else, had his own reasons for leaving the lower 48. He admitted that after thirty years
he was still discovering what kept him here. He also admitted to
finding the bleak, dark winter dreadfully frustrating. He drowned
himself in sunlamp therapy to hold back the SADs, the debilitating depression that descends every winter that Jane Haigh explained to me while describing her need to become a "snowbird."
Did John feel the same compulsion? "Sometimes," he confessed,
but he never acted upon it. He was too obsessed with the extremes of ice and rock, light and dark, the roaring aurora and
that incredibly mesmeric white silence.

As he was talking, he referred to his life in Alaska as a sojourn
in "the Big Lonely." It held him in its bone-numbing, icy grip and
would not let him leave no matter how he might rage against it.
He spoke of years spent walking in the wilderness and listening
to the "Arctic litanies" that sounded to him out of the earth and
air. From the time he'd first arrived in Alaska he had been acutely
aware of the "presence" of the place. It was something I too had

felt. This sense of a "presence" in the landscape had deepened as the years passed. It had propelled and challenged him. It was, for him, "the measure of everything we do and are." By way of explanation, he talked about a piece of music he had worked on for six years, until he was content with his composition and even sure there was real quality and merit in it. One morning he pulled back the curtains, looked out onto the Alaska Range and realized how insignificant the work was.

But he remained working and living in the wilderness. "The sonic geography of Alaska is so rich it requires a lifetime's devotion," he declared, and put on some of his CDs. Birdsong and the noise of wind, water and thunder floated around the room. Obviously John was no conventional composer, nor was his music melodic in the classical European sense. His harmonics were stark, disturbing and deeply penetrating. Inuit voices spoke from behind the music, calling out their native place names. The music was like the names the natives had given to the land—void of elaborate description yet full of the experience of the place. The ghostly voices resonated with ancestry and myth. As I listened, totally overwhelmed, John spoke about the "salvation of silence," that great mysterious quiet that wraps around you in the bush. I knew it from my own night on the lake. And when he spoke about music as a metaphor for silence I was with him all the way. There is a quality about silence that suspends time and makes every sound clear and precise. The composer's music was an echo of and a portal into that silence; it was not a representation of the place. It was its own landscape; it had moved beyond external reference. You didn't just hear the music, and it didn't throw up images of the wilderness, you felt it resonating from somewhere deep inside you. Describing landscape in words or music is limiting work. Like the Renaissance idea of perspective, it sets us at a distance from the object, detaches us from its organic being. It is a two-dimensional thing that misses something elemental.

I was becoming intoxicated with our talk, and with the music which elaborated on the words. But what was this "sonic geography"? Even as John was trying to define some kind of extraterrestrial terrain, somewhere at the crossroads of imagination and place, I was suddenly blasted into that place by the forceful, trance-like, driving rhythms of the drum. John's mountain music exploded at me like the first sight of the mountain ranges. It penetrated through my bones and rooted me into the stone as if I were petrified flesh. It was scary; I felt I could not escape it. Like the mountains, the terrifying noise of the drums was everywhere around me.

The music was removing the necessity for conversation, but when the composer spoke about the timeless place of forgetting and unknowing I knew what he meant, for that's where Alaska is, and John Luther Adams's music can take you there.

John had begun our conversation by trying to explain why he had come to Alaska. He was looking for a home place. But I felt he had discovered that home was within, and that home was also in his music. I left him sitting in the corner of his minimalist white room, gnome-like, his knees bent up to his chin, his long arms and fine-boned hands draped over the arms of his chair.

Big John arrived in a big, powerful 4 × 4 half truck that had the same roughshod appearance as its driver. I could hardly have expected anything else. We drove into the hills, exchanging easy conversation about Ireland and Alaska.

Big John didn't have the erudite intensity of John Luther Adams. However, like Adams, he had hitchhiked up from Florida, where he had been studying with a swimming scholarship, in his early twenties. He had come to Alaska for a "bit of an adventure" and hoped to pick up some money along the way. He never made the return journey and by his own admission had picked up a lot more than a few dollars. He really wasn't sure how much land he owned, but he knew it was a lot more than anyone else. He leased out several of his mines to local prospectors, and the "rental" on the lease was one tenth of the value of gold they extracted. How did he know how much each mine produced? "One thing you need to learn fast about miners," he informed me with a serious expression. "Never ask them too many questions, never ask how much they are digging, and absolutely never ask about the quantity or quality of the gold they process."

"So how do you know you are getting one tenth of their gold?" I persisted.

"I don't," he answered emphatically. "I take on trust what they give me." He paused for a moment. "I don't tell the IRS anything and they don't either, you understand?"

"Sure," I said. "It's a mutually beneficial conspiracy of trust."

"Exactly," he said, complimenting me on my understanding with a knowing wink.

A drive up into the hills at this time of the year confirmed to me just how fast summer was progressing. From a distance, the carpets of white mountain avens looked like the last remnants of snow, but as you looked closer you could see the pink blush of small clumps of moss campion and the deep purple of lupines, or an Alaskan breed of wild azalea. I mentioned to my companion the changing colors and how I understood what brought so many artists to Fairbanks. "Yeah, too damn many of them if you ask me. The place is coming down with artists, liberals and leftover hippies!"

Big John drove on to the mines and with macho redneck ebullience castigated anything that even smelled liberal or left wing. I listened and smiled quietly to myself. There wasn't a word coming out of his mouth that he or I believed.

"How did you make all your money?" I asked.

"Luck," he answered. "Like everybody else who made a little bankroll for themselves—luck, hard work and a lot of nervous energy."

Big John's bankroll was far from small, and he knew I knew it. When Big John realized you were not going to fall for his tall tales or that you saw through his redneck persona, he spoke openly. Apparently he made his money at the beginning of the oil boom. Having obtained the contract to supply the oil fields in the far north with everything from pencil sharpeners to giant propellers, he worked an eighteen-hour day organizing fleets of trucks on the haul roads and flotillas of Dakota freight planes flying from the lower 48 with heavy precision-engineered parts. "It was madness. I was ordering men and machines about like I was conducting the Second World War. Christ, I was only twenty-three at the time and before I was twenty-eight I had more millions in my bank account than I knew what to do with."

I was waiting for him to add some fantastic elaboration, but he didn't need to—the truth was fantastical enough. After the oil boom had settled and the pipeline was up and running, he looked around for something to do with his money. He had had a lot of fun with it in the meantime but was tired of fun. Because of luck and boredom, he bought up large mining companies that had ceased functioning. The price of gold on the world market was too erratic and the cost of extraction too high for the large companies to continue. Big John bought them not really knowing what they comprised. He laughed at the idea that he had become the largest private landowner in the state without knowing it. "Hell, I'm still trying to work out what the company owns, and where it is. Apparently, I now possess the fullest, most detailed and complete history of mining in America since I bought the company and all its records. The Smithsonian thinks I should donate it to them. But I keep telling them I had to pay a lot of money for them, and if they are that valuable to them they should do likewise. And if they don't, well, it's kind of nice to own a chunk of history." I remembered his machine shop in Fairbanks and how all the long-outdated machines were kept clean and in working order. I believed his sentiments about the value of owning history.

I was just about to ask him another question when he announced that we were on the site of one of the mines he had leased. I could see nothing but mile upon mile of heaped rock and earth, as if a huge urban motorway was under construction. Everywhere as far as the eye could see there were piles of spoil and ugly man-made lakes that had been created when the earth was scooped up in search of gold. John told me that the miners are supposed to return the land to its original state. "But no one ever sees, and no one ever makes them," he said. I had not expected one mine to cover such a vast tract of land, but my companion explained that the permafrost was too difficult to dig through and too cold and dangerous to work for long periods. "In Alaska, you just gotta scratch the surface to find gold," he announced, pointing to the giant digger trucks hauling away hundreds of tons of the land surface to be washed by a huge machine called a dredge. After that, the waste or spoil was carted off to be dumped wherever was handy. It only took three men to work seven million dollars' worth of earth-breaking machinery, and there were dozens and dozens of such mines. "Well," I thought to myself, "you don't have to go to the moon to see lunar landscapes."

We drove around for some twenty minutes as John explained to me how the operation worked. It was simple enough, and probably the one thing that had changed since Jack London's days was the number of men, giant trucks and earthmovers. I asked him if anyone mined underground. He said that only a few big corporations could afford the technology and machinery to make it profitable. I thought of the three men working this mine with their seven million dollars' worth of equipment. How could they ever afford to pay off the bank loan for such equipment? "Well," offered John, "the bank has no trouble lending it, so these guys must have no trouble paying it back." And with no more explanation than that he said there was one guy operating underground, in one of the abandoned mines that had belonged to the company he had bought. One or two men could still make a living in these old mines, but few men stuck it out for very long. It was very hard physical work in extremes of cold that are so profoundly invasive that part of you had to be already dead to stay there.

John addressed the man who was working the underground shaft only as Mark, an ex-Vietnam veteran who had arrived in Alaska a few years after his demob. Mark brought his AK 47, or something equivalent, with him from his homestead in the woods to the mine.

"Why?" I asked.

"It's a free country up here. A man can do what he wants. Anyway, with a man like Mark you don't ask too many questions."

"Why?" I persisted, imagining some psychotic backwoodsman or John Bircher, seeing the enemy behind every tree and shooting at imaginary ghosts.

"You'll see," John said. "Mark isn't much given to talking. He's kinda choosy about what he says and who he says it to. But he's the best goddamned miner in this part of Alaska."

I ventured some more questions about the man, but all John could tell me was that he had been living alone in the woods for twenty-eight years or more and only ventured into Fairbanks for essential supplies. The rest of the time either John or other miners working a few miles away collected whatever he needed for him.

"But if he is so good a miner and he has been living out in the bush for so long, what does he do with all the gold?"

The question was obvious enough, and I should have known the enigmatic answer John would give.

"Don't know, and don't ask," he said.

So we drove on, with me feeling edgy. I wondered how I might approach this recluse. John seemed to read my thinking. "You and him might have something in common, and I won't be surprised if you get more out of him in twenty minutes than anybody else has in twenty years!"

Mark's mining camp was a small, cramped affair with some items of heavy machinery heaving out black exhaust fumes and a pile of rusting metal parts, the hulks of several small trucks and several freshly deposited mounds of earth and rock. "Might be a few dollars in that lot," John said by way of a greeting as he slid out from the truck, gesturing for me to remain. Mark said nothing as his eyes wandered from John to me. I didn't want to engage his glance and stared about me, feigning complete indifference. John and Mark moved toward the cabin and talked for a few minutes. Once again Mark's face turned in my direction, but this time his eyes remained on me. I nodded my head and waved. Mark didn't return the gesture. Instead, John signaled for me to join them. I did so, slowly, as if I was approaching a wounded animal whose reactions I could only guess at.

John made the preliminary introduction and I held out my hand to Mark. He took it and nodded a silent acknowledgment. Then he looked at John again and asked, "Coffee?"

"Sure thing," said John as he and I followed Mark toward his shed.

"Only got two cups," Mark said quietly.

John, however, always carried a flask and a mug big enough to hold a pint of coffee with ease. He retrieved it from his truck, along with a half-finished quarter bottle of whiskey which he poured into the three cups once Mark had filled them with coffee. I thought it was a promising gesture and that perhaps John was right. Maybe Mark would be amenable to talking to a stranger. I already knew the taboo topics for miners and sensed a few others Mark might acutely shy away from.

The three of us exchanged some idle chitchat about the past winter and the amount of game in the hills. Mark was self-sufficient when it came to a meat supply, and out in the wilderness where he lived no one was going to argue whether he took a moose or any other game out of season. I asked Mark banal questions about working in extreme conditions and living for so many years out in the bush alone. His answers were courteous and sometimes monosyllabic. He had the most intriguing blue eyes, neither steely nor soft, but they had a light in them that forced you to look into his face. In a man who wanted to give little away, it made the exchange difficult.

Out of the blue, he asked, "You been in Alaska long?"

"No," I replied, "but it's my second visit."

"Ever been down a mine?"

"No," I answered again, realizing that he was happier asking the questions.

Big John, reading some signal I couldn't, made some excuse about going to check his cell phone and walked back to his truck. Mark and I walked to the entrance to his underground shaft. He handed me a bulky flashlight. "It's a long way down and very dark down there," he said. "You okay with that?" At first I wasn't sure if he was suggesting that perhaps he should come with me. But there was something in the way he said it that made me realize that Big John had maybe informed him of my own history in Lebanon.

"Been in worse places, I think," I said, emphasizing the last two words.

Mark nodded and walked back toward his shed. He was a lean, angular man. Everything about his movement was slow and precise. It was difficult to tell his age, apart from the fact that he was a Vietnam veteran. He handled his body easily and there was no fat on it. I certainly hadn't seen any whiskey veins in his face or any debauched look about him.

So I was left to my own devices, and I entered the gaping mouth of the shaft pleased that he had given me permission to enter his world but unsure of where it might take me. Less than twenty feet into this frozen artery into the earth, silence walks through you and hermetically seals you off from the world you have just left behind. I searched the ice-encased walls with my big flat-faced flashlight. I could see a tweedy mixture of rock, earth, pebble and, unbelievably, the twinkling white crusts of seashells. Everything was clear as crystal against the bright beam of the flashlight. Then, suddenly, the beam picked up a fury of white charging toward me. I couldn't see what it was. My breath left me and I fell in defensive fear against the entrance wall. Some irrational part of me thought I had disturbed some monster whose breath was roaring past me. Then it was gone in an instant. I turned to look at the sky-blue opening that framed the entrance to the mine. Several ptarmigan were skittering into the sky, furious at my presence.

I continued on down the mine, every part of me tingling with adrenaline. I imagined I could hear my heart beating back at me like an echo from the pitch dark in front of me. But the absolute chill of the place soon numbed my nervous reaction, and paradoxically at the same time comforted me. The permafrost held the hollow together harder than several layers of tempered steel. Then, panic. What if there was some sudden glacial shift along the ancient fault line the mine had penetrated? Such shifts occur daily in Alaska but are of little significance and register infinitesimally on the surface. But I was way below and the ceiling could collapse, or, worse, the walls and floor could be crushed together and I would be fossilized here like something out of a Hammer horror film!

I kept going, down into the ice-numbing, petrifying dark. Just one glint of gold would make this endurable, I told myself. But I saw nothing, only the beam getting brighter as the dark got darker. I had had enough. If there was air down here, I wasn't breathing it. Something greater than fear was smothering me.

I returned to the surface and walked back to where Mark and Big John stood examining the petrol generator that powered light into the mine. I tried to imitate the deliberate gait of Mark. "How anybody reckons that hell's a hot place is beyond me," I said, with macho suaveness. Neither man reacted, beyond acknowledging my presence. "Jesus, Mark," I continued, "you must have lead-lined bones to work down there, or maybe you have a centrally heated diving suit somewhere?" My jokes passed over their heads.

"There's more coffee over there, but the whiskey's all gone," John said.

I nodded, but I was sure there was nothing that could ease the coldness in my bones.

After a few minutes, both men joined me.

"How do you do it, Mark, year in and year out? There's got to be more than gold down there."

"Well, there weren't no topless ladies either, that's for sure," John chimed in. Maybe he was anxious I was about to break the taboo.

Mark smiled, ever so slightly. "You get used to it after a while and then it doesn't feel cold anymore. Sometimes it can be colder up here than down the mine."

Somehow Mark seemed to soften when he spoke about the mine. It was as if the mine was a place of refuge. We continued our conversation with more animation now. Mark asked me naïve questions about Beirut and Belfast, which was only to be expected from a man who had had his own fair share of violence and had lived so far from human habitation that few enough fragments of world affairs interested him or even reached him. The afternoon soon brought itself to an end, and John and I headed back toward Fairbanks.

"Well, he seemed to take to you," John ventured.

"Yes," I returned, and smiled. "I suppose you can't make up for a quarter of a century of solitary living in one afternoon. Do you reckon something bad happened to him in Vietnam?"

"Other miners around here say so, though nobody quite rightly knows exactly what, and if he hasn't said in twenty years he isn't intending to."

Big John was right, but a part of me felt that whatever it was that troubled Mark he took it with him into the dark cold of the mine and left it there. He seemed happy and at peace with his unspoken obsession. I wondered if John had much regular contact with the man, and asked him. He then launched into a story that threw all my observations up in the air.

Some time ago John had been "mooching around" up in the hills and had called on some of the miners working his leases.

Several of them mentioned that they had not seen Mark for almost a year. Miners keep pretty much to themselves, but independents like Mark usually run out of something or need a machine part eventually so they call at the other mines for help. The favor is returned whenever it is required. So the disappearance of Mark worried John. The man lived so far out in the bush that if anything serious had happened to him no one would have known.

John decided to pay him a visit, but found no sign of him at his mine. He knew where his cabin was but had only been there once, many years before. So he drove as far as his 4×4 would take him, then started walking to the cabin. Big John knew that the man he was going to check up on didn't appreciate unwanted visitors, so he kept shouting at the top of his voice as he approached the man's home. He emphasized that he did not want to be mistaken for a bear or a moose, and that Mark's reclusive nature plus his semiautomatic rifle wouldn't be too concerned to discriminate either way. "All the way up to his cabin I kept hollering and shouting and got no response. I had a mind more than once to turn back. Being out alone in the bush has a way of making you jumpy. This guy had been living half his life out there and there were enough stories and rumors about him and dozens of other 'crazies' to make me want to turn back every time I put a foot forward. I was so scared I didn't want to shout too loud in case he had gone off his head and decided I was the enemy coming to kill him."

I smiled at this point, but John was having none of it.

"I'll tell you, man, I wasn't smiling. I'm not what you would call a small man, and the trees up here are hardly thick enough to hide a brush pole behind. So if he started shooting I was dead meat for sure."

It was obvious that John was serious, so I listened more intently.

"The nearer I got to the cabin the more I told myself to turn back, and when I reached it I must have stood there for ten min-

utes or more calling out to him. But there was no answer. I didn't
know what to do. I thought, 'What if I go and knock on his door
and he's inside in some weird paranoid state?' He could come
flying out of that cabin firing on all cylinders and it would be
bye-bye, John. He could dump my body for the birds and the
bears to pick at and that would be the end of me. I would never
be found. And even if I was, who would know or could prove
anything?"

"Okay, John," I said, utterly intrigued. "You're here now, so
what happened?"

"Well, as I got near the cabin door I could hear loud music
playing. It was dance music, like a waltz or something. If he is
alive, no wonder he can't hear me, and if he's not in there, then
I'm clearing out of here faster than if a big Kodiak was running
after me. So I went up to his door making as much noise as I
could and stood there, waiting to see if it would open. I must
have stood for a couple of minutes more listening to this loud
waltz music, then, as I was about to bang the door with a big
lump of timber I had picked up, it suddenly swung open."

John paused for a long moment. "And?" I said, half screaming at him.

"Well, there he stood, dressed in an immaculate tuxedo complete with white shirt and bow tie." I was aghast, but John continued as if he hadn't noticed, "In one hand he had a full cocktail
glass with olives on a stick, and in the other a long, slim cigar.
'My dear John,' he said, 'do come and join me for an aperitif.' "

The story was so unreal it was almost believable. "And did
you?" I asked, trying to deflate my storyteller's imagination.

"Did I shit," John answered, looking at me as if I was crazier
than the man he was talking about. "I just mumbled something
about people not having seen him about for some time and that
if everything was okay with him I would head on back home,
and you know what? He just said, 'Gracious of you, John,' and
closed the door on me. I can tell you, I charged back through the

woods calling him so many names that ain't in the dictionary. I stopped at a bar on the way back and downed half a dozen shots of Jack Daniel's in double-quick time, asking myself if I had really seen what I had seen."

As he finished I was asking myself if I really believed what I had just heard.

"Have you ever asked him about it since?"

"No," John replied. "There ain't much point."

I thought about it for a moment and half agreed with him.

Perhaps because the story had put it in his mind, or the whiskey-laced coffee at the mine had given him a taste for it, John stopped at a roadside store while we were still in the hills and told me he wouldn't be long. He returned with two one-eighths of Jack Daniel's in tiny hip-pocket-sized bottles and threw one on my knee, gesturing for me to drink. His fantastic story had whetted my appetite, so I did.

We drove languidly back toward Fairbanks, John occasionally pointing out features of the landscape and telling me more stories. One was about an old prospector out in the woods who lived off the frozen remains of a woolly mammoth he had discovered.

"Come on, John, do you expect me to believe that?"

He smiled. "Well, I sold the whole package to the people who make *Northern Exposure* and they bought it."

I had to smile as I swallowed another mouthful of Jack Daniel's. "How rich are you, John? You don't need to sell ideas, do you?"

Then John launched into a quantification of his wealth. "I only discovered what I had bought when I began to look at the title. Then I saw that the navigation floodlights for Alaska Airlines were constructed along my new property. So I told them they should reimburse me for the use of my land. Their response was that they never had to pay the original company and that they didn't see why they had to pay me. Okay, I said, build a new airport because I'm gonna knock them down. You have fixtures on my land that you need to pay for, and it doesn't lose me no sleep to remove those lights."

I was enjoying the repartee the Jack Daniel's had opened up. "So what happened?" I asked.

"Well, they argued it, said that the mining company that had previously owned the land hadn't objected or cared. But I said to them, 'So what? You have flightpath lights constructed on my land. Pay for that or move your airport.' There was all sorta arguments, but they paid up in the end."

I laughed at the idea of Big John taking the airlines to task and winning. But it wasn't the only case.

"You know, I sold this idea to the oil companies of how they could soften their image and develop a tourist industry around the old dredges. We spent weeks talking about it and they seemed taken by the idea. Draw it out on paper, they said, and I did. The next thing was they went off with all the ideas and the blueprint I had given them and began to implement it. So I thought, 'What the hell's going on?' I contacted the oil company and said, 'Give me a couple of thousand dollars for the work I put in, delivering these ideas.' " Big John took another swallow from his eighth of Jack Daniel's. "I had given them the whole idea, displayed it on paper. They thanked me for my interesting ideas but said it wouldn't work. Then up they get and do it themselves, exactly as I had suggested and laid down for them. So I said to them, 'Come on, guys, this was my idea. Pay me a thousand dollars' recognition and carry on yourselves.' Well, they denied I had put the idea to them. And when I insisted and threatened legal action they responded with a statement like, 'Listen, we have got more money and more lawyers than you can count, so you need to think real hard before threatening us.' So I did think about it, and for their cheek I took them to court."

"Don't tell me," I said, laughing. "And what happened?" I asked, enjoying every minute of the story.

"Well, it went to court and the jury ruled in my favor. It was a case of the little guy against the big guys. They ruled forty million in my favor. But the oil company immediately appealed it. I'm not bothered. They owe me forty million and they can appeal all they want."

I was loving this story. Big John was probably worth more than that several times over, but his lawsuit was about the theft of ideas, intellectual property rights, and he had won.

"So you're an intellectual entrepreneur!" I said.

John just drove and sipped from his bottle, which I could hardly see behind his massive hands. "I wouldn't even know what those words meant," he said.

So we descended toward Fairbanks with John telling stories about the city dump and how if anyone wanted to know about the town they need only go there. "On Saturdays or Sundays it's like a church gathering. People come just to see what everybody else is throwing out, and instead of being embarrassed about taking someone else's throwaways they have coffee and sandwiches. The conversation is amazing. Everyone is talking and looking and waiting to grab something before anyone else does. You know, I could do a master's degree on a sociological study of the dumpsters and it would be the most brilliant piece on life in Alaska."

I laughed as I sipped from my own bottle, thinking that Big John was more of an intellectual entrepreneur than he thought.

He dropped me near my cabin with the parting remark from me that it had been a good day and that he was a fabulous liar. Big John just smiled and insisted we meet again when I was back in Fairbanks. He called out, "I got your book off Amazon!" and drove off. I wasn't sure what that was supposed to imply, but a line from Jimmy Dean—"everybody knew you didn't give no lip to big John"—emerged out of the ether. I liked Big John Reese, and I knew he liked me. I didn't believe half of what he told me; I believed everything.

On our way back through the hills on a road that had been cut through the tree line, a young wolf had padded unconcernedly across our path. John had just been saying that a person could walk five miles into the bush and be lost forever. The wolf passed across the roadway without feeling the need to slow or stop. "I have been here half my life and I have never seen that," John stated, genuinely astounded. "Wolves never, never, ever come this near anything that smells of man. You have just witnessed a rare thing, and so have I."

That night I went to bed thinking about Vladimir and Mark, John Luther Adams, John Reese and the wolf that had crossed our path. Maybe it was the Jack Daniel's, maybe it was the big raven that watched me walk up the path to my cabin, or maybe it was all the other maybes these few weeks had thrown up, but I was sure about no sense of reality. I opened my notebook and began with another maybe: "Maybe I'm on the Yellow Brick Road with the lion, the tin man, the scarecrow and whatever else the kingdom of Oz might throw up."

I had time only for a brief rendezvous with Debra about our trip into the Far North. I already accepted that she was a woman of exceptional gifts, with powers beyond my understanding. When she explained that during my travels she too had been traveling in the spirit realm, everything looked good around me. She informed me that her own "helpers" in the spirit realm were encouraging for her also. I couldn't question her on this, as I was in the dark about the physical journey we were intending to make as much as I was about the spirit world I had been dropped into.

We quickly agreed on dates, and Debra described a loose itinerary west from Fairbanks to Kotzebue on the Bering Strait and then south down the coast toward Nome. In Kotzebue we would meet up with some local Eskimos who would take us by boat through a network of sea inlets to find and stay with Charlie and Lena, an old shaman and his wife. "Eskimos are very laid back about things, so don't expect everything to work out to a prearranged schedule," Debra warned. I was okay with whatever she said. She was the guide, and I was more than an innocent abroad. I made a list of equipment and clothing that she suggested I should bring.

"Won't your family miss you while you're gone?" I asked.

She replied that her husband would be more than happy to see her go. As for her son, he was a very mature fourteen-year-old who loved being alone with his dad. That prompted me to think of my own family, whom I had left to their own devices in a mobile home.

"What's your son's name?" I asked automatically.

"Keenan," she replied, her face and voice passive as poured cream. Which was exactly the opposite of what her answer had caused in me.

"Keenan?" I exclaimed, although the word hardly came out of my mouth for my throat was dry with sudden nervous confusion. "How? Where from?" The words fell out of me like a blind man feeling his way along a cliff edge. I knew of only one other person in the world who had had Keenan as a first name, an old Hollywood actor named Keenan Wynn. "Why?" I insisted. "You have no family connections to the name, in your or your husband's history."

"No, none," she confirmed, that same stillness in her voice.

"But why, then?"

"It was given to me," she said.

There was silence between us. I looked at the woman, knowing that I didn't need to ask from where she had been given it. I did a quick calculation. At the time I would have been locked up in Lebanon doing my own traveling in the ether of the imagination, tumbling through planes of existence and finding myself looking down on extraordinary landscapes and places that both baffled and consoled me. I said nothing of this to Debra, but thought to myself about how people's lives are tied together across time and space without their knowing.

I left Debra bemused by the strange things that happened whenever we met, and part of me was swallowing down some apprehension about where it was all going to lead.

That evening I took out my notebook again. The comparison of the Land of Oz with Alaska wasn't as far-fetched as it appeared. Dorothy, the lion, the tin man and the scarecrow were all creatures in search of something that they hoped would be granted to them by the magnificent Wizard of Oz. In a similar way, I felt that in the past few days I had met some people who had come to Alaska in search of something. Each of them in their different way had been spellbound by the place and all of them had been "enchanted" by the landscape. I mean "enchanted" in the medieval sense of being bewitched or under a spell. All had decided to remain. Each of them had found something liberating, enriching and healing in their relationship to the wilderness. The composer was granted a unique creative energy. Big John lived life with ebullience and gusto. Behind all his bravado was a huge sensitive heart, richer than all his accidental wealth. Even Mark with his fathomless eyes, bluer than the bluest Alaskan landscape, was about to bury his troubles in the cold earth and be at peace with himself and whatever ghosts and fantasies reside in his outback home. Each of them was an outsider in his own way and "the Big Lonely" had befriended that part of them and had shaped it, giving it a meaning and context, and had even drained the hurt out of it. They had found their home place and were happy with it. I paused for a moment from my speculations, and smiled to myself. Did I really see Debra as another Dorothy, dancing me along the yellow brick road? And although I had not met him yet, Charlie, the Eskimo shaman, could not be another Wizard of Oz!

*

CHAPTER TWENTY-ONE

ARCTIC INUA

I was acutely aware that the Far North Arctic coast was some-thing I was unprepared for, so in the few days I had before catching a flight with my guide Debra I tried to glean some information that would make me feel more comfortable. But even as I attempted to read books on the Eskimo people, I realized how little I knew. I had to start from first principles. Debra explained that Inuit was an umbrella term, like its English equivalent, Eskimo. All Eskimos were Inuits. But the Inuits in this part of Alaska had a regional name, Inupiat. In another region they might be called Yupik.

I began to discover something of the cultural complexity of Alaska, and to learn the importance of affiliation and ancestry. In a formal situation, I gathered, a native Alaskan might introduce himself by outlining his English name, followed by his tribal name, then the moiety (say, eagle), then the specific clan. This would be further elaborated by the house to which he belongs (say, iceberg house and iron house). Then he would declare his crest, e.g., bear, iceberg and porpoise. In this elaborate introduction is encoded a wealth of history, myth and legend. When I considered this, I thought how impoverished my own reply would sound. My frenetic reading was throwing up other details that intrigued me, such as how to make Eskimo ice cream by whipping bear, moose or caribou fat, then leaving it until it cools. It is flavored with seal oil, meat or fish and sweetened with honey, sugar or berries. The thought of such a delicacy did not excite me, but it did highlight just how little I knew.

And I discovered another curious fact. One of the many stories that have been collected out of the "Eskimo" folk tradition is described as the longest story ever told. The *Epic of Quyaq* chronicles the journeys of a young man. It's a mythological tale that originally took over a month to narrate and is more than a thousand years old.

So here I was trying to absorb the culture of a people that had explained themselves from the complex mythology of Quyaq's epic to the curiosity of Eskimo ice cream. This was indeed a long way from igloos on ice floes and men in bearskin parkas peering patiently into holes in the ice waiting to catch a seal for supper. Against these ice cream and myth makers my own experience seemed a lot less colorful, maybe even mundane. It was useless to attempt to become acquainted with this alien cultural repository; I would just have to take it as I found it, and they would have to take me as they found me.

Kotzebue was our point of arrival and, I suppose, our point of departure into the Inupiat wilderness. The village is almost directly in the path of what is known as the Bering Land Bridge, a thousand-mile-wide ridge of dry land that is thought to have existed between Asia and North America during the ice age (it is now submerged). According to the land bridge theory, humans followed migratory animals from Asia into North America thousands of years ago.

I wasn't sure what to expect an Eskimo village to be like, but whatever it was, Kotzebue was not it. What you see, after flying over millions of acres of tundra, is the end of a narrow spit that looks as if it has been leveled with a bulldozer and then constructed on a street grid laid on poured gravel. Kotzebue is estimated to be the oldest settlement in Alaska, but it is also a modern technological miracle. You land on an airstrip, for example, that floats on a six-inch layer of Styrofoam-type material over permafrost that is 2,240 feet deep. At first glance, as the plane taxis down the runway, the place more closely resembles an industrial park or a laborers' encampment than a town.

We had to wait for our boatmen to arrive and take us by skiff across the Kotzebue Sound, then up through a mosaic of sloughs where the Noatak River breaks out into the sea. Debra could not be specific about where we were going; only the boatmen knew. When I inquired how long we might have to wait for them, she informed me again that only the boatmen knew. She did, however, know a relative of Charlie and Lena's who lived in the town so we could wait at her cabin until the boatmen collected us.

Fanny Mendenhall was in her early nineties (she wasn't sure exactly), but she looked twenty-five years younger. She lived alone in one of the prefabricated wooden cabins that the whole town seemed to consist of. Even in her old age Fanny was alert and an able conversationalist. There was another passenger who had been on our flight in Fanny's house when we arrived. I assumed she was a relative, and sat quietly in the Eskimo home as Debra, Fanny and the other visitor chatted. Fanny did not know the woman any more than she knew me, but as I was learning, strangers are never made to feel unwelcome in an Eskimo home. The inbred ethic of respect for all beings is effortlessly upheld without ceremony or affectation. The Eskimo will share their home, their food and their company as if they had known you forever.

Fanny's living room would easily have been big enough for us all except that it, like her kitchen and hallway, was overflowing with clothes, boots, magazines, books and cardboard boxes of all shapes and sizes. I put it down to her age: it must be difficult for her to pack things away. Debra again corrected me. Order and tidiness are not a prerequisite in the Eskimo way of life. Things are valued for what can be done with them and how they assist in making life easier. Where they are left or how they are stored is of no consequence. The Eskimo has a visual capacity far superior to a white person's, but "they don't see clutter!" Having spent many years treating Eskimo people during her time as a nurse in Nome, Debra knew much about their day-to-day life.

There was a cloying odor of fish hanging in the air, and the whole house felt like an oven. I said so to Debra and remarked that I might go for a walk around the town. She walked me to the door, explaining that Fanny and the other woman were talking about Fanny's home. Fanny was complaining that she had never been warm since she moved into it. She had apparently spent her young life growing up in a sod and whalebone home, part of which was underground. She always remembers being warm there. The cabin let in too many Arctic drafts and winds, even though it was centrally heated by oil. I remember the two women laughing as Fanny joked that before the Christians came the Inupiat people lived underground, where it was warm, and buried their dead on the surface, where it was cold. "Now the Christians have us all living up here with our long-dead ancestors," she quipped.

While walking around the town I came across a signpost telling me I was 180 miles from Russia, 4,000 miles from Washington, 6,000 miles from Greenland and 1,500 miles from the North Pole. There were two blank spaces beside the words "Sunset" and "Sunrise." I tried to work out if the spaces were blank because at this time of year there was neither a sunrise nor a sunset worth talking about, or if it was simply another wry Eskimo joke, much like Fanny's.

I walked on, smiling, through the block sections of unpaved roads, past the Quaker church established in 1897. I couldn't imagine who had brought the Quakers here over a hundred years ago, but I could imagine how bleak and desolate it must have been. Many of the cabins along these roads seemed to rise out from a midden of over-wintering debris. Dogsleds lay on the roof alongside racks of caribou antlers. The ground was piled with driftwood; rib cages of seal or perhaps walrus lay yellowing amid barrels, snow machines' outboard motors, and mountains of netting and oil drums, and every household had a long wooden rack for drying fish. Occasionally the remains of such fish hung black and shriveled like melted rubber tire, unrecognizable as fish.

I walked past a huge wooden structure uplifted on spars with a sign that read "Alaska Commercial Company." I climbed the ramp to the entrance and went inside. It was a supermarket chocka-block with everything you would expect to be in a supermarket and lots and lots of all the necessary items that living in this extreme place required: Gore-Tex clothing, rubber boots, engine parts, fishing tackle of monstrous proportions, hand-held harpoons and harpoon guns, shotguns, rifles and ammunition to suit, knives of every description—the list could go on. Looking at all this, I wondered just how far these people had come from the Eskimo hunter who'd fished with tackle made of whale baleen, bone, bear claw and sharpened ivory, and who'd used braided sinew instead of nylon-coated lines of incredible strength.

As I walked out of the shop and down the ramp two old women approached me wearing fur-lined parkas and heavy baggy trousers tied into traditional Eskimo boots. Sled mittens hung round their necks and dangled at their waist. Their faces were buried in the huge cowl of their parkas and were wrinkled and lined to such an incredible degree that they looked like images in a daguerreotype photo. They pressed some money into my hands and asked me to go and buy some "soda pop" for them. I laughed and told them to go and buy it for themselves, but they were insistent, and I did as I was bid. When I returned with the cans of soft drink, they shuffled off in gratitude and delight. I don't know why these women didn't want to go into the store, but something about them informed me that no matter what modernism had brought to these people, they still inhabited their own very different world.

I still had time to call at the Museum of the Arctic. I caught the end of a slide show illustrating the changing seasons in this corner of the Arctic. I was trying to imagine this world when the screen faded to black and a single seal-oil lamp lit the place. Out of that soft dark emerged images of the bowhead whale, walrus and seal. Dall sheep, moose, caribou and musk ox appeared and disappeared like ghost creatures, and behind them the Inupiat drums beat and dancers arose. But this dancing was so different from the raw, shuffling, bestial energy of the Gwich'in and their caribou dance. These dances are almost Oriental or Hindu. The story is told through the movement of handheld fans trimmed with fur and feathers. The gestures, creating accentuated features, unfold the tale. The dancer's body moving to the rhythm of a drumbeat adds to the fascination.

On the way out, I studied some old black-and-white prints of the Eskimo people who had inhabited this land long before I was born. Their enigmatic Asiatic faces told of hardship and endurance that few other humans on the planet could have survived, and as they looked out across endless windswept whiteness you sensed that they could see something more than the blasted whiteness. Out in the street again I thought about the two old women who had stopped me and come and gone in an instant with their bottles of soda pop. They could have walked out of any of the old photos I had been looking at. But just because I had seen them and spoken with them didn't make them real. The Inupiat other world had already invaded my consciousness without my knowing. Was this a preparation for what was to come, or was it a warning? These thoughts were rolling round in the back of my head as I headed back to Fanny Mendenhall's cabin.

Debra was with the two boatmen, who were already packing our gear onto their truck to run it down to the beach. They said nothing as we drove the short distance to where an aluminum skiff with a powerful outboard motor lay on the boulder-and-rock shoreline of the Kotzebue Sound. I wondered if Debra had any more ideas about where we would be going. No. It had been many years since her last visit to Charlie's fish camp and she would never be able to find it again. In any case, although families return to the same camp year after year for generations to stock up on fish, wild berries, duck, seal and caribou, sometimes natural disaster forces them to move. However, unlike the rest of their people, Charlie and Lena chose to live at their fish camp all year round. These fish camps are in such remote locations that people work them only in the summer, when the salmon are running. In the depths of an Arctic winter they are impossible to get to.

Debra questioned the boatmen, who were relatives of Charlie's. They confirmed that he was still at the same place, though the route to reach him was different from the last time she had visited. "Seasons are all changing and it's changing the river course too. Charlie thinks he's gonna stay at the fish camp forever. Charlie's old man now, will have to move into town soon." As he finished speaking and loading the last of our bags, and some supplies for Charlie, the boatman looked at me. "You best put something warm on. It' gonna get cold out on the sound until we get across." It was said matter-of-factly, and he and his friend began to shove the boat into the water. I looked out at the murky stretch of ocean that was already throwing up wind-tossed whites. The boat suddenly seemed very small with its load; with the addition of the four of us it would look pathetic. I know nothing about boats, and I never learned to swim, so what the hell was I doing heading out into the Chukchi Sea in a tiny tin boat that sat so low in the water? The sea was already lapping at my fingertips as I clung to the sides before we had even moved off.

As the small boat pushed out into the choppy waters of the Kotzebue Sound, I noticed how carefully the boatmen had loaded us and our cargo of supplies and belongings. The larger of the two men sat up front with some of the heavier baggage behind him; I squatted in the middle with the light bags behind me; Debra and the other boatman took up the rear as the outboard roared us out across the waters. I quickly learned the reason for all this meticulous storage as the boat bucked in the choppy ocean and slapped back down into the troughs between waves. It was cold and intimidating way out in the middle of the sound. The sea was murky and ugly, as if ten million tons of earth had been stirred up. It was tiresomely slow, too, perhaps because you had nothing to look at but the soupy ocean and the waves banging against the hull. "If it was wintertime we would be crossing with a dog team," Debra volunteered. I looked out on the expanse of heaving water and found it hard to imagine it frozen solid. Nor could I really imagine a cold so intense that it could freeze an ocean. I had seen images of icebreakers moving through icebound seas on TV, but sitting in this tiny skiff with the cold numbing me and the waves wanting to tumble us all into its seething emptiness I was finding it difficult to believe what I knew to be fact.

There seemed no end to the tedium of the uncomfortable journey. Apart from Debra's one statement, no one spoke. The man in front of me sat in silence and never took his eyes off the water; the erratic rise and fall of the boat had no impact on his stillness. I tried to imitate his impervious demeanor, but the icy sea was only inches from me and we were miles from anywhere. I looked behind me at Debra and the helmsman, but she had turned her back to me to take the brunt of the wind. The man at the motor had fastened his parka up to the bridge of his nose and his face had disappeared into the dark folds of his fur-lined hood. A human voice would have been comforting, or some kind gesture to let me know where these speechless, faceless men were taking me, or even how much longer we would have to endure the dreadful journey. But everyone had turned into themselves. I pulled the collar of my coat about my ears. All my

questions about what I was doing, where I was going and why
fell into the sea or were blown away by the wind.

It seemed to take forever to reach the far side, but eventually
a perceptible lessening in the bouncing of the boat woke me from
my oblivion. Now we were moving easily up a wide river slough.
The banks on either side were steep, and I stood up to appreciate the lie of the land. Rolling away on both sides was endless
tundra as far as the eye could see. Not a tree grew to break up the
remoteness of the blasted heath. I sat down again. The high
banks provided a shelter and I was beginning to warm up again,
but still no one spoke; only the outboard droned softly as we
glided over the dark, still waters and penetrated deeper into the
wild. For about another three quarters of an hour we followed
the river course, and through all that time I watched anxiously
as cloud upon cloud of mosquitoes gathered into dizzying spiral
columns and hovered like sentinels, each no more than a few
yards from the next and some of them reaching fifteen to twenty
feet in height. There had to be millions of them in each of these
seething black pillars. I knew that my supply of repellents would
be useless against this infernal plague. I tried to convince myself
that perhaps they would remain near the river and that Charlie
and Lena's place would be sensibly placed far back from it.

And that was exactly how we found it. Charlie and Lena's
"fish camp" was marked by a large white tent erected on the
riverbank. Beside and adjacent to it was a long, rough table sitting on a platform of old timber boards. Around the table sat a
collection of plastic basins and buckets along with barrels, tin oil
drums and aluminum baths. Beside the work table and stretching out along the bank were several fish racks and a skinning
horse—basically a plank of timber turned into its narrow end
and held up at either end by timber supports. Over this, the skin
of a seal was stretched. As it dried, the excess fatty membranes
could be scraped off with an ulu, that famous half-moon-shaped
cutting edge that native peoples in this region use for every
task that requires a sharp edge. About 150 yards back from the

river, perched on a high bluff that overlooked the river and the endless tundra plain, Charlie and Lena's wooden cabin sat low and squat. A welcome windbreak of trees and bushes sheltered it, though its summer smoke belched out of the short pipe chimney.

We hauled our bags across a stepping-stone path made in the marshy tundra and climbed up the thirty-foot incline to our new home. Apart from the cabin, there were three outhouses. One was the toilet, a replica of many all over Alaska. Two wooden planks had had a semicircle cut from the center of them and had been placed side by side across two large drum containers at either side of a large, deep hole in the ground. The other small outhouses consisted of a workshop full of tools and parts of snow machines, and a tanning shed for hides. Flung across a long cargo sled was the hide of a brown bear. Later, I discovered the body parts of animals in very advanced stages of decomposition hanging from the branches of trees at the perimeter of the camp. Only one tree had been left to grow in the center of Charlie's enclosed camp; all the others had been cut and cleared to let the wind blow through.

It was a bright day, and the Arctic sun was heating up the place. Lena was overjoyed to see Debra and made a great fuss of her. When I was introduced she looked me up and down intently, then whispered something to Debra. Both women giggled as they regarded me again. Charlie, the old shaman healer, unlike his wife, made no fuss over our presence. Instead he sat on an old tubular-framed chair like a Buddha under his bodhi tree. I knew Charlie was an old man, somewhere in his nineties, but his lean frame and drawn face were not purely the results of aging. His narrow, angular face looked as if the skin had been stretched across his skull and left to dry there like the sealskin on the skinning horse. He walked with a stick, and it was obvious he was suffering some discomfort, but his hands still looked strong and his forearms displayed long strands of muscle under his skin. When we shook hands, his grasp confirmed what I suspected. As I looked from Charlie to Lena, I decided that you could only discern the classic Eskimo features in Charlie at a second glance. Charlie may have been living in this Arctic coast when few white men ever thought of coming here, but I was sure there was some white Russian or Scandinavian blood in his ancestry, maybe from the whaling ships or the fur traders who came here in the 1800s. But then, when I looked at him again, I thought he looked like a little old Japanese fisherman. There was an impassive stillness in his face that did not let you penetrate behind his exterior presence.

Lena, on the other hand, was ethnically beautiful. She had the tiny round face of the true Inupiat. Her small, dark eyes glowed out from the Asian slant in which they were set. Though she was in her mid-sixties, her long black hair shone in the sun and the first traces of silver were only just beginning to show. Her face was full of life, spirit and fun, the way her husband's was not. The lines on her face could have suggested that she was much older, but even her lack of teeth did not detract from the femininity that radiated from her. She laughed coyly behind her hands like a geisha, yet had no fear of the camera and posed effortlessly. I was mesmerized by her gorgeous, warm, womanly face, and by her infectious sense of girlish fun.

Charlie hobbled inside his cabin on his aluminum hospital-issue walking stick. It was one of the few concessions to modernity I could see in this wilderness homestead. The curious irony struck me: here was this reputed shaman healer who had worked attested and medically inexplicable "healing" on thousands of people supporting himself on this medically designed crutch. But the thought left me as soon as I entertained it. The people who live in these extreme regions are the ultimate pragmatists. They have survived for untold centuries by utilizing anything and everything. Charlie's metal stick was light and adaptable to his height, and it would not rot, nor snap, forcing him to go and cut another piece of wood. It served him well.

We entered the cabin through the kitchen area. There was no

running water or cozy modern appliances; a small cooker running on bottled gas was the only concession to modern living. Pots and pans, bowls, plates, knives and forks were littered everywhere. The open shelves held an assortment of tins and dried foods. Underneath, the worktop revealed a plethora of containers, buckets and basins. Opposite the kitchen was a small storage area that was even more littered with too many things for me to decipher what exactly they were. The rest of the cabin comprised one large living-room area with two smaller rooms sectioned off as sleeping quarters, I assumed. Charlie's big, handmade bed was set off to one side of the living area opposite a huge woodburning stove. The heat it was throwing into the room was suffocating. It was high summer, but Charlie insisted on burning his woodstove.

For an instant I imagined snowdrifts engulfing the tiny cabin, Arctic windstorms howling across the tundra, the moon lighting up a wintery whiteout landscape that would make you feel that you were the only person alive on the earth. The constant darkness, and the below-freezing temperatures so severe that to go even a few feet outside for firewood could mean risking your life, and to expose your hands for a few minutes longer than you should would certainly mean frostbite of such severity that you might have to amputate your own fingers to stop gangrene killing you. Even as I was thinking this I saw the huge CB radio system that was Charlie and Lena's only connection to the outside world. In the worst of the winter months they might be able to contact someone in an emergency, but there was no guarantee that anyone could reach them.

There was a big old sofa a few feet from the bedside. It looked as if it had been around a long time. There were also a couple of armchairs of different design, one by the radio and the other near the stove. These two seemed the worse for wear, but as Charlie and Lena had had thirteen children and God knows how many grandchildren who would have visited them over many summers, I could understand their disheveled, rickety appearance.

In any case, it was a long way to go to the nearest furniture store! I noticed little in the way of decoration on the walls. I was sure neither of my hosts put much thought into the appearance of things.

Behind one of the easy chairs was an old TV set. Piled in columns behind that were dozens of videocassette boxes and dozens more books. A bank of heavy-duty car batteries on the floor beside the radio confirmed the power source. Neither the titles of the books nor the films told me much about these people, except that they would read or watch whatever came their way. Years of living and raising a family in the wilderness had not allowed Charlie or his wife to develop any discerning tastes in literature or film. But then, that was my world, and it had no application here.

Charlie had taken to his bed as soon as we had come into the room; he sat propped up with pillows and was explaining to Debra that he had had a bad fall from his snow machine last winter and had broken and fractured a few ribs and bones in his wrist and arm. He had been unable to get back to his cabin, as the machine was too damaged and injuries to his foot and leg meant that he couldn't walk. He had had to spend several days and nights out on the frozen wilderness waiting until his son picked up his trail and brought him back. I thought that anyone else would have given up and died out there. I stood at the window beside his bed and looked down on the river we had traveled along and out over the vast tundra beyond. I could imagine how this panorama changed with the seasons and even how the huge sky enfolding the horizon line could change daily. I could even imagine Charlie and Lena sitting at this window looking out over plains of snow with the aurora fusing and unfolding above them.

As if she was reading my thinking, Debra informed me how during early autumn you could watch small herds of caribou and their young crossing the river and heading south. They sometimes stayed for days out on the tundra, filling up on the last long shoots of winter grass. I had noticed several racks of antlers piled up between the cabin and the fish camp. I asked Charlie about these, wondering if he had acquired his injury while out hunting caribou. He explained he never needed to travel after the animal; they came to him. He always shot the caribou in the water, where it was easier to retrieve; a wounded animal was also easier to finish off in the water, rather than having to run across the tundra. Charlie said he didn't eat much caribou meat anyway during the autumn migration. The bull flesh was still strong from the rut, but their hides were at their best. Caribou hide was unequaled for warmth and made the finest winter clothing and sled blankets. Charlie declared that the caribou was a nomad like himself, and now that he was too old to travel much he had less reason to take a caribou.

I left Charlie and Debra to talk and went outside again. The land rose up from the site of the cabin in a long, slow incline. There were lots of spruce trees with good-sized girths, which obviously fed Charlie's stove. I kicked around the buildings taking perspectives from different positions that its elevated site had thrown up. But whatever spectacular vista was set before me, I was not taking it in. I had traveled this far ostensibly to learn and attempt to understand the spirit world of these people through this old shaman. Their profound belief in the "spirit" of the land, or "inua" (a Gaelic and native Alaskan word for spirit), is why they survive here. But now, having come so far, I suddenly didn't feel so determined to inquire into this world. There was some kind of futility in walking into people's homes and lives in pursuit of old stories, as if in coming to this extreme place the door of the spirit world would blow open. And what if it did? Would I be able to look into it and understand its reality? If I was hardly taking in the landscape in front of me, how could I hope to see into the other world that lay both in it and on the other side of it?

That evening and for the rest of my stay all of us except Lena slept in the big living room with Charlie. Even two of Charlie's grown sons, who stayed most of the day in the fish-camp tent or went off in a small boat, returning late in the evening, occasionally joined us in our communal slumbers. They never spoke and were gone again in the morning. Sometimes one of them would come up to the cabin during the day, make himself something to eat, then leave again without much more than a nod of acknowledgment, and only then if I had initiated the exchange. At first I thought it was embarrassment, or even surliness, but I later learned it was neither. The silence of the Arctic is overwhelming, but it is neither unsettling nor disturbing. It certainly blew away the cobwebs in your senses and could be deeply rewarding. I was beginning to understand its sonic qualities, about which the composer John Luther Adams had spoken to me. The great empty silence that blew around the cabin was, to me, comforting, and sometimes, I thought, idyllic; Charlie's sons had simply subsumed this silence into themselves. They had both spent nearly forty years living within it, and the clutter of words or banal though well-intentioned exchanges were alien inconveniences.

Charlie was also uncommunicative. His injury and severe lack of mobility had tied him to the cabin and his bed. I found it difficult to speak with him. Sometimes I thought he was cranky. He seemed to want a lot of attention from Lena and Debra. But I suppose that's true of any older person who finds him- or herself so debilitated that they no longer have any function in life. I gathered from his conversations with Debra that his own reputed healing powers had diminished, prolonging his own self-administered recuperation. Debra spent many hours working with him, massaging and exercising his withered muscles. In the evening she would perform a shamanistic healing ceremony, calling up the spirits to the ritual of drum and chant as she whisked incense about him with a feather-and-bone rattle. Charlie seemed to enjoy this attention, and my own attention was drawn constantly to learn whatever power Charlie and Debra were attuned to. Lena radiated something else. I could sit in silence with her with no awkwardness or discomfort, but I didn't have to. Lena conversed with easy grace, occasional seriousness and much mischief. She made me laugh at the devilment in her small black eyes, dazzling like polished onyx.

Lena grew up traveling from camp to camp with her family in the Kobuk Lake area, and every summer, when she was thirteen or fourteen, "there was this young man out there," as she put it. Her mother told her about him. He kept coming round. Then she and her two sisters were in Kotzebue (which was an extremely small place at the time) and Charlie showed up again, looking for pups for his dog team. The girls took him to someone who had pups for sale. He gave them each a puppy, which made them very happy. Then he started showing up in the winter, which was unusual because it was more difficult to travel in the winter, especially just for a social visit. At some point that winter, when she was seventeen, she went home with him by dog team for two or three months. They went back to her parents for three months after that and her mother asked why they weren't married. They eventually married when Lena was eighteen and Charlie said he was twenty-eight. She laughed, saying she did not believe him. Charlie told me basically the same story but from his viewpoint, which was that he too was moving around from camp to camp and would visit Lena's family. He said he noticed that she did real good work, and he thought she would make a good wife, so he decided to marry her.

I remembered Charlie's remark about being a nomad like the caribou and could only imagine the incredible hardship of surviving half a century in the Arctic outback, living out of a dogsled and eking out a living against incredible odds. Only the Inupiak, the Yupik and those born into it could have endured it.

They had thirteen children, two of whom died in infancy and one as an adult. Lena raised these kids while moving and traveling from camp to camp. It was a lifestyle even more difficult than the way they lived now, which was basic enough but in comparison to those years on the tundra quite plush. During the winter Charlie made a living making log houses, and eventually boats as well. When he was in his thirties he suffered a stroke that left him debilitated. That's when he became a healer. He healed himself by massaging and moving his body, bringing himself back to complete recovery. That was the beginning of his unique and particular brand of healing. He continued by helping others. Soon he became well known and sought after. Apparently, some years later Charlie sustained a second, more severe stroke, which again he overcame by his own healing methods. Both strokes, Debra explained, had been confirmed by doctors at the medical center in Kotzebue. Those same doctors could not explain how Charlie had managed his own recovery twice, but they were content to let him treat other patients for whom their own skills and medicines had little effect. It was several evenings before I got to talk to Charlie about this.

I kept thinking about their early life together, giving birth to and bringing up thirteen babies while constantly on the move in the northwest of Arctic Alaska. This was, for me, the greater miracle. When Lena was a young mother there were no doctor's clinics or trained midwives; there were no medicines or epidural injections. Lena's labor pains and the screams that accompanied them would have been blown away in the howling winter winds that brought storms and temperatures no human being was supposed to survive in, never mind give birth in.

It was inevitable that I should spend more time with Lena than with Charlie. Lena was up every morning at around five to stoke the fire for the day. She ate little and was gone to the fish camp by 5:30. I followed her, like a lost pup, and spent as much time as I could with her. At first she was bemused by my presence and all my questions, but after a while, instead of answering my insistent "what's this for" or "why do you do that," she simply showed me and then told me to do things. In those first few days she soon had me tanning sealskins, preparing seal meat for the winter, cleaning and racking fish, and preparing blubber to be rendered into oil. Lena worked me hard. Apart from meal breaks she would work the fish camp until 6 or 7 p.m., and then she would either continue working on the hides in her tanning shed or sew mukluks—Eskimo boots made from moose hide, wolf and sealskins—and decorate them with the most intricate embroidery.

Her energy was phenomenal, her humor infectious. She was constantly teasing me about being lazy, and that if I wasn't so lazy I would have more than two sons. Then she would pity my wife and me because I was "too old." I teased her back, and she laughed her shy laugh, her head averted and her hands at her mouth.

Soon I had progressed from the fish camp and she showed me her hide shed. Pelts of wolf and wolverine, bear, moose and caribou hung everywhere. The snow-white fur of the arctic hare and fox lay draped over wooden trestles. But it was the whole skins that impressed me. Lena had carefully removed the hide so that the face mask of the creature was intact. They were beautiful things, and I couldn't resist brushing my face against her wolf as I walked among the hanging pelts. I fingered them delicately. The wolf paw was as big as my hand. Deftly I threw one of the wolf hides over my shoulder and inset my head under its face mask. I wasn't sure, but as I turned to look at Debra and Lena, who were talking behind me, they suddenly stopped and looked at me with expressionless faces. After a few moments Lena invited me to come and help in the shed the next day. Only it wasn't an invitation, it was an instruction, with a further command to ensure that I closed the door and bolted it after me.

I was left alone in what I mentally registered as this "hide-hung house of the dead." Holding the wolf skin I had dressed myself in, I walked slowly around the small shed, touching, smelling, stroking and allowing these wild creatures to caress my face. I thought for a moment of the wolves in Jack London's *White Fang*. I remembered the strange feelings and thoughts I had had about the wolf pack in Denali, and I recalled too the wolf that had crossed our path as John Reese and I drove down through the hills above Fairbanks. It seemed the wolf had been stalking me all these years, a shadow creature at the edge of my life's horizon. In

London's books, and in my young imagination, the creature was a metaphor for nobility, justice and freedom. If it was bloody, savage and remorseless, it was also intelligent, social and lovingly defensive of its own. The native peoples believed the wolf was "very human," and in much of their literature the wolf is indeed depicted as a disordered reflection of the human psyche. The man-beast, the werewolf, embodies all the conflict of good and evil that is a part of Jack London's landscape, just as it is in each of us if we honestly examine our own souls.

Alone with these thoughts, I donned the skin again, pulling the wolf's face down over mine. I looked out through the eye sockets at all the other hides around me. I was part of the pack, and I could imagine myself running through the bush with my brothers and sisters panting and howling beside me. I was looking out through the eyes of death, intoxicated with blood lust. The moment passed, and I pulled the wolf from my shoulders and skulked out of the "hide-hung house," locking the wild creatures inside.

The next morning, I returned again with Lena. She sorted through the various pelts to find me something to work on. I asked her if she skinned the animals herself. She explained that mostly her sons did this while she prepared the hides after they had been left hanging for some months. Her sons traveled far into the bush on snow machines during the winter months when the wolf trail was easy to follow and their fur was always at its thickest. Sometimes they were away for several days. She explained that the wolf skin I had dressed myself in was taken from an animal that had come right into the compound of the cabin. "He came to give himself to us," she said. I couldn't argue, but I remembered the ranger in Denali explaining how wolves sought no correspondence with human beings.

Did she know how to skin the wolf, I asked? Without answering she spread the pelt, then, lifting up the headpiece, she gestured with backward slash marks using her thumb as a knife. She made the gesture of hooking her fingers under the nose, yanking her hand upward and backward simultaneously. I never asked why the process begins with the head. I knew that native peoples always treated their kill with respect and that it was not good to look a dead creature directly in the eye. Its spirit was still present, watching you. I suppose that by removing its facial mask, the creature's identity was gone and its dignity was maintained. To simply decapitate the creature would have been a gross insult. Lena then made cutting marks with her thumbs circling her wrists, afterward drawing long lines up the inside of her arm. Deftly she made a snapping gesture with her two hands while pointing at the carcass where the paws would have been. "Then we have to hang him upside down to take the overcoat off, and that is why a man must do this work." I listened and smiled at her words. I sensed that this was only half true, for I knew there were many ritual taboos about women and the preparation of these powerful spirit creatures. In any case, the last few days had shown me that Lena was as fit and able as any man, certainly fitter and abler than me.

With the imaginary beast hung before me, Lena mimicked the action of teasing and pulling the thick, shining coat from the animal. I could imagine the red-blue sinewy shape peeled of its luxurious skin. Lena lifted the hide and explained how the ears are pushed inside out with a short stump of wood so that they will dry in the upright alert position. What happened to the rest of this magnificent animal? "The body is burned way out far from the houses," she replied. Sometimes the sweat glands from the corpse were extracted to produce a lure for the traps. Years ago, people would sell wolf feet and skulls to buyers from the city, but mostly the buyers wanted the fur for shoes or parkahood lining.

I looked at the wolf skin stretched out before me. It was longer than I was tall. Lena's elaborate mime had dismantled the creature with silent efficiency, but it could not diminish its enigma. Its spirit was as real to me as it was to those who believe in the supernatural power of the animals. I knew Lena believed it too. I suppose anyone who hunts such creatures must come to the same conclusion, for their relationship with their fellow animals is a complicated one. They "take" the animal's life because their own well-being and survival depend on it, and more especially for the regard they hold for these creatures. Once you have developed a physical and spiritual dependence on or even fellowship with them, then "taking" them does not become a self-indulgence, rather a fitting acknowledgment of the creature's being. The human and the wolf world are deeply intertwined.

Lena said, "This one is for you," and spread out a pelt on the ground for me. She squatted down on her knees with her scraping tool—a piece of copper pipe rammed into a short scrap of wood. She proceeded in short backward and forward movements to scrape the dried rind of flesh from the hide.

"I can do that, Lena," I said. Debra had joined us, and Lena said something to her and began to laugh. "What is it?" I asked, seeing that the upturned hide was too small to be a wolf.

"This work is for old men," she said, still laughing.

"It's a wolverine," Debra told me, and then she explained the joke that Lena had shared with her. "The wolverines are real recluses, and they wander a lot. I think Lena might be telling you something!" Debra was smiling, and I smiled too at being given an old man's work.

I set to my task with vigor while Lena and Debra watched. They both smiled down at me as if I was a child discovering a new toy. After a while they left me, and soon I learned what backbreaking work this was. Sweat lashed out of me, and mosquitoes buzzed around me. My shoulders ached and my wrists and forearms burned. My reading about Eskimo folklore had informed me that the wolverine was the most powerful spirit animal, and Lena was making sure that I did it justice. Perhaps I was a mystery and a stranger to Charlie and Lena in the same way the wolverine is. Anyway, I scraped and shoved and sweated with the wolves watching me. I stopped often out of sheer exhaustion and looked at them.

Since my experience in Denali I had picked up bits and pieces of information about the wolf whenever they had come my way. One interesting fact was that more wolves die of starvation than are eaten by their own kind or trapped or shot. Maybe that was part of the enigma. The wolf preys on itself. It is the predator, and ironically it is the prey. Was this the natural circle of life? There was something vaguely eucharistic about it. Life and death were wheeling about me. Here I was with the wolverine below my knees and the dead eyes of the wolf, the bear and all the other creatures watching me. I toiled away, sweating and swatting mosquitoes in the Arctic sunlight. I was alone in this tiny shed, not knowing where I was or how I could map my way out of here with the spirit of the wild everywhere around me. I was deliriously happy.

The days passed, and I felt more content by the hour. I learned much from Lena, apart from working in the hide house or down at the fish camp. We went with Charlie in his small boat to collect water, which simply meant filling as many containers as we could with snow from the many remaining snowbanks. On another occasion we went to check and repair Charlie's salmon traps. Lena took great delight in showing us the various wild plants she collected and used in her cooking. I supposed she could have grown vegetables during these long months of continual sunlight, but why would she need to? The wilderness offered her all she wanted.

During one of our collecting trips we came upon a small herd of musk ox. When they saw us approach they charged through the tundra and collected together, the adult animals forming a tight circle around their young. There they stood rock solid, the steam flaring from their nostrils, their chests heaving, their black, boulder-like heads with a crown of solid horn sweeping down below their ears turning outward to face whatever threatened them. This primordial phalanx of bone and muscle fixed us in its stare; the twenty or so animals seemed to have fused into one mass. It stood there silent and unmoving. Like a primed explosion, it declared, "Go away!" Only their great fur overcoats of black, brown and creamy beige blowing in the wind told you that this was a living thing. The adults were about half the size of a plains bison, but their coats were twice as long. I relished their iron will. I marveled at their instinctive collective defiance. I knew what a rare sight stood eyeballing me thirty yards away. The musk ox had all but disappeared but was very slowly reclaiming its species and its territory. I remembered the circling caribou dance, and my blood lust in the wolf skin. I wished these creatures well. My stay in the Arctic had been made very special by meeting such creatures, and I knew I would think about this moment often and tell my sons of the powwow of the musk ox.

That evening Charlie seemed more amenable, perhaps because he had got out of the cabin and was driving his boat and tending to his fish and seal traps. As we all wearily languished around Charlie's bedroom–cum–living room, I broached the subject of his unique power of healing and how he had learned it. Charlie said something about the power of the blood, about how the journey of the blood through the body must be allowed to take its course. It was rudimentary medical science, but Charlie was not a scientist. He had no formal education apart from a few years in a mission school as a child. He explained that he had been a nomad and a hunter all his life. He had taken many creatures because he had to, and had used their bodies for many things. In all his years of cutting up and dissecting so many different creatures he had become something of an anatomist. He knew the function of every organ and the bloodlines and arteries of every bird or beast. He knew the cause of illness in animals and could diagnose the cause of illness from the carcass of his kills. No books had taught him this; only the life he'd lived and his close observation of the network and cycle of cause and effect had led him to certain fundamental conclusions about how the body worked and why it might cease to work.

I wanted to be pushy with Charlie. He had not been so open to questions before. "But where does the power come from?

What is the magic you possess that enables you to heal people others have failed with?" When I asked these questions I slightly emphasized the word "power" but did not highlight the word "magic." After all, these were my words and Charlie's Inupiat language and culture understood them in a very different, even more mundane way.

Charlie answered quietly that he had had visitations from the spirit to guide him in his understanding.

"What spirit?" I asked softly, not really knowing what to expect but assuming he might make some reference to an animistic spirit world.

"The Holy Spirit."

His answer was just as softly delivered. This was not what I'd expected and I felt I couldn't pursue the matter further. I sat silent for a moment. Debra was obviously aware of my plight and asked Charlie about what he was doing when he was performing a healing. I listened, trying to follow him. Charlie was not only a uniquely gifted and renowned healer, he was also an elder and therefore was entitled to the utmost respect. Even though he knew I was writing a book about my travels, I felt uncomfortable with notebooks and tape recorders. I felt they might diminish him somehow by "stealing" his power. These were the artifacts of my art, but talking with Charlie I felt I would have been happier with a handful of bones and feathers.

Through the conversation between him and Debra, I gathered that Charlie's "power" lay in how he manipulated the body so that the blood's trajectory to the heart was not impeded. Charlie had evolved and had been "shown" by the Holy Spirit how to manipulate and massage the whole body to release the dammed-up "power" in the blood to energize the heart. The heart was at the center of all healing and all pain. And just as humans had a physical body, they also had a spiritual or a nonphysical body. Illness in the physical body was often caused by distress in the spirit, so Charlie sometimes treated the spiritual body to relieve the physical. I knew of Charlie's reputation among his own people, and among the medical doctors who had referred patients to him. His spiritual healing had been powerful with patients suffering from varying degrees of what is in the modern world described as mental health problems. I could only sit and listen, picking up the fragments that I understood. But Charlie tired quickly, and I got the impression that trying to explain these things to me was burdensome to him.

I went to sleep that night thinking over what he had said. His reference to the Holy Spirit had stopped me dead in my tracks. This was a Christian concept, out of place in the vocabulary of a shaman. I thought what a clever old wolf trapper Charlie must have been in his time. The best trappers know how preternaturally intelligent the wolf is. Anything different or unnatural troubles him. To be ahead of the wolf you have to use his intelligence against him. So hunters will leave something on the wolf's trails that will make the animal turn immediately from its chosen path and veer into the bush, where several trap lines are set for it. I wondered if Charlie had done the same thing by laying the Holy Spirit in my path, thus making me veer away from the subject of the spirit world entirely. Could I blame him if he had?

The next morning Debra and I went for a walk and I brought up the subject of the Holy Spirit with her. She smiled at my confusion. She explained that many native peoples accepted the ethics of the Christian world because they were close to their own, but they never relinquished their own spiritual understanding. Charlie spoke of the Holy Spirit because he saw me as a Christian; the idea of the Holy Spirit was the nearest he could come to help me understand. "Charlie was being polite and helpful," Debra said. "He felt you might not understand if he explained openly and honestly according to his own tradition and experience. Charlie has lived and worked in the white man's world for a long time. He knows it as well as he knows his own." Many white people think of the native spiritual understanding as primitive and unevolved, but it is really the reverse. They absolutely know by experience that there is an invisible reality out there that coincides and interacts with our own. In comparison, the Christian view of spirituality is far removed.

We walked on, talking about our hosts. Debra was concerned about Charlie's demeanor. "He is really not himself," she said. "Old age and being cooped up like a battery hen does not suit him. I suppose, for a man like Charlie to feel a loss of his 'power' must be deeply frustrating." Debra signaled inverted commas with her fingers in the air at the word "power."

I had noticed that Debra had openly referred to Lena as her "other mother," or "my second mother." At first I'd thought it was simply an affectionate name, given that the two women had not seen each other for a long time and that Lena was indeed old enough to be her mother, but as the days passed I sensed there was something deeper to the exchange. I asked Debra about this.

"I called Lena my other mother because of the link to my childhood and the homestead," she answered. "I grew up very much like what you see at Charlie and Lena's minus the cultural difference and the rotting meat lying around. Lena is very much like the image I had of an ideal woman as a child. Women who knew how to dress and put on makeup never, ever impressed me. But a woman who can do what Lena does impresses me greatly. She is also a warm, smiling woman, and if I had a choice I would choose her before anyone else to be my mother. Imagine, a woman who can truly clothe you (by cleaning, tanning and sewing hides), truly feed you (by fishing, hunting and picking plants) and cook for you (she can cook on anything)—she doesn't even use, let alone have, tinfoil! She's the kind of woman I grew up around, and there aren't that many of them in the world. They are very precious."

I thought I understood what she meant by Lena's being "very precious"; I too had spent days in her dazzling company utterly bewitched by her. She was a seamless part of the fabric of this landscape. She lived a life of joyous equanimity in it, existing in intuitive harmony with the world she inhabited. You sensed that there was an invisible light shining around her and everything she did, the same way light catches a precious stone.

I continued talking with Debra about her own growing up in Alaska. She was very precise about her childhood and spoke of it with a sense of wonder. I could appreciate her connections with Lena.

"As a child, starting at two years old, I had some pretty amazing numinous visions, but when I tried to tell anyone about them they didn't know what I was talking about. My mother just laughed. When I finally realized that no one could help explain them to me, I resigned myself to becoming a child. I didn't feel like one at the time. I shut down the visions and made an oath that when I was old enough I would return to them to find out what they meant. The visions retreated, recurring occasionally to keep me from forgetting.

"During that time, every time we drove to our house in Anchorage we had a magnificent view of Mount Susitna, the Sleepy Lady in the distance on the far side of Cook Inlet. Somehow I came to believe that the land of the Fairy was on the other side of the mountain. I really believed it. When I was seven we built our homestead out in the bush on a land grant scheme for incoming settlers. We piled our gear in a boat and Joe Reddington took us across the inlet to the mouth of the Big Susitna River, which flows directly in front of the mountain. I had been so busy looking at everything along the banks that I didn't realize we were so close to the mountain. When I finally looked up and saw her, she was at an odd angle and I got it into my head that we were passing around the mountain and entering the far side, the land of the Fairy. I was amazed and delighted because I really believed it. I believed that Joe was one of those magical people who conducted people from the regular world into the land of the Fairy. I knew not just anyone could do it, and I was in awe.

"It got better. We left the river for a small, winding creek that eventually took us into the lake, Flathorn Lake, and the most amazing moment of my life took place. Stretched out along the lake, the mountain was mirrored perfectly by the lake. It was a stunning sight, and I knew that the lake was linked magically to the mountain and we were going to live there. It was years before I realized what had happened, but what arose from that was a firm belief in magic and fairies. Because I believed the world I lived in was the land of the Fairy and magic, it was magical. It still is. Everyone needs to realize that the world they live in is magical. A spiritual realm coexists with our own. It acts upon ours and we can enter into it. So nature was my constant companion, and I regularly talked to the mountain about all my problems and feelings. She was my confidante. I knew she watched over me and kept me safe. I sent her lots of love and she sent a coverlet of love back to me. I regularly talked to all of nature—the lake, the plants, the bugs, the sand and dirt. It wasn't as if I saw any spirits, it was more like a communion. Everything was alive and friendly. I never thought I could come to harm in that place because the world itself protected me. I hated to leave it."

Though she spoke with such warmth about her childhood, I wanted to know more. What else could she recall about life on a homestead? She remembered how hard life was. But that was forty years ago. Her parents had practically no money. They took whatever work they could find, which was little enough at that time. The homestead was so far into the bush that it meant her father would be away for weeks at a time. When he returned, he worked long hours trying to build their home, which was no more than a cabin with compartments for cooking and sleeping. She had brothers and sisters and they all slept together. Because they were older than her and had no idea of the world she inhabited, she was left pretty much to herself.

I pictured her remote cabin way out in the bush with no radio or communication link to the rest of the world. Her brothers would have had no time for their "dreaming" little sister. Alone with a young family, the burden of survival must have been a great hardship to her mother. I imagined I could see Debra as a young child standing alone at the edge of the tree line her father had cut as a firebreak. Her mother would be too busy washing clothes in an old aluminum bath in which they also took turns washing. Father was away, and the boys were off trying to catch fish to eat. Young Debra looked back on this human world from the edge of her own special world.

"Were you very lonely?" I asked.

"No," she answered, her soft voice breaking with my reverie. "I was always alone, but I was never lonely. I don't even remember having new clothes or special presents. But that was the way life was. I didn't know anyone else, so I thought everyone was like us."

She explained more about the struggle to survive the winters and how the family lived off the land for shelter and sustenance. I kept thinking of the people who inhabited John Steinbeck's novels: families pushed economically and emotionally to the margins of existence; people who were more shadow than substance, walking skeletons, clothed in destitution and despair. But Debra and her family finally made it. The family has long since left the homestead and created new lives for themselves far removed from the hardships of those early years. Her brothers are successful fishermen in Sitka, her father has retired to Hawaii and her mother and married sister live in Anchorage. Debra trained as a nurse and worked for many years with Third World charities. But only Debra ever returns to the homestead. It's still there, just as she remembers it from her childhood. She likes it there, and she likes to be alone there. The magic is still there, more real and more tangible than in the past. And this time she knows and understands the veil through which she often passed. The homestead remains her home in more ways than one.

Debra and I decided to take a long hike inland, climbing up the gently sweeping landscape that led us away from the coastal fringe and Charlie's fish camp. It was new territory for her, as it was for me. Our conversation hopped from one thing to another; it was like feeling out stepping-stones to cross a strange river. We crossed soggy tundra from which it was almost impossible to extricate your feet. We walked through a long tract of woodland that I was surprised to find so far north. When we cleared the trees the ground cover revealed a patchwork of exposed rock, dwarf conifers and swaths of low-growing sedges. Tussocks of cotton grass and the flowers of crowberry and bearberry bushes added texture and color. The openness blew away the scavenging swarms of mosquitoes. The climb up through the trees had been more demanding than I'd expected. The strain on my legs and thigh muscles from dragging myself through the down-sucking wetlands had taken a lot out of me; the next climb through this patch of boreal forest with its bands of marauding mosquitoes had me suffocating in my own sweat.

We both sat on a great boulder with years of lichen and decay growing on it. It looked like a very faded old map that years of Arctic weathering had left almost indecipherable. It told us nothing of where we were or where we were going, only ghostly outlines of headlands, mountain ranges, dried-up courses of river-beds and blue patches where imaginary seasonal lakes might have been.

"Do you know where we are, or better still, how to get back?" I asked.

Debra answered that she was pretty sure that if we returned by this route—she pointed at a different direction to the one we had taken—we should arrive back at the camp without too many problems. "You've just got to know your limitations in the wild," she added. "That way you always find your way back. Never believe that you are bigger than the bush. It can swallow you up faster than you can blink."

I confessed I was glad she was with me. Navigating was something I was hopeless at.

For a while we sat still, letting the cool breeze fan us. The land-scape stretched out before us was magnificent, the colors blurring up from it like strange fire, the burning reds and hot oranges and yellows of the forest floor; then out across the empty expanse of russet, soft browns and blends of green, and beyond the black blur of spruce stand the snow-covered mountains with their hints of pink and smoky blue. It was as if the aurora had dissolved down into the earth and was staining everything with its presence.

"You haven't told me where you want to go with this," Debra said out of the blue.

For a moment her query threw me. It seemed not in her nature to put herself forward with questions, but I sensed that what she was asking me was not about where our hike was taking us. We had been discussing many things as we negotiated our way upland; now here we were with the way ahead clear and inviting. It was still an upward climb, but the air was cooler and we could see the distance in front of us.

Debra and I had not really had much time to talk during our stay. She was always talking and "working" on Charlie, or I was working for Lena or else off on my own, tramping around the place. In the evening we all sat together sharing food and stories. Yet something beyond my knowing or planning had impelled me to come to this place. And here I was, as lost psychologically and intellectually as I was geographically. I had planned to come here to live with the Eskimo and learn something about their life and cultural understanding, but now the focus was away from them and on me.

"I don't really know, Debra," I said. "You are my guide on this trip in more ways than one." It was all I could think to say, and I knew Debra would understand.

"Okay," she responded. "Maybe if I begin first with a healing it may help."

I knew Debra's proposal was only a step on this journey. She had remarked to me days ago that she saw I had some trouble with my back. It was true. I had had back pains come and go for a long time and had simply put it down to age, lack of fitness and being overweight. I jokingly remarked that maybe Lena was not working me hard enough.

"I have seen you with her. You enjoy doing anything she asks, so don't blame Lena. And all those things you mention might contribute to your problems. Remember, I was a nurse in another life, Brian."

Humor was not going to let me off the hook, and before I could say anything else Debra suggested we find a place somewhere. I had no idea what kind of place might be suitable for a healing ceremony, but I suggested we climb further.

The going was easier now, without fallen trees or the dense growth of high summer to impede us. But, noticeably, a raven stalked us as we climbed. Occasionally I thought it was trying to attack us, making sweeping dives out of the sky and screaming some abuse just feet above our heads before flapping off to some rocky outcrop to monitor our ascent. Then he would be up in the air again, cawing out to us, before settling back down once more to watch. He did this several times over and I forgot my ideas about him attacking us. He seemed rather to be continually calling us onward. Every time we approached him he flapped up into the air and flew about backward and forward in front of us, as if tracing out an imaginary path while all the time seeming to be calling out with his throaty cackle, "C'mon, c'mon, slowpokes, c'mon, c'mon!" We climbed after him and his antics reduced our effort and speeded our progress.

Then, as suddenly as he had arrived, he was gone. His disappearance amplified the silence incredibly. We had reached an area where the hillside leveled out. We were above the tree line, and even the dwarf trees and bushes seemed to have long ago ceased trying to colonize where we stood. After a few minutes' resting and taking in the land rolling away into eternity, Debra suggested that it might be a good place to work on me. I looked around. In front of us, the hill continued to rise but only for what seemed like another few hundred yards. "No, let's carry on to the top," I said, hardly knowing why. So we climbed on to see what was on the other side.

The top of the hill proved to be as barren and bleak a place as anywhere you could imagine in the Arctic. Nothing grew here beyond a tight skin of tundra grass. Here and there, rocks broke through the surface. It was a superb natural crow's nest from which you could look out on thousands upon thousands of miles of emptiness in that strange Arctic sunlight that seemed to multiply your normal horizon. At one side of me, the huge ocean glinted like polished pewter; the other three quarters of my vision, at each side and behind me, threw up the endless Arctic. It was profound and magical and terrifying all at once, and for a moment it wasn't a place at all, but rather the allegory of a place—somewhere imagined, the backdrop of fairy tales and myths.

"Where is that?" I asked, pointing to the boiling gray ocean.

Deborah's soft voice beside me answered, "That's where the Chukchi Sea and the Arctic Ocean meet."

I looked round at the land. The tree line below us seemed to be waiting in a semicircle, afraid to come any further. Beyond that, the endless tracery of mountain and valley. "This seems like a good place, let's do it here," I announced. I hadn't a clue why; the words seemed to have been sucked out of me.

Debra looked at me for several seconds saying nothing, then walked in a slow circle around me, studying the place as if she was absorbing something from it. I watched her briefly, and then looked back at the sea. This might be a meeting place of the oceans, but the sky and the sea also seemed to flow into each other. The liquid gray of the water and the metallic blue of the sky were in perfect harmony. The silence of the place was rushing up from all around me.

"Come, come over here, Brian," came Debra's voice out of the quiet.

I turned and saw her standing beside a cleft of rock that had pushed itself out of the earth, as if waiting to receive me. I walked toward it.

"Your Celtic intuition is very strong in you," Debra said. "This is a powerful place. The winds from the four quarters blow right through here and will carry away anything that needs to be got rid of."

"Which way shall I face?" I asked.

"Whichever direction you wish," she replied.

I chose to look out on the elemental fusion of sky and sea. I could throw myself into its tranquil emptiness.

"Best remove your coat and shirt, but leave on one layer as it's cold up here."

I did as I was bid, like a child undressing for a doctor's examination, half curious, half fearful.

"I'll work on your back first, as that's what we both know about. But let me first look at the problem."

I sat on my altar of Arctic stone while Debra squatted invisibly behind me. A sense of approaching somewhere quite profound was strong in me. Here I was, a million light years away from anything I had previously experienced, in an alien landscape, yet one I had instinctively chosen, as if there was some correspondence between it and me. What had I really gotten to know of Debra in the few days we had spoken together? Practically nothing. But at the same time, everything I needed to know to hand myself over to her ministrations.

I sat, as oblivious as the stone that supported me, while Debra's hand searched and manipulated my back. We said nothing to each other. Then she stopped and walked around to my side where I could see her. She spoke softly but matter of factly, explaining that she had been doing much "traveling" in the spirit realm, consulting with her advisers about me and this trip. There were certain things she could not ask as she had not been given permission, and there were many things she didn't know as she had been unsure about what I sought from her. She now understood my back pain, but it was worse than she had speculated. I looked at her, my curiosity and fear levels shooting up several points. She read my anxiety instantaneously, though I was sure my features had not changed in any way. I was still half entranced by the supernatural magic of the place.

"Do not worry," Debra said. "I can help you and take this thing away from you and you will feel no pain. Do you still want me to continue?"

She was not so much asking me as reassuring me, so I nodded and answered, "Do what you have to."

She looked at me for a moment, then explained that what she had diagnosed was that my back was covered in scales. They were not scales such as you find on a fish. They were huge, and they had been growing on me for many, many years. Many of them protruded up and out like porcupine quills, only much larger; others were large, solid formations the shape of shark fins, only bigger and thicker, like a dinosaur's skin. I looked at her, beginning to feel a mixture of fear and shame at the hideous creature she had seen. Again, she must have read my thoughts. "Do not let this worry you. This has been your armor for many, many years, even since childhood. It has protected you and kept you safe. It has made you strong and unafraid. But the dinosaurs have gone away now and your dinosaur must go too. You do not need it now. It is old and burdensome. But maybe you do not want to let it go. This is what is causing your pain. You must let this go or it will get heavier and more hurtful. I can take this from you. You must not be afraid."

"Yes," I said, my voice almost inaudible.

There was the smallest flicker of a smile on Debra's face and then she was gone again behind my back.

I sat breathlessly, trying to cope with what I had been told. Then I heard a voice behind me mumble something. It was an incredibly old voice and it sounded very unearthly. Slowly, the sound and the cry of the ancient hag's voice rose in tempo. This primordial thing behind me was wailing and moaning. The pain of this being reverberated inside me. The anguish that was semaphoring behind me was almost unendurable. I couldn't have turned to look at this thing even if I'd wanted to. Something was happening inside me and behind me that held me where I sat. The power of it immobilized me. I didn't experience any fear,

only that awful pain associated with what was happening behind me.

Then Debra's hands were on my back—strong, muscular
hands. I could feel her making ripping gestures and sighing with
the effort. Then she was tearing and wrenching. The voice I
could now hear was not the voice I had heard only moments ago.
This was Debra's voice, straining with effort and moaning with
pain and exhaustion. It was dreadful, and I could barely endure
it. Great sighs of relief and sympathy sounded up from within
me. Tears flooded out of me, though I felt no pain. For the next
twenty minutes or more Debra invisibly flayed me. Toward the
end of this bloody work I could still hear the incredible strain in
her voice. She was almost screaming. There was no other living
soul to witness her pain, and I could do nothing but sit there
stunned and endure the psychic recoil coming off it.

Then it was over. I could sense Debra standing behind me, her
hands resting heavily on my shoulders.

"It's finished," she said in a quavering voice. I could feel the
whole weight of her body leaning on me. Then she pulled back
and I stood up.

"Are you okay?" I could only ask, my voice low with anxiety.

"Yes, yes," she answered. "Now, go and do whatever you have
to do. I need to go away for a few minutes to do something."
And with that she walked off.

Respect, courtesy, apprehension and confusion washed over
me and I walked off in the opposite direction, not daring to let
my eyes follow her. I didn't know what I was expected to do. I
possessed no well-defined spiritual understanding or ability to
deal with what had just happened between us. I walked toward
the shining emptiness where the sea and the sky met, hoping
that maybe it would expunge all the conflicting emotions that
were circling around me. When I thought I was far enough away
from that stone post on which I had been exorcised, I stopped. I
remembered Debra's comments about the winds of the four
quarters. For a few moments I stood and faced the polar ex-

tremes. It was some kind of obeisance, and I let the winds of the north, south, east and west blow over me in turn. But there were no winds. I can recall only the constancy of a balmy breeze at every point of my salutation.

I waited for a moment after this rudimentary ritual, then walked back. Debra was already there, and she asked me to sit again. I hunkered down on the stone and buried my head in my hands. Debra brushed me down with a handful of spruce, telling me only that there were healing properties in the branches.

Everything had changed. All the unbearable tensions and agonizing distress were gone from me. Whatever had taken place on this stone, I was not the victim.

Debra's mood was light. "How do you feel?" she asked.

"Like I have just had a bath," I answered, without trying to analyze my response.

"Well, that is exactly what you did have," she confirmed, and suggested that we should go back soon. I knew what she meant. We needed a chance to catch our breath and maybe let things embed themselves. We talked easily, sure of this safe place.

"A Spirit Bear came almost immediately we began," Debra explained. "It had white flashes across its maw. It was a creature of much power. Normally things don't happen with such powerful immediacy. My hands were burned almost to the bone."

I didn't want to question what had happened. Words often get in the way of experience, or they transmute it. Both Debra and I knew that. I just wanted to sit and soak up everything, let everything find its own place.

"I want you to come and see something," I said. "There is a very curious arrangement of stones over here, as if someone had been writing." Debra followed me as I retraced my steps to where I had stood facing the winds. "You see, look at this. That's no natural occurrence."

Debra looked down at the collection of fist-sized stones. "I think it says 'oneson,' " she said.

The rubric of the lettering was not precisely outlined as winds or passing animals had disturbed it, but the formation clearly spelled out the word "oneson." The lettering was approximately nine inches to a foot long and was about three and a half to four feet in width. I foolishly thought it might have been a land marker for a helicopter. I knew how far Charlie and Lena's camp was from civilization, but because of his reputation many people knew where he was. If he or Lena were ill, a helicopter would be the fastest way to get them to a hospital. Debra soon put my thinking straight. This hill would be so deep in snow for ten months of the year that nobody would be able to find it from the air, let alone read these words. In the winter, if it was necessary, a dogsled and driver could get to the camp and get people out quicker than a helicopter. If either of them was so ill as to require evacuation during the winter, how could they have got up this hill anyway? I gave up. My urban thinking had easily been swept away. We walked around for perhaps another hour looking for something else that might explain the imprint of the stones. All we discovered were animal bones, the debris of wolf or bear kills.

It was time to descend the windswept hill. We stumbled and tripped our way through the woods, then pulled ourselves limb by limb through the soggy tundra. I felt more able now, and I was anxious to learn what Charlie or Lena might be able to tell us about the stony cipher. Debra fell in behind me. At times when I seemed utterly lost, she would point out the direction we should take. All the time I heard her voice behind me explaining the power of the spirit world. She was convinced by her own travels in this alternative realm, and from our early conversations in Fairbanks, that I too had been introduced and initiated into this other reality.

"Is that why you contacted me so many years ago with those letters about the Dreamwalker?" I asked, beginning to see things falling into place.

"Perhaps," she answered. "I'm not sure exactly. I only remember that I had to contact you. Sometimes there are requests laid upon us from the spirit people that you simply have to follow through on blind faith and trust."

"But the timing was so perfect. Your letters were like a light shining in a dark place. They were the key that enabled me to complete my book."

Before, she had simply listened. Now, she responded, "Well, there you are, you have your answer, and maybe there's one for me too."

Throughout our descent Debra's disembodied voice behind me explained many different aspects of working with the other-world spirits. It was a powerful place, and also a dangerous zone. It must never be taken lightly nor misused. It was a contract between the individual and his or her spirit adviser; it in no way impaired our freedom or our life in this world, though it would unquestionably redirect its course. She spoke of the persons one might encounter in the spirit world. All would not be helpful because some of them are lost themselves. She hinted at changes or sacrifices I might have to make. She was passionate about how the ego was the greatest impediment to understanding, to progressing one's understanding, and to the ability to "travel" in the spirit world.

I listened to her talking over the hour and a half it took to reach the camp. It was as if all the information she was feeding me was coming from somewhere other than herself. I may have been the leader on the descent, but Debra was still the guide. As I tried to comprehend all this different thinking and new understanding that was pouring in on me, I realized just how in need of a guide I was.

At last we reached the clearing that marked our destination and the camp. The cabin was billowing smoke that curled up into the air, then disappeared. The thoughts inside my head were like Charlie's chimney, full of thick smoke that was dissipating before I could see what it might mean.

As we approached the cabin door, Debra came up alongside me, as if to confirm her reality. "You should wash your back when you get a chance," she said. It was another way of telling me just how close the two worlds are.

Later that evening, Debra and I sat in the kitchen with Lena, drinking herb tea. We asked her about the cryptic stonework we had found. For a few moments she sat silently, though there was much animation in her eyes. Then she walked off and rummaged through some books piled on a shelf. She discovered what she was looking for and handed us a small photo. It was of a small boy about eight or nine years old. He was smiling out at the camera, obviously fond of the person who was taking the picture.

"This is Oneson," she said.

As I passed the photo on to Debra, Lena continued, the animation in her eyes now brightening with tears. "Poor Oneson, poor, poor Oneson. It was very sad for him."

Both Debra and I knew what was coming, and for a moment I wished we had not unearthed this memory. But Lena didn't weep. Instead she told us about one of her daughters (the mother of the child in the photo) who had died from diphtheria, leaving her only child to be cared for by its grandparents. Lena and Charlie named the infant Oneson, as he was the one and only son of their daughter. The name became the child's given name. He spent several years with Lena and Charlie before going to attend school. As a child he learned quickly and was very athletic. He was a favorite with many of his teachers, and the other kids were all drawn to him. Lena called him a special child, and I was sure she was being more than a fond grandmother when she said it.

One day Oneson was out playing with another boy, but after a few hours the other child came home to his parents alone. Everyone thought Oneson was still playing with the other children or had gone home. It was not until many hours later that Charlie and Lena became anxious about Oneson's whereabouts and people realized he was missing. The young boy he had been playing with said he did not know where Oneson had gone, but the child was withdrawn and uncooperative. Everyone knew a bad thing had happened. Lena declared that there were many bad omens about that day.

Before many more hours had passed Oneson's body was found with a hunting rifle beside it. The boy was dead. There were no witnesses to what had happened, but the demeanor of his playmate over the next few days suggested much. The boy became more withdrawn; even when he was told of Oneson's death he kept asking where he had gone. Everyone accepted that a tragic accident had occurred.

It wasn't until some days after Oneson's funeral that the truth became apparent. The playmate had constantly been telling everyone that they must never be jealous of other friends. Slowly, it became obvious that some childish jealousy had caused one child to shoot his friend. Now his friend had left him forever, and sadness and guilt had left the child morose and withdrawn. That was how everyone understood the death of Oneson. But it was an affair of innocence, and Lena and Charlie wanted no more suffering. Oneson was buried where we found the stones. Lena hadn't been up there for many years. She was too old to go there alone, but she asked if she could go with us the next day.

The remoteness of the camp and the image of the child in the photo made this tragic story very poignant for me, and the quiet stoicism of Lena's telling of it reinforced it. I thought of my own sons and how they would have loved it here, just like Oneson. But would I have had the practical courage of Lena to endure one tragedy compounded on another? First her daughter, then her daughter's son. As if she was reading my thoughts, Lena announced, "He's not gone far. I think he heard his mother calling him and he went home to her."

The next morning Lena made it to the top of Oneson's hill with less effort than me. She read Oneson's name in the stone quietly to herself, her head all the time nodding as if she was agreeing with someone. Then she sat down and let the sunlight and the wind caress her. Once she turned her face up toward the light. She looked beautiful. The great earth mother, queen of heaven—all the names of the divine were only names for something that radiated out of her. I took her photo, and I have it still, to remind me of her and that such divine beings can still be found in the extreme wilderness. As I studied her, I thought how life and death are at such people's doorstep every day. They deal with mortality daily. Lena's sealskins, her fish racks and her hide house were testimony to the fact. But they respect the animal they kill. A host of rituals are played out to its spirit. They know the spirit has power over them greater than death could ever have.

I walked off to be alone, and to leave Lena to her thoughts. Debra also went off on her own. I saw her hunkered down collecting something, then she walked even further away from us and studied the land like an animal scenting the breeze. When I reached the spot where I had stood the day before in contemplation of the confluence of earth, sea and sky, I sat down. We would be leaving the next day, so I opened my mind to allow whatever memories, emotions or impressions that were buried there to swim to the surface.

I thought of the hours I had spent with Lena, teaching me how to skin and tan her hides. I laughed at how I had draped them around me and the impulse I had felt while trapped in the wolf skin. Then I remembered that only yesterday I too had been "skinned" on a rack up here. It was some kind of complicated metaphysical irony I could not work out. I also thought of Oneson and why I chose his place. I couldn't work that out either. The old raven had called us up the hill, but something else had made me stop there. Was it the spirit of Oneson, happy that we had come? The child who caused Oneson's death had continually scolded others about the dangers of jealousy and wanting what others have. In the end he got what Oneson had now, loneliness. But there was something else that struck me. I recalled the almost eerie voice of Debra warning me about the danger of the ego as we had descended from this place yesterday. Was finding

Oneson's grave and learning his story a way of reemphasizing her admonishments? In a way, Oneson's death was the result of someone else's, albeit innocent, ego.

But maybe my intellect was working overtime. I lay back and closed my eyes. The sun and the breeze washed over me like Lena's luxurious furs. I sank into the exquisite quiet like a dream. I heard voices, but knew it was only my imagination. It sounded like Jack and Cal calling out to me from way off. I was remembering the story I had read to them so often about going on a bear hunt. Suddenly, I thought how the story had acted itself out with me yesterday. I had indeed walked through the swishy-swashy grass, splish-sploshed through mud, stumble-tripped through the dark forest, climbed the hill where the wind woo-hooed and had an encounter with a bear. Then I had run back, retreading the path I had journeyed up on, with the bear following me, speaking through the body of Debra. In the original story the escaping children lock themselves in their cabin. The bear cannot get to them and is left to wander off alone along a gold-dappled ocean—just like the one before me now. I had always insisted to Jack and Cal that the bear in the story didn't want to hurt the children, only to make friends and play with them. My spirit bear also was a great fearsome creature, according to Debra, but he too was lonely and wanted to make friends and help. I laughed at the association I was making. It was irresistible, and I could only conclude that I had indeed been on a bear hunt. And that the bear had found me!

Just then a voice called out my name. This time it was not my imagination. From the top of the hill Debra and Lena were waving. I climbed up to them. While I had been away, Debra had asked Lena if she would like her to perform a blessing, and Lena had agreed. The three of us sat in a crude circle holding hands while Debra called on the spirit world to look after and bless the life of Charlie and Lena. It was a simple thing in that simple place. And I wished it for Charlie and Lena also.

As we were standing to leave, Debra gave me a handful of

bones which she thought might be finger bones and some feathers. This was shaman stuff and I asked what they were for. "You will know in time," she said. Then she asked Lena if she knew of any violent deaths that might have happened here long before Oneson was buried. Lena confided that the bones of a young child, a girl, had been found "way over there" and that many, many years ago, "in older time," there was much fighting and killing. I looked at Debra as Lena walked slowly a few feet in front of us. "I knew it," she whispered. "I could feel lots of them way over there."

On our way back Lena seemed in high spirits. She skipped through the undergrowth like a teenager. She was smiling and full of laughter. The visit to Oneson and the blessing had worked quicker than I could have imagined.

When we got back to the cabin Lena went in to make something for Charlie. Debra and I walked round to the other side and sat in the shade of a few trees. I explained to her that I was still trying to sort through my responses to all that had happened, to get to the substance of what she had been explaining to me. Debra was consoling. "You must learn to walk before you can run," she commented. Without thinking, I announced that my youngest son Cal had learned to walk since we arrived in Alaska. She smiled. "Baby steps first, Brian, right?"

"Okay," I answered.

But she was insistent. "You really have to be sure about taking this further."

I was only sure that the way to understand this stuff was to take it further. By way of helping me, Debra explained her own early encounters with the "other world."

"I remember how stunned I felt when I came back to this world. I didn't have a lot to latch on to because the symbolism was so different from my spiritual practice of the Hebrew mystical path that I didn't know where to go or what to think. I felt a little crazy, but I knew what I wanted. I knew it was all real and I wasn't crazy.

"I didn't know what it all meant until I found a book that had been given to me ten years earlier by a friend that I had never read. It was called *Shamanic Visions*, by Joan Halifax. The wonder of the book was that it was a compilation of firsthand accounts by shamans from all over the world instead of scholarly, anthropological accounts. Each shaman described in his own words the experience he'd had of being initiated into shamanism. Several accounts, the northern and Arctic ones, were almost exactly like mine, so when I read them I knew what had happened to me. It explained a lot to me and helped me move on. For several months, every time I closed my eyes to meditate, the animal was there, no matter how hard I tried to have a "regular" meditation. My animal always led me back to my grandfather teacher, who kept teaching me and telling me that I needed to shamanize. I couldn't imagine how I could do that, being a white middle-class woman, but he assured me I could and if I accepted the gifts they would take care of the rest. So I thought, "Okay, I'll do it," and to my amazement people started coming to me for healing work almost immediately.

"A series of events occurred that led me to the Foundation for Shamanic Studies, which then led me to teaching as well. To me, the most telling was that I live in a very conservative town and I had received hate calls from fundamental Christians about my mystical path, but to this very day I have never received one about my shamanizing. After ten years I finally was curious enough to ask my spirit teacher why, and he said because I was doing healing work, they have protected me all these years by throwing a cloak of invisibility over me so that I can do my work unseen. It actually makes sense to me. It explains why I've been able to do this work without any problems, and even why it's been so easy. I've had very few obstacles put in my way. In fact, it all seems to happen easily, as long as I remain committed to the work, stay impeccable, maintain my ethics and don't take it personally. In other words, it isn't really me in this, so I have to be very careful about not bringing my ego into it. When I slip and the ego gets involved, the work starts to become difficult. It is a path, and one can inadvertently start to wander. I always know when I'm being impeccable because all this shamanic work goes well for me. When I start to wander, it doesn't. It's really not so hard to stay on it when the path is so clear. It has not been that difficult a journey, and in the beginning, when I felt crazy, it was the most difficult. Now I don't worry at all about shamanizing. If it is correct, the veil protects me."

"And do you still need the veil?" I asked.

"No," she answered. "I have spent so much time crisscrossing worlds that I know who I am and what I have to do. If I remain true to that, then the powers give me all the support I require. But enough of me. I have been 'working' on you since we left the hill yesterday. I have something to tell you. It's bad news, but you need to know it."

"Okay," I said, trying to hide the apprehension flaring up inside me.

"The scales have grown back. There are lots of them like small buds on your back. I don't know why that has happened."

I saw Debra look at me. The shock and the fear on my face must have been very apparent.

"Don't worry about this. It is often not easy to fix things at one go, and it was incredibly strenuous work for me yesterday. But perhaps this has happened for a reason. Perhaps you still need your armor for a while. We shall see. But always remember you have great allies in the spirit world. I knew from yesterday and what I have been learning since. We will work together again. You can be my son for a while and I will teach you to walk on your own."

*

CHAPTER TWENTY-TWO

NO PLACE LIKE NOME

The day of our leave-taking was bright and hot. We were packed and ready to leave long before our boat arrived to ferry us back to Kotzebue. I wandered about the campsite and ranged about the land where we had climbed to Oneson's hill. Then I took myself down to the river. The sealskin Lena had taught me to tan was still stretched in its wooden frame. Anyway, now the fish rack would be full of salmon hanging like dripping candles. All Lena's buckets and basins were piled under the gutting table. Several of her ulus lay on the table with their queer half-moon-shaped blades, which she handled with such dexterity and finesse. I remembered the mischievous look on her face when she sliced a piece of raw seal flesh for me to eat. Life was simple and very hard, but I had loved being here and I would miss it. It had been nothing like what I'd expected, yet it had been everything and more. I tried to find a suitable phrase to encapsulate my time here but I couldn't. I had been blissfully content. I was about to leave this little piece of paradise and I knew that I would never return. I would not find anything to replace it, nor would I want to.

As I walked back to the cabin, I spied a particularly fine rack of caribou antlers still attached to the bleached skull of the beast. I walked over to it and took it back with me. When I reached the cabin our bags were stacked outside, waiting to be carted onto the boat. Charlie was sitting under his tree, just as he had been when I arrived. I was a bit apprehensive as I approached him with my find. It was like being caught in the orchard with an armful of apples. Before I could say anything, Charlie nodded sagely with the tiniest hint of a smile.

"You take to your home," he said.

I noticed Lena and Debra standing in the doorway. "I would rather take Lena, she is a great worker," I said aloud, mimicking what Charlie had first said about Lena when he met her. Charlie just kept nodding as if he hadn't heard me while Debra smiled and Lena chuckled.

Inside the cabin the CB radio crackled and a squeaky voice said something I couldn't understand. Lena rushed in to answer the call and came back within a few minutes to declare that the boat would be with us in ten minutes. There was little else to do but say our good-byes. Charlie stood leaning heavily on his stick and shook hands. His arm was still giving him a lot of pain, so our handshake was brief, and I hugged him slightly, remembering his damaged ribs. But for Lena I reserved the biggest, most affectionate bear hug, and unashamedly confessed just how much I would miss her.

"Maybe you come back sometime," she said with the kind of invitation that you know is a final good-bye.

"Maybe," I returned, keeping up the pretense but speaking with heartfelt yearning.

The boat to take us back was not an open scull like the one that brought us. It had a small cabin area to the front, mainly as a windbreak and nothing more. We were soon loaded and waving our good-byes to Charlie and Lena on their hilltop position. As the boat motored downriver and toward the open sea, I felt lost for words. Joe, the boat's skipper, was in good humor and bantered us "white guys" about going native.

"It's such a pity to be leaving so soon," was all I could manage.

"Yes," answered Debra. "It's always a pity to be leaving." She hesitated before adding, "It could be years before I see them again and Charlie is in such a state."

The fact that she used the word "state" rather than refer to Charlie's illness or his injury suggested that perhaps she was hinting at something I could sense but hardly understand. I didn't want to pursue the matter because I didn't want these dreamy days to be blown away so soon.

Back in Kotzebue we stowed our bags in the back of Joe's truck. He took one look at my antlers and asked where I intended taking them.

"To Ireland," I replied innocently.

Joe just looked at me quizzically. Debra volunteered an explanation. "We are going to catch a flight to Nome for a few days and then fly back to Fairbanks. We were hoping to ship them on to Fairbanks."

Joe studied the antlers. "They ain't gonna carry them. They have gotta bit particular lately. Won't ship any antlers unless you have got them specially packed."

I was heartbroken. These antlers were very, very special to me. Debra checked with the cargo handlers when we got to the airport. Joe was right. I walked out of the corrugated-iron shed, dumped the antlers on the ground and walked over to collect the rest of our baggage from Joe's truck.

Suddenly I had an idea. "Joe," I said, grasping excitedly at straws, "if I pay you, would you pack the antlers and send them on to me in Fairbanks?"

Joe was still unsure. "Maybe you paid me and I packed them and they still didn't take them."

"Well, then I won't have lost anything as I'm going to have to dump them anyway," I said.

"Except a few dollars," Joe was quick to remind me.

I shrugged my shoulders. "At least I would have tried."

Joe lifted the last of our belongings out of the truck and carried them into the departures area, where he deposited them with the rest. "Okay," he said. "Write down your address in Fairbanks and I will try and get them shipped to you. I know some of these guys who work here."

I was almost ecstatic. "Great, Joe. Now, how much do I owe you?"

"Nothing. If they get to you, you send me a case of Bud."

I looked at Debra, unhappy to be shipping alcohol to a native community. She just shrugged her shoulders, understanding my dilemma. So I gave Joe a contact address in Fairbanks, still insisting that I should pay for the shipping in advance. The case of Budweiser I would send on to him as a thank-you anyway. But he was insistent that he would take no money in advance. I concluded that the case of Bud was just as important to him as the antlers were to me. So I left them with him and passed through the departure gates.

As we waited, Debra spoke again about her work on Oneson's hill.

"I know you thought it was a difficult job, my working on you, but the truth is, all the pain I felt was your pain. I felt a tremendous amount of sadness and I cried because I felt it, but it wasn't my sadness, my pain, it was yours. It did take me over, but that was part of the healing. I took it on for your benefit and then I could let it go because I wasn't attached to it. It was a long and major healing; you had kept so much for so long and needed to release it all. A lot happened. I remember I brought back at least one if not more soul pieces, lost parts of yourself. I can't remember them all, it was all too much like a dream, so it fades. There were many spirits watching, mainly spirits of that place, of the hill, the tundra, the wind, and many animals. They were all there to support you, to bear witness to your healing. It was a tremendous experience to have all of nature watching and supporting us. Mostly I was pulling dark energy from you and throwing it to the wind. So much old energy, old sad stuff that needed to go.

"I knew I received a lot of info for you. I was told to teach you to journey, that you were a Dreamwalker too but a lost one. I remember the bear and how it came over the hill from the north and tried to keep hidden in the bushes, not coming out all the way. It growled and acted feisty but was immensely powerful and was willing to share its power with you. A very good thing.

"Remember the bones? You were practically lying on them and when you sat up we saw them. They were a sign from your ancestors that they were with you, and would be your future allies. That's why I told you to take them."

There was nothing dramatic in Debra's voice as she spoke, but I was filled with wonder and awe. I could have been my son listening to a fairy story. But I never doubted for a moment what my guide was telling me.

The drone of the plane's engines and the flashing seat-belt signs ushered us back into another world. In ten minutes we would be on the earth again.

Mike Murphy, a retired sergeant in the Nome Police Department, was an old friend of Debra's and had kindly offered to put us up. Nome's short but colorful history unearthed a community that had been burned almost to the ground and pounded by Arctic gales blowing in off the ocean. Its population had been decimated by epidemics of influenza and diphtheria, and on occasion its extreme location had it on the verge of starvation. In 1900, Nome was the biggest boomtown in Alaska, with a population of more than twenty thousand. In the good old days of the gold rush, anybody could pick up a fortune off the beach and thousands of dreamers flocked here from all over the Americas and Europe. But now, Nome is like any other well-settled small town in rural America. It looks staid and settled, but you just know there are hundreds of stories here waiting to be picked up and dusted down. I looked out of the window of Mike's powerful Jeep. It could have been Punta Arenas set in Connemara countryside!

Mike soon had us settled in at his home. He was a big man in height and in girth. The walls of his home were draped in bearskins and the hides from musk ox. He brewed his own beer in his cellar and we enjoyed a few glasses as we chatted about our travels and intentions. Mike smiled in admiration as I told him of my travels to date and my last few weeks, when I intended traveling down through the southwest peninsula.

"You've seen more of Alaska in a few months than most Alaskans have in their lifetime," he commented.

I nodded, explaining that he wasn't the first person to have told me that.

"What have you made of it so far?"

I told him I wasn't quite sure. It was too big to be quickly summed up. In any case, most Alaskans to whom I had put that question had been stumped for an answer. "In a way, it's a conundrum," I said, attempting an answer I knew would be hopelessly inadequate. "Sometimes it feels smaller than its actual size. And there are so many layers to it. Sometimes moving between different locations is like moving between unknown worlds. No wonder the writers of *Star Trek* stole the phrase "the Final Frontier" from Alaska. There's a lot of worlds out there, and sometimes when I arrive in them I feel just like Captain Kirk, that I have boldly gone where no man has gone before." I saw Mike and his wife and Debra looking at me in silence. "It's your home brew that's doing the talking, Mike," I quickly added, trying to lighten the situation.

"In vino veritas," Mike said with a laugh, filling my glass.

"Well, the core of the conundrum is that it's big but it's small. It's American but it's not culturally part of the lower 48. It's one country yet full of different worlds. There is little consensus about the big issues, yet every Alaskan declares themselves Alaskans to the bone." I realized that the beer was having the precise effect on me I had said, so I decided to cut the monologue short. "It's about transcendence. You can lose yourself and you can find yourself in the Big Lonely, and that is the biggest conundrum of all." I paused for a moment. "And I'm not drinking any more of this rocket fuel, Mike, okay!" By now everyone was laughing, including me.

The next day, Mike drove us around the town and the outlying area. It looked more like Connemara than I had first thought. He informed us that some people had reported sighting a polar bear only a few days ago. By all accounts it was a young one. It was unusual to find such creatures in and around Nome in summertime. He hoped the game and wildlife rangers found it before someone with a bellyful of booze decided to make a trophy out of it. In over twenty years as a police officer, Mike assured me that there had been no real serious crime. The community was too small and too long established. Everybody knew everybody else's business. But there were many funny and sad stories, and some that were not so funny, like finding the bodies of young kids who have committed suicide or have gone off on their snow-mobiles without the right gear and no bush savvy. "You need to teach survival skills very young here. Bringing home some young kid who has died from exposure after a few days in the bush is very disturbing. You probably know the kid and its family. It is a very unpleasant and upsetting day's work. Thankfully, it doesn't happen too often." Mike paused for a moment, then stated that it wasn't so much a police force they needed in Nome as a force of psychiatrists and social workers.

Then he related another story about his first months on the job. He was in the station house when a call came in from a woman claiming that there were intruders in her home and they were trying to kill her. When she gave her name and address, the rest of the officers were reluctant to go to her assistance. She had made many similar calls before, and as the "new kid on the block" Mike was sent to deal with the situation. The woman lived on her own in a large wooden house about forty-five minutes by car from town and miles from anyone else. Mike had some trouble finding the place but eventually made it. He remembered the woman's big, staring eyes and her whispering voice. She ushered him in, signaling for him to be quiet. Mike obeyed, and she whispered to him that she could hear "them" talking about her and how they were going to kill her. They wanted her house all to themselves. Mike knew immediately that the woman was insane but went through the house checking all the rooms, looking under beds and into wardrobes to assure her no one was there. But she insisted she could still hear voices. She pointed to the electric sockets and told Mike to listen. He did, and then, putting on a conspiratorial face, he nodded. Yes, he could hear them. He told her to wait while he went out to his car, from which he returned with a home battery charger. Saying nothing but signaling with his finger for her to stay silent, he went through the house plugging in the charger at every socket and pointing to the needle on the gauge as it reflected the electric charge. After he had "sucked the voices" out of the sockets the lady was greatly impressed. She couldn't hear them any longer. Mike left with the woman singing his praises and thanking him profusely for saving her life! As he was about to drive off, she suddenly asked what she should do if they returned. "Just change your lightbulbs, madam," Mike informed her, "that should take care of things. They don't like new bright lights."

"How did you work that one out?" I asked him.

"I didn't," he answered. "It was the first thing that came into my head."

"And what became of the woman?"

"We didn't really have many more calls from her. As I recall, she died a few years later. She was found in her house with all the lights on and enough boxes of new bulbs to light up Nome at Christmastime."

We both laughed, and I conceded to myself that Nome was as I had imagined—a place full of stories.

Later that day we ascertained that it might be several days before we could get a small plane to fly us to the Serpentine hot springs, and we would have to overnight there. But that was impossible. It would throw my whole schedule completely out, and I had been away from Audrey and the kids for long enough. We decided to leave the next day, which was earlier than we had planned, as there was little point in remaining.

While heading back to the town, we passed a small semi-derelict cottage.

"That's Wyatt Earp's old home," Mike informed us. I knew from some background reading that the famous frontier marshal had amassed a fortune in Nome in just a few years and had headed back to the States. I was surprised the cottage was in such a state and wondered why. "Image isn't everything," Mike replied, "and a lot of folk up here don't look too kindly on Mr. Earp. The truth is, he arrived here in 1898, a bald, bespectacled, paunchy man in his fifties. Well past his prime. He was mean, tightfisted and malicious, and his wife was as ugly in looks as he was in personality. He built the Dextor Saloon in town and he sucked the life's blood out of the twenty thousand miners and their families who shivered and died in tents trying to scrape a few ounces of gold off the beach. He bailed out after two years with an absolute fortune. If Nome was ever a seedy, ruthless and ugly place to be in, it was because of professional con men like Wyatt Earp and many like him."

"Well, I guess that puts paid to Wyatt Earp's romantic reputation," I said.

"Yeah," said Mike. "And good riddance to all sewer rats!"

Front Street had been the heart and business center of Nome since the gold rush. Apart from tacky neon lights naming the bars, it still had the feel of a street that grew up on the drunken dreams of gold-hungry men and is still hanging on long after they and their dreams have died. There are no longer forty-four saloons; there's only a handful left. Only two were open when I arrived. There were some shops and a hotel too, but there was little activity, except in the Board of Trade Saloon, where half a dozen Eskimo men were hanging about, shifty and obvious. I tried not to look into their eyes as I passed, for I knew there was nothing in them. These men are pathetic shadows, but still I tried to say a cheering "Hi guys" as I passed. It was a hollow attempt at offering them some sense of identity. They returned my greeting with morose politeness and I went into their bar. Was I trying to show them that I hadn't dismissed them, or was I too embarrassed by my own fear and pity for these washed-up wrecks of men?

Inside, the bar was seedy and depressing, as I knew it would be. About a dozen or so men and women were sprawled around the room in various stages of intoxication. They were all Eskimo. I was the lone white man, and they eyed me with a mix of contempt and curiosity. I ordered a beer in a loud voice from the Eskimo woman behind the bar. It was a dead giveaway about my anxiety. Their eyes stayed on me as I drank. I felt like an exotic butterfly skewered in a display case. A poster behind the bar declared it "The Sin Capital of Nome." I smiled, pretending to be real casual.

A man was sitting at a table with two women a few feet from me. "Hey, man, you looking for some sin?"

I thought to myself how the whole moment could have been a scene in a very poor B movie. I didn't bother to look at him because I knew he would see the apprehension in my eyes, and I answered with a bullshit remark straight out of the B movie I was making in my head: "No thanks. I've done enough sinning in my life, don't need any more."

The remark must have impressed another customer standing at the bar who laughed openly and said, "Ain't we all, brother, and ain't that why we're all here!"

I finished my beer and ordered another one. I immediately regretted it. I knew that their curiosity was becoming greater than their contempt. I thought to myself, "Soon, one of them will want to start a conversation in the hope that I will buy him a drink. I have to find a way to get out of here without making my panic apparent."

I noticed some ivory carving lined up on the shelf behind the bar.

"Those for sale?" I asked.

"Yeah, but not here," the barmaid answered. "You gotta talk with him back there in the shop." She pointed into an archway that led from behind the bar into the shop next door. Then she placed her body in the archway and called out for Jim, gesturing with her hand for me to come behind the bar and go through the arch. I complied, and took my drink with me in case one of them drank it while I was away, forcing me to complain or quietly buy another. Whichever I chose, they would have me tighter in their grasp.

The shop was a tiny room about eight feet by ten. There was a small showcase counter with an empty revolving chair. The walls were shelved and lined with various pieces of ivory carvings and scrimshaw work. Jim appeared from behind a curtain that led into another room. He was in his fifties and wore a red plaid shirt and cheap denim work trousers. His hair was yellow and gray, and his fingers had black nicotine stains on them.

I pointed out a few pieces and asked their price. He told me, but when I didn't offer to buy he suggested that "everything was negotiable." I told him there was a large piece behind the bar that interested me. "Okay, show me," he said, and pointed me back through the arch.

I pointed to a long piece of what I thought was ivory with an animal head carved at each end. "What is it?" I asked.

Before he could answer, one of the customers shouted out "An Eskimo dildo!" in a voice full of derision and laughter. Jim suggested that perhaps the man himself should buy it. The sarcasm was softly delivered, but everyone else in the bar was enjoying it, even the man himself. While the customers were guffawing at him, he nodded his head in the direction of the shop. As I passed him to enter the arch, he said, "A man should never do business in a bar, even if he owns it."

He seated himself in his chair and explained that the carving I had asked about was the penis bone of a walrus and the heads at either end were carved from the tusk. He made me a good price for this item and I asked if this too was negotiable. He thought for a moment, then explained that the same item in a native crafts shop in Anchorage would cost me five times what he was charging.

I smiled. "I'm not in Anchorage, Jim, and I'm not a gullible tourist either."

Jim nodded his head. "Okay, I can see that, so we can talk about it. What are you doing in Nome anyway?"

I explained that I was researching a book and that maybe he could tell me some stories that may be of use to me. I suggested that he might even get a mention if they were any good and the price for the walrus bone was right. Jim smiled, then said that henceforth he intended to change his advice about not doing business in a bar. "From now on I will be saying never do business in your own bar with a talkative Irishman."

I let another remark pass and asked him about himself. He was from Arkansas originally and had been in Alaska about thirty-three years. He was a painter by trade and had come to Nome on a painting contract with the military. There was a lot of work around and he made a lot of money at one thing and another when there weren't so many rules and regulations. The latter phrase suggested that the "one thing and another" might well have been illegal or at least dubious. He eventually bought the bar and established his ivory trade business. He also ran a bingo hall business for the Eskimos above the saloon. He made a point of telling me he fed the Eskimos for free when they came to his bingo hall.

As he was talking, a young Eskimo man in his late twenties came in. I browsed around the room while Jim and he did business. The young man had brought along some small ivory carvings of musk ox. Jim studied them, then asked how much he wanted. The young man named his price and Jim agreed without question or negotiation. He went into the back room to get some money. While he was away I admired the proportion and detail of the work, which the young Eskimo told me he had done himself. He had only been carving for a year, which I found hard to believe, given the craftsmanship of the work. Then Jim came back in and handed over the money. The young man thanked him politely and left.

"Nice work for such an amateur," I observed.

"Yes, he's good, but they all are. There's something about these people. They've just got to see something once, even for a few minutes, and they have it. They can reproduce it to scale perfection." Jim was obviously impressed by the intuitive artistry of the Eskimo. "You noticed, I paid him exactly what he asked for. I always do. They don't try to cheat me and I don't cheat them."

I looked at the wad of money in his hand. I believed what he told me but his honesty seemed to be paying off, for him at least. I was sure that Jim had been involved in all sorts of dubious activities over the years, but I liked him. I was equally sure that he had hundreds of stories to tell, but when I pushed him on the subject he sidestepped. "Sometimes telling stories can get you into trouble in this town," he said. I was baffled as to what he meant, but before I could ask he waved me through the curtain into his back room.

"There are some things I won't sell," he continued. "This piece is a special favorite of mine." He lifted up a beautiful scrimshawed ivory box, which slid open like a matchbox. He explained that it had been made by an old one-legged carver who was probably the best of his generation. Jim had bought many pieces from him over the years, but this piece the old man had made for himself. "You see," Jim added, "all this old man ever wanted was a woman like himself. But a one-legged man is no good to any Eskimo woman. He can't work, can't drive a dog team, can't hunt or fish. He never found his woman. So he did for himself what he did better than anyone else. He made for himself his perfect woman. Look."

I looked as Jim slid open the box. Inside, lying on a silk bed, was a small carving of a naked woman. The ivory was obviously prehistoric. It was the same soft brown and red color as the samples John Reese had shown me. The tiny face was as beautifully ethnic as my lovely Lena, but the reclining figure had only one leg.

"Beautiful, isn't it?"

"Yes," I agreed, thinking that the story and the carving formed an exquisite symmetry. "How did you come to buy it if he made it for himself?"

Jim closed the box and wrapped it in a square of black velvet. "He came in to me one day and gave it to me. He had shown it to me before and refused to sell it when I offered him good money. But that day he just gave it to me and refused any money for it. He said that I had looked after him for many years when no one else was too interested in him. He hoped she would comfort me the way she had him. The next time I saw him was a few weeks later in a coffin in the undertaker's. He had just gone off and died quietly. There were only a handful of people at the funeral. But at least me and his wife were there to say good-bye."

"Are you married, Jim?" I asked.

"No," he replied. "Not anymore, leastways."

"Okay," I said, "I'll think over some of these things and get back to you before I leave tomorrow."

"You'll know where to find me," he called after me as I walked out the door.

I walked up the street reminding myself that even Satan was born an angel and that Jim West, proprietor of the Sin Capital of Nome, was truly the Eskimo Godfather.

✳

CHAPTER TWENTY-THREE

SOUL BEARS

Back in Fairbanks, two days in advance of schedule, it was like coming home except that Audrey and the boys wouldn't be there. I had contacted them and asked Audrey to drive the *Pequod* up from Anchorage to meet us. I couldn't wait, but was glad all the same of the day and a half's breathing space.

After I had deposited my belongings in my cabin in the woods, Debra suggested I should come out to her home. She only lived a few miles away and would pick me up. I was glad of the invitation. Being alone in this borrowed cabin I had come to think of as my own didn't seem so attractive. I knew there were unfinished things that twenty-four hours alone in my cabin would not resolve, and I knew that Debra's invitation carried with it an understanding of that. We had talked much during our time together, but there were still lots of empty spaces. There were several questions I felt the need of answers for, but I didn't have the right formulation of words to ask them. Sometimes words get in the way. They put more trees into the wilderness when you are trying to see your way through. I had sensed that Debra intuitively knew what was running around in my head.

Debra's home was a splendid octagonal log structure. She and her husband, Dennis, had designed it themselves and had built it in a wooded setting. Years ago, Dennis had built a large two-story annex on one side. Outside were the inevitable outhouses. The smallest of these housed cut timber for heating, and there was a much larger enclosed shed for "all the stuff we need to survive up here," Debra explained. The largest of the outhouses contained cars, four in all, each of them vintage classics. "But," Debra continued, "he keeps telling me there is room for two more and the jury is still out on that one."

I thought of the roads I had driven in the RV, then commented, "There's not enough roads here for anyone to need any more than one vehicle, unless it's a giant bulldozer with snow-shifting attachments."

"Exactly!" Debra concurred.

I knew that one could really only use the roads for three months of the year. Each of Dennis's superbly restored vehicles would probably only get an outing a few weeks a year. Still, I loved this Alaskan eccentricity, and the fact that everyone was a collector or a hoarder. Obviously Dennis had refined this curiously Alaskan preoccupation. I admired him and his collection, and was curious about what he intended to fill the two empty spaces with. But I also felt it would not be a good conversation piece with Debra.

Inside the octagon, Debra showed me around. I was impressed by her and her husband's art collection. Dennis's taste in line and color had been apparent in his vintage car collection, and it obviously did not stop there. Debra also had an extremely interesting collection of native artifacts. I remarked how her present home was a huge difference from her first. She agreed, but at the same time explained that the original homestead was still there and she still visited it when she could. She hinted that the spirit world was really her true home, and she increasingly found herself traveling in the spirit plane. She looked casually at me as she insisted that deciding to go on such a journey was not a decision that should be lightly taken. Nor is it one we can turn back from. We may refuse the call for a while, but inevitably, if we are true to ourselves and to what is meant for us, we will be empowered to achieve this end. I sensed again that she was not simply passing the time of day with me. It seemed a good opportunity to discuss things further with her.

I remembered her telling me that she had chosen to leave the visionary world of her childhood as she was growing up but had promised herself that she would return to it when she was older and perhaps better able to understand it. I was always anxious with Debra. I did not want her to feel concerned by my questions, or that I was prying, but I should have known better. Debra probably knew me better than I knew myself. She complied with my request with no more hesitation than it took to collect her thoughts.

"Shortly after my son Keenan was born my life started to not go so well. Not from anything external—Dennis was grand, my life looked good. What was wrong was all internal; I just had a profound sense that something was wrong in my life. I started to be sick all the time, I was becoming chronically tired and depressed, not my normal self. I became worried because I knew it was not a disease of the body but a dis-ease of the heart, and I didn't know what to do about it. Then I saw some Japanese drummers and I walked away knowing that if I made a drum I would be healed. I didn't know how or why, I just knew it. It took me two years to make a drum, something I can do now in one evening.

"As soon as the drum was completed I started having waking visions and unusual dreams even though I still didn't know what to do with the drum. This went on for months. Finally, I waited for when Dennis went on a hunting trip and I had a whole week to myself. I shut myself away, lit candles and spent the time meditating and asking for guidance. About two days into this, I sat down to meditate, closed my eyes and saw an animal staring me in the face. I opened my eyes and it was gone. I closed my eyes and it was back again. No matter what I did, whenever I closed my eyes there was the animal looking at me. I knew immediately that this was not like any meditating I had ever done before. The animal turned and made motions for me to follow it. After this happened several times, I decided to follow. This was my first shaman's journey, before I even knew what that was. It was completely beyond anything I had ever experienced, and I had been meditating for twenty years at the time.

"I followed the animal for three days and two nights. We spent the night out in the cold huddled against the wind until finally we climbed a high mesa, and at the top was an old man seated at a campfire. I cannot say everything that went on there, but he did leave me with four gifts and he said they were not given to me for my own glory but to be used to help others. He said if I used the gifts to help others I would be healed, but if I didn't, I would get worse and worse and maybe even die. At the time I thought, "Well, that's not much of a choice!" I was completely confused by it all. I even wondered a bit if I was going crazy, though I thought I knew in my heart that I wasn't.

"I had a rough couple of months after that trying to figure out what happened to me and what it was all about. It was so unlike my usual thinking and knowledge and so foreign to the imagery and concepts that I had to go outside myself, to other sources, to help me. But because I chose to go for it, everything fell into place. Everything went smoothly when I let go and let it all happen without trying to stop it or block it. I just said, 'Okay, I feel a little bit crazy but I'm going for it,' and it all worked. I did get better. Every time I shamanize I feel well and good, and when I stop shamanizing I start to feel bad again and my life doesn't go as well, even until this day. People think I am helping them, but I am really helping myself. It's a win-win situation! When we work with powers of the universe it should always be a win-win situation."

At first I was struck by my friend's openness; after all, we had only known each other a few weeks. But then I corrected my thinking. Debra had contacted me, a complete stranger, over seven years ago. She had an interest in the psychic powers of the blind musician I had written about, had read about my university lecture in the local paper and had attempted to contact me in pursuit of her interest. And after all that time we had met up again. My friend Pat Walsh knew of her interest in the spirit world of the Inuit and had contacted her about becoming my guide, even though Pat had known nothing of Debra's letters to me. Debra was my guide into the Arctic North, but she was also another kind of guide, and her candor was as much instruction as it was storytelling.

I was studying a beautiful skull Debra had shown me as she spoke. She must have been watching me as I tried to take in what she had set out for me. Then I heard her suggest that we might do some more "work." "You will be leaving tomorrow and there is much that needs to be done," she said. "It is unfortunate because I usually have more sessions with people." Debra had a way about herself. Maybe it was the openness with which she spoke of her spiritual life amid all the other curious coincidences that made me trust her completely.

I agreed, and we passed from the octagon into the great hall-like structure that had been annexed onto the main building. At the far end of the room Debra spread out a small blanket then left, leaving me to "prepare myself" in whatever way I thought fit. I kept thinking about how quietly serious she was. I thought about something she had spoken to me about: "Maybe you don't need to shamanize like I do, but the universe has called you to a task and it will make you well if you choose to do it. Carolan was the spirit that called you to your task, but as we move through our life we must never forget our allies, our helpers, like Carolan, who guide us and call us to our true tasks. And we mustn't ever forget that when we are called by the universe to do a task, it is never for our own glory but for the 'upliftment' of man. In the process we become uplifted ourselves. That's a pretty neat situation, don't you think? We all win on this one!"

Debra returned with a bag and a wooden box. From these she extracted a collection of feathers, some bones and incense. In the bag was her drum. She also showed me her shaman face veil, which was tied across the forehead and covered the eyes and nose. She also produced a rattle and some stones, explaining them away as "aids" and "props." In reality, she didn't need them, but they were traditional tools for her work. She compared them with a psychiatrist's "Rorschach card, word association or even hypnotherapy." Some native people with whom she had "worked" were happy with her shaman's tool kit. She continued to use them because she always had, and they made the transfer from this reality to the spirit realm more immediate and intense. They were familiar to her, and in her own words, "what works best for you is what you work with." But I was sure it was as much about honor and respect for the tradition of shamanism as it was about creating altered states of consciousness.

We spoke for some minutes about what things I might seek assistance from the spirit world about, so that we could focus our journey. Debra wanted to give me some basic instruction on how to begin to locate my "own power and animal spirits." I sensed that Debra was anxious over what she was about to do. "It really needs more time and more sessions to set this up right, but today is all we have so we shall have to make do."

She placed her props around the blanket. The incense was already perfuming the room. Debra donned her face veil and told me to lie back and empty my mind. After a few minutes she would give me some instructions to focus on and hopefully I could take my first small step into the unknown. I listened to Debra's instructions and followed them. I knew we were sensing out a portal, a place where two worlds cross. From there I could go and return on my spiritual quests.

Out of the quiet I heard the dull chink of bones, then the sharp noise of her rattle. Debra's voice was low behind me. Then the emphatic rhythm of her drum reverberated around the room; Debra's power chanting accompanied it. I lay back and let whatever was about to happen, happen.

Suddenly my guide's voice changed. It was clear and bright, completely different from the soft, melodic voice that had been building up the power chant. I knew immediately that she was speaking in a disassociated state, speaking her vision to me. She spoke of seeing a young child. He was alone, and seemed profoundly sad. Then she saw a frightened adult hiding behind the corner of a wall. At moments her voice became low and strained, as if the effort to speak was too much or what she was "seeing" was painful to articulate. I tried to listen intently but could make out little. Still, I sensed the pain and distress of it. It wasn't frightening or unnerving, but it did make me feel very close to my guide. I wanted to help but didn't know how.

Just when the whole thing seemed too unbearable, Debra's voice called. This time she saw another bear. It was a huge creature. Now it was carrying a child and the lone boy. It was very protective and caring. A moment's silence followed, and Debra's voice changed again. This time it was full of wonder and enchantment. The place she was in was variously described as being beautiful, peaceful, filled with such content, and radiating with such harmony. The words themselves tended toward the banal and sentimental, but I could feel the heat coming off them as Debra spoke. She fell silent, and for a few moments I could only hear her languorous sighs. Then it was over, and we sat in silence, letting the moment retreat from us.

When the room had calmed and reality returned, we shared our experience, trying to piece together what we had separately seen and felt. Normally such otherworldly intimacies can be awkward, but neither of us felt that. The power of the moment had been reassuring. "When I do soul retrieval," Debra explained, "I actually see the soul piece at the age it was lost, many times in the very setting where the loss occurred. When, say, I find a four-year-old in a certain place doing a certain thing, I actually see it as if I were there and it is very real. Sometimes those journeys are very long. The big bear was carrying yourself, the child, to protect the child/you. You had a need to feel safe, which was carried over into your adulthood and was exacerbated by your "lockup." In actuality, the bear was a type of power wrap, a lorica from Celtic wisdom that you could call to you. You were very much in need of this." I looked at Debra questioningly and she looked up at my unspoken query. "Yes, Brian, you are carrying a lot of pain and have been for a long time. But I know you intently understand this as I say, ultimately we heal ourselves with the help and advice that is given to us. Really we should be doing more work together on this. But it seems as if it is not to be. I can still watch out for you, but only if you give me permission." I knew Debra was not making any demands. The best of guides don't only show the way, they help you when you stumble. Debra had given me a lot to think about, and though I knew as I left her home that we would be unlikely to meet again, I also knew it was not the last time we would speak.

Back at my cabin I sat on the porch. I thought I could see the tiny pinpricks of distant stars. The seasons were on the turn again and I still had some traveling to do. I had already been to places that were on no map. Now I was heading southwest to Dillingham to catch the shoals of salmon as they return home to spawn and then to die in the waters in which they were born. There was some kind of metaphor for myself in this. I kept thinking of what Jack London said about being prepared to forsake your old ways, belief systems and old gods when you come to Alaska. But it was too much to take in just now. I have never been convinced by Damascus Road experiences, and in any case, my life was not my own. Tomorrow, Audrey and the boys would be back with me.

I looked out at the strands of fireweed growing by the track up to the cabin. Seedpods were beginning to ripen at the bottom of the stem; at the top, the remaining purple petals. Soon those seedpods would split and the seeds with their downy parachutes would float off in the breeze to root and grow again. Winter was already drawing near. But for now the fireweed was resting in the night, and I wasn't sure where my dreams would take me.

Audrey and the kids made good time traveling from Anchorage. The first thing that struck me when I saw them was that Cal was walking more steadily than I remembered. He seemed happy to make adventuresome forays on his own without having to hang on to one of us or whatever was at the ready. I was taken by the idea that my youngest child had learned to walk in Alaska while his father was learning to walk in another reality that Alaska had opened up. Jack was even happier to see me. I had lots of stories to tell, but they could wait.

The next morning we deposited the *Pequod* with the rental agency after we'd bought an extra baby carriage and stocked up on baby supplies. Pat would take care of the goods we had to leave behind. That afternoon, I watched as a V-shaped flight of geese flew over us heading southwest, the same direction as us. They always seemed to be turning up at such moments. Now here we were, leaving, like the birds, on our homeward leg. Our flight out of Fairbanks would only take a few hours on a commercial jet.

When we arrived in Dillingham a fisherman friend of Pat's called Mike and his fishing partner, Olaf, met us. I observed to myself that this was the third Alaskan named Mike I had stayed with, and I had met plenty of others on my travels.

Mike Davis had arrived in Alaska some thirty years ago to work on a volunteer scheme as a teacher. Like most of the people I had met, he had found himself staying for one more year, then another and another. Over those years Mike had worked as a journalist, a teacher and a union representative, and had even served a term of office in the legislature as a Democratic representative. Now he worked for the University of Alaska's rural development program in Dillingham, and spent the summer break fishing the Bristol Bay area during its massive seasonal salmon run. Olaf was a postgraduate of the same university doing research into the walrus. He and Mike partnered up during the fishing season, but, as they explained during the drive to our cabin, it was one of the poorest seasons on record. The salmon numbers were exceptionally low and the price of fish per kilo the canneries and the buyers were offering was also the lowest it had ever been. As we drove past, Mike pointed out the harbor. It was jam-packed with the chunky, silver gray aluminum fishing boats that were unique to the Bristol Bay fleet. "This time last year that harbor was empty. It's going to be a long, hungry winter for some fisherfolk." By the time we'd got ourselves installed in our cabin, Mike was still talking salmon. The disastrous season was having a major impact on everyone in this lively but isolated bush town. Dillingham was, as Mike proclaimed, the salmon capital of the world. Sometimes more than fifteen thousand tons of salmon are hauled out of Bristol Bay in a six-week salmon run. During that time, the population doubles with seasonal fishermen and cannery workers.

The majority of the resident population were native, a mix of Eskimos, Aleuts and Athabascan Indians. The whites who had settled here were well assimilated. The greetings hailed across the street to Mike declared that he was a well-liked resident. A glance at the map explained why the majority of the population was native. The names of the small villages clearly declared that this was Yupik territory. Quinnhagak, Togiak, Aleknagik, Ewok, Koliganek, Iquigig and Kokhanok all made the name Dillingham appear ludicrously cumbersome and totally inappropriate.

In spite of its name, Dillingham was a good place to stay, but it was the countryside around it that made it so attractive. This was still the Alaskan bush. The only stretch of road out of Dillingham ran for approximately twenty-three kilometers to Aleknagik Lake and back again. The countryside beyond and around this road was virgin bush, teeming with mountain lakes and rivers that were the spawning waters of millions of Pacific salmon every year. A cursory glance at the map confirmed that everything here was dependent on water. The salmon were born in icy mountain lakes, then swam through the labyrinthine network of rivers to mature into fabulous majestic fish far out in the ocean, only to return some three or four years later to the exact spot of their birth to start the cycle all over again. Dillingham could have been Killybegs in Donegal to me, except that the fishermen in Donegal would not believe that such a place as Dillingham existed. It was part of the dreams of old men and drunken deckhands. In fishy terms, it was El Dorado.

On the second evening of our stay, Mike invited me to a "steam," which I was happy to agree to. A "steam" in Alaska means a steam bath. It is a ritual in every native community, the traditional way of getting clean but also something more than that. It's a bit like going to the pub, or even to church. It's where men gather at the end of the day to contemplate life and gossip about the fortunes and misfortunes of friends and enemies. It's where you can cleanse yourself, ease the aching in your bones and put the world to rights with a few other naked men in the space of a few hours in a tiny wooden hut in the back of beyond. The steam is where you purge yourself, body and soul.

The steam Mike took me to was a rickety old plywood and plank structure erected a few meters from his fisherman's cabin. There were a few other cabins whose inhabitants shared the premises. The steam house was never fired up without first inviting the other fishermen. There were several boats resting on trailers and various piles of boat parts and fishing gear lying around. In fact, the steam looked more like a repair shed than a bathhouse. It was divided in two, with a changing area and a sauna. The changing room comprised two plank benches running along each facing wall. At several intervals at about head height, cup hooks or an occasional nail had been driven into the wall to hang one's clothes on. The place could not have held more than about eight men.

There were already three "steamers" there when we arrived,

and all of them sat unconcernedly naked as they talked intensely to one another. Mike introduced me, and we undressed. There was no formality and little ritual in this freemasonry of the steam. Another man arrived with a bag of beers, and after being introduced to me he too got naked like the rest of us and slipped into conversation without further ado.

The poor season was the big issue, and as the men bemoaned the insignificant catches they were making one or two of them would disappear into the sauna and reappear ten minutes later, red and sweating, to join us. Each man wiped the excess sweat off his face and the back of his neck like a penitent about to enter a house of prayer. A single bare bulb lit the place, and ghostly wafts of steam bellowed in every time someone entered or emerged from the sauna.

As the only non-fisherman, I was soon informed by my companions about the finer details of the Pacific salmon. The Chinook or king salmon was where the real money was. These fish could weigh up to eighty pounds and more. In a good season, you could fill your boat three or four times a day if you had the energy and a good crew. Then there was the sockeye salmon and the humpy, a much smaller fish at about two and a half feet in length and weighing up to twelve or fourteen pounds. The coho was a better fish: it could grow to over three feet and weigh in at some thirty pounds. It tasted a lot like the Chinook as it fed on the same basic diet. There was an argument about whether the curiously named Dolly Varden was a trout or a char. But, like the steelhead, it was really a sport fish, and the sport fishermen were welcome to them.

With this debate going on, I asked what fish they didn't like to catch. There was a moment of quiet thought, then one of the naked confederacy laughed out loud. "I hope you won't take any offense at this, but there is one fish that ain't worth the effort unhooking it. It's called the 'Irish lord,' and if you're a sports fisherman and can't catch nothing else, then you're sure to catch a lord. They are ugly brutes with big mouths and bulging eyes and you can't fail to catch them because they will take any kind of bait. Anything from shrimp or spinners, banana peel and cigar butts to bologna sandwiches and potato salad, if you can get it to stay on your hook." I laughed along with everyone else as the storyteller spun out his improbable list. Again he apologized if he was offending my Irish sensibility. I explained that I wasn't the slightest bit bothered as there were no "lords" in Ireland. The only time the Irish had had lords that fitted his description was when the English imposed them on us. Another round of laughter went up, and I took my bow by taking a turn in the sauna.

It was about half the size of the changing room, and the heat emanated from a fifty-gallon oil drum that had been cut and laid on its side. A door had been constructed in the top of it that was covered with a blanket of rocks, and a long metal chimney stack carried the smoke out through the roof. Near the fire sat a large bucket filled with water. A ladle constructed of pieces of timber with a tin can on the end was used to pitch water onto the hot stones. The benches that faced each other beside the fire could only hold four people. The room was dark from years of wood smoke and lit by one small window in the wall. Underneath the bench were a few basins, each with a helping of cold water for dipping your washcloth.

I quickly learned the ritual rhythm of the steam. The easygoing camaraderie of the changing room changed in the sauna. Here, the macho element of the freemasonry kicked in. This was very much a testing room, and I was sure my companions in the steam room were determined to test my pale suburban flesh against their own hardiness. I have little time for such shows of prowess. As the water hit the stone, exploding into slow-moving clouds of steam, I lowered my face into a washcloth and hoped that the dampness would cool the roaring air that was barbecuing the back of my throat. When the gold chain I had forgotten to remove from around my neck started to burn through my flesh, I'd had enough.

Back in the easy atmosphere of the changing room someone

handed me a beer and the conversation carried on—sometimes about boats, or engines, sometimes about different fishing practices in other countries. A lot of the talk was about their dependence on the canneries and the Japanese fish market, which ultimately determined the price. At this time of year the season was coming to a close. Men were calculating how they would get through the winter without having laid down a big supply of fish in their freezers. The talk turned to hunting and trapping. Some of the men were considering getting out from the worst of the winter. The talk was all "men talk." I had half expected a bunch of guys swigging beer in a sauna to crack a few jokes about women, but the subject never came up.

As we walked back to the cabin, I asked Mike what people did in the winter. After all, I thought, you can't hunt every day. Mike wasn't troubled by the question. "It doesn't get as cold here as up north. So when we get snowed in we just have fun. The countryside is great for cross-country skiing and people still like to run their dog teams. Though most prefer to load up a trailer on their snow machines and head through the mountains to the villages. Alaska is a place that keeps you busy even when you think there is nothing to do." Before parting, we planned a trip to one of the nearest villages, called Togiak, some fifty miles west of Dillingham.

"How was your evening out with the boys?" Audrey asked mockingly when I returned to the cabin.

"It's a male thing," I answered teasingly, "and unless you want to come and join us I can't tell you. After all, this is the Brotherhood of the Steam."

But she would not be drawn in. She and the kids enjoyed Dillingham—not that there was much to do or see, but the small town was homely and uncomplicated. Cal was getting stronger on his legs and wanted to go "walkabout" everywhere. Jack wanted to go fishing, but Mike wasn't entirely happy about that. You had to be several hours out on the ocean to lay the nets, then you either hung about and waited or came back ashore for a

while before going out again for a few more hours of heavy hauling work. Mike worked from a big, long, open boat powered by
a large outboard. It was cold and bleak out on the bay and there
was noplace to shelter from the cold or a mass of three-foot-long
fish thrashing around in the boat. However, he did lay out a
beach net one morning. Jack and I watched as he walked into the
sea with enormous rubber boots on that allowed him to wade
into the ocean up to his chest, whereupon he anchored the net to
the seabed. "Don't expect much, these subsistence nets haven't
been catching much," he'd informed us.

In the meantime, we all went off to church and the potluck afterward. I was beginning to think that we were not in Alaska at
all. We stayed longer at the potluck than we had intended. The
food was good and everyone wanted to welcome and help the
new Irish family. The only thing was, Mike suddenly realized
he had forgotten about the net on the beach and we had to leave
in a hurry. It was just as well. The tide had come and gone and
fish lay entangled in Mike's beached net. "Oh my God!" he said.
I was amazed at the number of fish. Jack was running up and
down the length of the net deliriously calling out, "Daddy,
Daddy, look, here's more fish!" I don't believe he had ever seen
so many real fish, even on a fishmonger's table. "Look at the size
of this one!" he called out again.

Mike decided we needed boxes and some help to get the fish
untangled before the tide started moving again. He also quietly
confessed that although he was surprised at the number of fish,
he really wanted to get them out of the net before any of the villagers saw what had happened. I looked at him, puzzled. Nobody ever allowed fish to lie on the beach like this. The people
here have a thing about taking fish then forgetting about them.
Subsistence is a big issue here, and food is too valuable to leave
for the birds or the bears to pick at. And things like this have a
habit of becoming a joke at the steam. I swore myself to silence
as I pulled another big salmon out of the net while Mike headed
off. Within minutes he was back with Olaf and a truckload of fish

boxes. After a few hours with four of us working we dropped the last fish into a box. I now understood why Mike thought Jack might not enjoy being on the ocean, laboriously untangling thrashing fish in a rolling boat.

Back at a shed near the steam, Mike enlisted a few neighbors' help to fillet the fish. In the meantime he phoned some native families to come and share his catch. Obviously Mike had a long time ago understood the Eskimo ethic of sharing.

The next day, Mike and I drove the two and a half miles to the airstrip. There were three other passengers, all young and in various stages of inebriation. The pilot was an Indiana Jones look-alike with a brown leather jacket and carefully crushed fedora. I got the feeling that his attire was chosen to give the impression of a cool, risqué bush pilot who had long since learned to ride the storms of Bristol Bay and didn't care too much about the rules of aviation or recommended flight paths. When we were all safely buckled into our seats the swashbuckling pilot informed us to expect a few bumps and that if anyone was feeling sick to make sure they used the sick bag in front of them. We knew he was reinforcing the message to one passenger in particular, and he wasn't being too diplomatic about it.

We were only airborne a few minutes when the radio crackled and the pilot turned to Mike, who was sitting nearest to him, and said, "We're gonna have to go in low. There's a big heavy cloud formation above us and a big blow coming off the bay." The pilot must have believed he had been an eagle in another life, for the plane dipped and swooped, powered in and out of crosscurrents of air, and flew so low over the tundra that you would have thought the pilot was looking for something he'd dropped on a previous flight. Even Mike, who had made this journey many times, thought the pilot was pushing his luck way beyond the safety limits.

Mike leaned forward and tapped the flyer on his shoulder. The pilot removed the headphones from one ear and leaned back to hear what Mike had to say. "I've never been to Togiak this way before," he said, but the implication of his words was, "Do you know what you're doing, flyboy?" The pilot's answer couldn't have been less encouraging: "No, neither have I." To which Mike could only smile and shrug.

Meanwhile, the least inebriated of the passengers who sat directly behind us leaned over the back of the seat and began to massage Mike's shoulder blades. Mike nervously thanked the lady and suggested that he was just fine. She in turn insisted on striking up a conversation, which Mike found hard to detach himself from. He looked at me pleadingly and I winked back at him, enjoying his discomfort. At one point he tried to extricate himself by pointing out the landscape below, saying it was "one vast protein soup," to which I could only teasingly remark that it wasn't half as thick as the soup he had currently got himself into!

The young lady showering attention on Mike didn't seem to be intoxicated like her two companions. They were obviously Eskimos from the village. But the lady in question was very questionable. She was immaculately made up, with plucked eyebrows and shiny black hair that was coiffed to give it body and depth. However, her clothes were straightforwardly masculine. Alaska was a country that didn't discriminate between the sexes and even in the summer it had neither climate nor culture for the latest haute couture. I left Mike to his dilemma and smiled quietly to myself. However feminine "he" may have made "herself" appear, I knew for sure that this "lady" was definitely a man.

We were late arriving at Togiak. Flyboy admitted that he had got lost and couldn't find the string of small plane wrecks that all the local pilots use to plot their flight path. Mike explained that the storms and hurricane winds that blast in off the ocean tossed light aircraft about like straws in the wind. "Parts get snapped off and the plane goes down like a clay pigeon," he explained.

I was pondering whether or not to thank him for telling me this when his friend who lived in the village pulled up in his truck. As we stowed my bags, Mike asked about the woman who had traveled with us. His friend, the village schoolteacher for twenty years, looked at our three traveling companions, then back at Mike. "No women on that flight, Mike," he answered with a deadpan expression. Mike was aghast as I laughed aloud and commented, "Too many hours sitting in that sauna or out at sea. You've lost it, Mike." This time Mike laughed, but when I teasingly asked him if this was another incident that he didn't want brought up in the hallowed confines of "the steam," he answered with a seriously affirmative "No way!"

We only had a few hours before our return flight, so we deposited our gear with the local schoolteacher and had a coffee before heading off. The man's name was Bill. He'd arrived in Alaska on the same volunteer program as Mike, and, like Mike, had chosen to remain. He admitted he didn't rightly know why after all these years. Then, after a pensive moment, he said that as a young man life hadn't seemed to have the same edge to it back home. "I suppose you take on the values of the people you live among without knowing it. You share so much with these people that they become family. Also you learn a lot about yourself and what you want to do with life."

We finished our coffee, and after a brief chat about fishing quotas left to look around. We walked around the village of sturdy wooden cabins that stretched out behind a bank of dunes along the seafront. Boats of every size and description were everywhere. The village contained a well-stocked supermarket, a school and a youth facility and community center. As villages go, Togiak was enterprising. On the outskirts was the cemetery. A few of the graves had carved marble headstones, many were wooden, and many more were simply marked by a large boulder. In a close-knit community such as this, everyone knew who was buried where; names and dates were an irrelevancy. Mike explained that there had been many more smaller communities in the Bristol Bay area, but that epidemics of influenza and diphtheria had reduced the population and created thousands of orphans. Many people remembered these epidemics and the orphans, although they were pensioners now and were living proof of the tragedy. "It almost wiped out the culture of this area completely," said one. "I survived, but now these epidemics and the controls of the fish and game department on local hunting and fishing have all got lumped together by some aggressive young Eskimo rights activists. The traditional way of life had functioned here for thousands of years, but now, with the coming of the white man and his system of government, it's being changed out of all proportion."

On our way back to pick up our gear and catch our flight, we called on one of the village's oldest residents, Moses Nick. Mike had not spoken to him for maybe fifteen or sixteen years, and it was obvious old Moses was not sure who Mike was, but we were welcomed into his house and offered tea and boiled eggs. Moses understood English, but his age and his accent made it difficult for me to follow as he talked about Togiak and how he remembered growing up. He showed us some ivory carvings he was doing, and when Mike asked him if he still played the accordion his eyes lit up and he answered, "You betcha." He hauled himself out of his chair and went out of the room, returning within minutes with a gleaming red and white accordion. Mike had been explaining how early Russian trappers had frequently visited this part of the southwest before the Russian government sold Alaska to America. The mention of the Alaska purchase did not pass by Moses Nick. "I ain't never seen no bill of sale with any Eskimo name on that sold any part of Alaska to the Russians in the first place. So how they could sell it to America is way beyond my understanding." Moses Nick was making it plain to the two white men in his house that the Eskimos owned Alaska and everything in it. There was no piece of paper, title deed or proclamation of any government anywhere that could prove otherwise.

"Now, what you wanna hear?" Moses asked. I left the choice up to him, and without further ado he squeezed out a note-perfect "Lilli Marlene" and followed it up with a few more German waltzes. His playing might have attracted an old friend who called in. He and Moses chatted away in their Yupik tongue, and as the visitor spoke little English we thanked Moses, took our leave and walked back to Bill's place, to the strains of "The Blue Danube."

On board our flight back to Dillingham, Mike jokingly asked the pilot if he still intended taking the "lost" way back. Indiana Jones was unruffled by the jest. "No, sir," he said. "The wind blew the cloud cover clean away, so it's blue skies straight home." The engines fired up, and within no time we were homeward bound.

I asked Mike about Moses and his accordion. "Music was not intrinsic to their culture," he said. "They had the drum and the chant and even dance, but music in the European sense was alien to their culture. The Eskimos have something much cleverer than music. They have this uncanny skill of studying something by simply looking at it and watching it work or how it moves. Leave them alone with it for long enough and they will dismantle it and put it back together in perfect order. They are superb fixers of things." He went on to relate how Moses Nick had once seen an accordion being played when he was a very young man working in the cannery. He had been mesmerized by the instrument and had sworn that one day he too would have one. Many years later he bought one in Juneau or Anchorage. He knew nothing about the thing or how it worked. He preserved it for a while until some German tourists sent him some tapes, and within months he could play every tune on the tapes as if he had been playing all his life. I understood what he meant, having spoken to the ivory carver in Nome. It was a short flight, and I had opened up the question about his "lady friend."

"Mike, what would you have done if we had crashed on the trip out? I mean, that 'lady' was extremely taken by you." Mike looked me directly in the eye. "What woman are you talking about? There weren't any women on the flight!"

During the drive back to the cabin I asked Mike about the chance of seeing some bears. I explained to him how I had told my son Jack before we left Ireland that we were all going on a bear hunt. I told him how *We're Going on a Bear Hunt* was my son's favorite bedtime story, and that although we had seen some bears in Denali, I wanted something a bit more experiential than looking out of a tour-bus window. His answer was immediate: "Go to Katmai. You'll see plenty of bears there and you'll have to do it on foot. There are no buses. But it's the best time to catch them. Whole families of bears will be feeding at the river falls and in the lakes, piling on the fat for the long hibernation." It seemed the perfect place.

That evening, Audrey and I pored over the map. We could take a short flight to a place called King Salmon and from there catch a seaplane to land us on one of the several lakes in the Aleutian Range of mountains that ran through the Katmai Reserve. From there, we would have to return to King Salmon, dogleg back to Anchorage, then over the Alexander Archipelago to stay over in Juneau and Sitka. We were both conscious of the changing weather and the need to complete the last quarter before the first snows returned. It all seemed so hectic.

"It's a lot of hopping on and off planes," Audrey pointed out, "especially with all our bags, the two of us, two kids, two sets of baby carriages—"

"And two sets of antlers."

Audrey stopped dead in her tracks. "Two sets? What do you mean, two sets?"

"Well, there's a set of moose antlers waiting for me in Anchorage. I'll arrange to have them shipped on to Juneau and from there to Dublin. I picked them up while I was up north, just forgot to mention it," I said sheepishly.

Audrey looked at me with a long, silent glare, then slowly shook her head.

✳

CHAPTER TWENTY-FOUR

THE FINAL QUARTER

As our small six-seater seaplane descended on the mountain lake I turned to Jack and Cal. "Look, boys, there's a bear standing by the edge of the water."

Our pilot instantly asked, "Where?"

When I pointed out the large brown bear ambling peacefully along the lakeshore he immediately hoisted the plane into an ascent and circled over the lake, quickly explaining to me that Katmai was brown bear country and the bear always had right of way. As the bear was near where he intended mooring the seaplane, we had to hang around until he moved on. It didn't take long. The brown bear looked over his shoulder twice as he moved lazily along the lakeshore. We were an alien irritant in his world and he dismissed us with appropriate disdain. Eventually we landed on the still waters with all the grace of a snow goose and motored to our mooring pier. Babies, baby carriages and bags were all unloaded and we set off into bear country.

But there was something even bigger than bears in Katmai,

for running parallel with the Shelikof Strait were fifteen active volcanoes. Flying across these incredible snow-covered Aleutian mountains that seem to go on forever, it's hard to believe that below their forbiddingly cold, granite-hard surfaces molten rock lies boiling and bubbling. Steam plumes still rise from Mounts Mageck, Martin and Trident, declaring that creation is unfinished in Katmai.

The June 1912 eruption of the Novarupta volcano altered the Katmai area dramatically. Severe earthquakes rocked the area for a week before Novarupta exploded with cataclysmic force. Enormous quantities of hot, glowing pumice and ash were ejected from the mountaintop and nearby fissures. This material flowed over the terrain, destroying all life in its path. Trees upslope were snapped off and carbonized by the blasts of hot wind and gas. For several days ash, pumice and gas were ejected and a haze darkened the sky over most of the northern hemisphere. When it was over, more than sixty-five square kilometers (forty square miles) of lush green land lay buried beneath volcanic deposits as much as two hundred meters (seven hundred feet) deep. At nearby Kodiak, for two days a person could not see a lantern held at arm's length. Acid rain caused clothes to disintegrate on clotheslines in distant Vancouver, Canada. The eruption was ten times more forceful than the 1980 eruption of Mount St. Helens. Only one eruption in historic times, Greece's Santorini in 1500 B.C., displaced more volcanic matter than Novarupta. The terrible 1883 eruption of Indonesia's Krakatoa belched out little more than half as much, yet killed thirty-five thousand people. Vastly isolated Novarupta killed no one. Had the eruption occurred on Manhattan Island in New York City, the writer Robert Griggs calculated, residents of Chicago would have heard it. The fumes would have tarnished brass in Denver. Acid raindrops would have burned your skin in Toronto. In Philadelphia, the ash would have lain waist deep, and no one would have been left alive in Manhattan.

Our short-lived flight over the Katmai Reserve confirmed that what Griggs wrote almost a century ago was as true today, if not more so. The apocalyptic energies of nature do not bring about disasters as much as recreations. The theory of tectonics may explain why such things occur, but it does not capture the austere and terrible beauty that Katmai has become. Maybe because of its cataclysmic eruptions and its remoteness, there are no roads or railways to fetch you here. Nature has been allowed to heal herself in her own unique way. Looking at a map during our flight, then trying to comprehend Katmai's bulk with my own feeble eyes, I began to understand how the true nature of wilderness eludes us. We were looking out on mountains I only wanted to bow before. Beneath me were enormous lakes and island-studded bays. There were hundreds of rushing rivers and open waterways that would take a lifetime to navigate. There were mountain passes and valleys windswept by gales in excess of a hundred miles an hour. No pilot will go near them, and even the most determined backwoods hiker gives them a wide berth.

I looked along the lakeshore before we left it. The big brown bear had gone. "Must have been seven hundred pounds and more," said our pilot as he lashed the last ropes to the pier.

At Brooks Lake, where we had landed, it was compulsory to sign in at the ranger center, confirming when you would be leaving. There was only one way in and one way out, and if you didn't show up at the time of your departure it meant Katmai had got you. To ensure this didn't happen, everyone had to sit through a fifteen-minute safety talk. We were given a small hand-printed map showing distinct pathways through the woods and along the lakeshore. These were not tourist routes as much as safety routes. All led away from and back to the ranger station. On these paths no one could get lost, and in emergencies everyone could be found. "Remember, just because you don't see anything doesn't mean you are not being watched," the map declared. It then encouraged hikers to "talk loudly or sing in the forest. Creatures of the wild do not like to be disturbed suddenly." I am no singer, and walking through the Aleutian Range singing songs or rhyming fairy tales did not tally with my idea of an Alaskan experience. But the sight of the seven-hundred-pound bear as we arrived made me forget my inhibitions. As an extra precaution, we bought several small bells and tied them to the buggies. Then we set off on the Great Alaska Bear Hunt.

After ten minutes, I conceded I was happy to have the baby carriages, the bells and the narrow hikers' path that would eventually bring us to the Brooks Falls. From our seaplane, the awe-inspiring geography of Katmai had been added to by the lavish autumnal colors that were beginning to burn up through the foliage. But now, as we walked through it, there was a different kind of awe. The kind that made your eyes sweat so that you saw things that weren't there. A silence that made you sing, whether you could or not, so that you felt less vulnerable and alone. But you were never alone. In this wilderness through which we were walking, caribou, fox, lynx, wolverine, porcupine and squirrel moved silent and unseen.

So we rehearsed our bedtime story aloud. We chanted together as the little brass bells rattled against the side of the baby carriages. After a few more miles we finally made it. The falls dropped water some thirty feet in a gentle descent broken by huge boulders and rock shelves. The river at this point must have been fifty feet or more wide and the roar of its white water hit you before you saw it. A long raised platform had been built to allow travelers to view the falls from a safe distance and at a height no bear would think of climbing. The spectacle it presented was the fairy-tale fantasy come true. At first six, then eight bears of varying age and size were wallowing in the water, making occasional dives at the salmon that swam past them. Older and wiser bears stood solidly on rock platforms and waited for the leaping salmon simply to jump into their mouths, or so it seemed. Jack sat on my shoulders, silent and fascinated. Then he excitedly pointed out each new bear as he spotted it.

One juvenile bear attempting to gain a fishing ledge like the mature bears was swept off his feet and carried ignominiously downstream by the torrent of water. Jack was concerned by his plight, but my reassurance calmed him.

For almost two hours, we sat and watched. The bigger bears could fillet a large salmon in seconds, and the carcasses they threw away were immediately set upon by a squabbling pack of gulls. Further downstream, far from the falls, other birds circled and swooped down on the fish-filled stream. It was difficult to distinguish what kind of birds they were, for bald eagle, falcon and hawk all inhabit Katmai.

I took time to study Jack as we lingered, knowing that we would probably never return to this magical place. I had told him as much as I could explain to his young mind about where we were and about the Eskimos and the Indians I had gone to live with. I had shown him photos of these people and the landscape they lived in. I noticed how tall he had grown and knew that as a young man he would be much taller than me. He is a bright boy, full of questions. There is a tenderness in him; sometimes I think he is too like me. I sat and watched him as he studied the bears and for a moment I knew that the fairy tales had overtaken the fact. Jack was staring beyond the fishing bears into a land of his own. For an instant, he looked back at me. I was sure he knew what I was thinking. But it was not knowledge, more a shared sense of something. I remembered carrying him from his mother the moment he was born. He was only minutes old, but even then he knew what I was feeling. I waved to him, and he waved back.

But Cal, having found his legs in Alaska, was determined to walk all over it, so we walked up and down the platform, pointing out the bears. When I'd had enough of walking I played at being a bear, scooping salmon out of the air and biting off their heads. After a few minutes of watching me as if I was demented, Cal tugged at my hand and commanded me to "Wak!"

We headed back the way we came, reversing the story while bounding along the pathway, the baby carriages bouncing off it and the bells jingling erratically. "Run, run, here he comes, the bear, the big brown bear. Maybe he thinks we're a fish!" The boys squealed with laughter. Then it suddenly poured with rain, so we ran faster and the boys laughed louder as we squishy-squelched through the mud.

Back at the ranger station we dried off and ate a quick lunch as the short monsoon abated. It was a rapturous day. One of those days that you know will go on forever because it was so unforgettable.

As we sat on the jetty waiting for our pilot, I watched Audrey and the boys talk excitedly about the bears at the falls. A part of me wonders if Jack and Cal will ever understand why I brought them here. Yes, it was to see great mountains that go on forever, to stand beside rivers that frighten you with their roar and speed, to catch fish bigger than you would dream of, to fly like an eagle over ice fields and glaciers, and to see bears and wildlife not imprisoned in a TV screen. But it was more than that. It was to let them experience in their innocence that life is more majestic than fairy tales. I wanted them to be touched somewhere inside themselves with the magnitude of such wonder that life could never crush or diminish. In short, I wanted to enlarge their spirit in the only way I knew. But would they remember all this? Yes, for I know that above all things the mind forgets nothing. In the majestic landscape of the mind and the imagination, they could return here, to this special place, when they wished. It would always be magical, and it would nourish their spirit like the salmon and the bear.

We bundled ourselves back into our seaplane and headed back to King Salmon, then on to Anchorage to connect to Juneau en route to Sitka. Juneau was to be the jump-off point for Jack London's Yukon, where I imagined I might catch up with and befriend the ghost who had brought me here. But I had been thinking long and hard about heading in Jack London's Yukon footsteps. Certainly it was in the Klondike that the author declared he had got his perspective. I kept thinking about his other statement about Alaska: "When a man journeys into a far country, he must be prepared to forget many things he has learned, he must abandon the old ideals and the old gods and often times he must reverse the very codes by which his conduct has hitherto been shaped." Something inside me was telling me to jettison my ghost hunt in the Yukon. If I was to take London's imperative to heart and abandon the old ideals and the old gods, then that might also mean abandoning my Yukon trip.

In any case, finding perspective is about distance, about creating a mental landscape in which we might evaluate the relative importance of things. My travels in this compelling land, the experiences and thoughts it had induced, my stay with the Gwich'in and with Lena and Charlie, the "otherness" of the land itself, and especially the portal Debra had opened up for me, all required that I extract from these things a new set of compass bearings for my life's trajectory. As I thought over these ideas, more than a little unbalanced by the dizzying perspectives they threw up, I remembered my own words written years ago on the night train from Temuco to Santiago in Chile: "there was another landscape to be discovered and negotiated, the landscape of the heart. The emotions and the imagination had to be opened up and new route maps planned." My travels in Alaska had been a confirmation of that and more. They had given me a sense of direction. Jack London, I determined, was one of the old gods that had to be cast off. My own spiritual life had to be nurtured, and I had been instructed in the method of achieving this. A great sense of urgency was married with an exhilarating feeling of liberation and well-being.

When I apprised Audrey of my thinking as we awaited our flight to Juneau, she was both surprised and relieved. Though she admitted she hadn't been looking forward to many more weeks living out of a suitcase, she was perplexed at my sudden decision to abandon Jack London. "I'm too old to believe in ghosts," I said. Audrey looked at me, knowing there was always a lot more behind my throwaway remarks. "We all need a holiday anyway. And I need to stop somewhere for a while to get my perspective."

The idea behind staying in Juneau was so that we could collect all our baggage together in one place and store it there while we did whatever traveling we chose to do, then return for a last overnight before leaving the Final Frontier. The small two-story travelers' hotel we booked into was centrally located, and it had sent a courtesy bus to pick us up from the airport.

Juneau looked like nowhere else I had been in Alaska. The city rises steeply up from the waterfront to cling onto the mountains behind it. It is a cross between a mini San Francisco and a Swiss mountain village. It has all the cozy sophistication of a state capital without forgetting what manner of state that is. It was all summed up for me one day as we strolled through the downtown area to be confronted by a "typical" Alaskan dressed in cowboy boots, worn denims and a checked shirt with heavy lumberjack braces. He was leading a young but fully grown timber wolf on a strong leather leash. I stopped to talk to him, but the eerie yellow twilight in the animal's eyes spoke more to me. I thought of the creatures in *The Call of the Wild*, Buck leaping above the pack and howling at the moon, crying out his unearthly paean to the wilderness. This wolf was also beautiful, but there was something pathetically hideous about it as well. Its eyes were empty and soulless. The owner had acquired the animal as a weaning pup from a trapper friend and had raised it as a pet. I wondered if he had ever read Jack London's books. Then I realized the owner had obviously had too much to drink. What kind of relationship could there be between this caricature of a man and this beautiful creature with its haunting, empty eyes?

The evenings were colder now and the staircase streets of the city were frequently slicked with downpours of showers. I was enjoying the comforts of hot showers, flushing toilets, restaurants that served good wine and the supremely fine local beer, Alaskan Amber. But after a few days I was getting edgy. Maybe I had been too long in the bush. Juneau was too settled and enclosed. A guidebook note informed me that it is the only capital in North America you can't reach by road. It has more than a hundred miles of pavement road around it, but none of it goes anywhere. Every year two hundred scheduled flights never make it because of bad weather. I could feel the bad weather in the air and the pressure of a place confined within itself.

Another incident confirmed for me the need to move on. During one of the frequent rainy spells we crashed our baby carriages into the state capitol building for shelter. On the first floor there is an almost life-sized photo/mural of the representatives of Alaska's first territorial legislature in 1913. The all-male representatives looked exactly like what they were—ragged pioneers and frontiersmen whose life experience was about doing and surviving in the great outdoors rather than sitting and talking about legislative regulation. I studied their bearded faces and staring eyes. They looked distinctly uncomfortable, even lost. In their starched collars, tight ties and dress suits that looked two sizes too small, they looked more like people who had had the life wrung out of them. Behind the bravado smiles and the puffed-out chests I had a sense that some of them looked more like condemned men than committed legislators. I sympathized with them. Civilized society is about more than signatures on policy documents or the codification of laws. It is also about the loss of individual freedom, for something as vague as the greater good. There were no native names or faces among the legislators. I remembered reading somewhere that the native peoples should not set up as native corporations or be given special ownership of vast tracts of Alaskan territory but should rather be as "the minds over the land," for they alone knew the land and the natural laws that emanated from it. I looked again at the photo and felt once more a shared discomfort passing between me and these pictures of the dead. Finally, the rain ceased and we departed.

Of all the places I had been to in Alaska, Sitka appeared to be the loveliest. There was a serene kind of beauty about the town and its location that was almost oriental. The town sits facing the Pacific and is overshadowed by the Mount Fuji–like features of Mount Edgecombe, an extinct volcano. The waters offshore are broken up by an amazing archipelago of small islands, all with their own growths of pine and hemlock. When you look out on the silhouette that forms at sunset, you can almost feel the tranquillity rising up from them. Sitka is the only town in all of southeast Alaska that fronts onto the ocean, and with the backdrop of snowy peaks behind you can believe that you are actually standing in the most exquisite Japanese landscape etching.

I was far away from the Arctic with its Eskimos and Athabascan bush, and, I suppose, far away from all the awkward questions my travels in the Big Lonely had thrown up. But Sitka was idyllic, maybe because I knew it was the end of a long journey and I was unconsciously reacting to it. Still, there was a distinct ambience about Sitka that was restful and quiet. There was a palpable sense of harmony and easygoing good humor, and I wallowed in it. I had spent so long in the bush or on the harsh Arctic coast that I had forgotten how consoling a nearness to the sea could be. I had also forgotten about the "real" trees. For months I had seen only the eerie, spindly trunks of black spruce or gangly silver white birch. But here, the trees were magnificent. Western hemlock, Sitka spruce and red and yellow cedar added a sense of muscular vitality to the landscape. They were huge and lushly green, and inside their forests you felt small and humble but at the same time safe and reassured. The summer was ending with glorious haste, and under the green canopy of the evergreen forest autumn colors were setting the hillsides ablaze. It was a time for recollection, and Sitka was perfect for it.

For the first few days we stayed in an old, comfortable, run-down hotel. I could imagine it in an earlier life being the grand home of some whaling captain. Its rooms and layout were not those of a hotel. The bar was tiny, and it was the meeting place for many skippers from the fleet of working boats that lay out on the sound.

I thought of our days spent in the *Pequod*. In my own way I too, like Captain Ahab, had been chasing a metaphorical white whale. An article by Chris Bernard in the free summer visitor guide published by the local newspaper, the *Daily Sitka Sentinel*, made me think about my journey:

> When Ward Eldridge kayaked back to his beloved schooner **Merlin**, he found the boat resting quietly, exactly where he had left it in Still harbour, about 35 miles south of Sitka. But only the top of the mast was showing; the keel was sitting on the ocean bottom. The 73-foot **Merlin**, said to be the oldest working American-built vessel on the West Coast, had weathered a lot of storms in her 111 years. But something had brought her down.
>
> After the **Merlin** was raised, the cause of its sinking became clear: a collision with a humpback whale. Although such seemed unlikely— the last documented case of a whale sinking a boat in the area occurred at the turn of the century—proof was found. Several strips of baleen were wedged in the planks at the edge of the 5-foot hole in the boat.

I thought of my own *Pequod*, finally beached in Fairbanks. At first I had been enchanted with the idea of "sailing" across Alaska, stopping wherever we chose to explore and live in the wilderness. But it wasn't long before the cramped confines and the lack of navigable road made the "Dreamboat" irksome, and often an encumbrance. But that's the way it goes with dreams. Sometimes pursuing them distorts reality and often causes us to shipwreck our lives on the subject of such dreams. The obsessions of Captain Ahab and Chris McCandless had ultimately destroyed them.

I read another article in the *Anchorage Daily News* I had picked up somewhere along my travels, a scientific report about whales written by Ned Rozell. It pointed out that "Scientists previously thought that bowheads had a lifespan similar to other whales, but the old harpoon points hint that some of the whales alive today were swimming in the cold waters of the circumpolar oceans more than 100 years ago . . . One whale was 91, one was 135, one 159, one 172, and the oldest whale was 211 years old at the time of death . . . That whale, alive during the term of President Clinton, was also gliding slowly and gracefully through the Bering, Chukchi and Beaufort seas when Thomas Jefferson was president."

My fascination with Alaska was not quite as old as these ancient fish, but in a way it had been following me around all my life, like Moby Dick. For a moment I thought of Debra wrenching the scales from my back, as old as dinosaurs or ancient whales. Alaska had revealed much to me, and it was time to cast off old obsessions along with that ancient armor that had protected and defended me. Rid of its cumbersome weight, I could let the heart breathe and live more fully, nurturing my inner life and creativity. I may have many miles more to go, but the road was opening up before me.

That evening Audrey and I sat on the balcony of the small seafront motel we had moved to. The sunsets were divine. Sometimes we sat for hours, hardly speaking. Often we watched the salmon carried in on the sea tides as they thrashed and splashed over the rock-strewn foreshore where a tiny river entered the sea. From here they would swim up to the mountain lakes where they were born, give birth themselves, then die. It seemed an impossible task to battle their way up through water my flattened hand would not submerge in. When they had entered the sea from this same river maybe four years ago they would only have been a matter of inches long; now they could be up to two feet long with the bulk to match. Often I wanted to go and lift them and carry them to the river they so desperately sought. So we sat and watched, humbled by the salmon and the sunset.

It is said that the Clan House of the Tlingit people is a representation of the cosmos, and it always faces the water. The fire pit in its center symbolizes the center of the universe and is the intersection to the middle world dominated by man, the under world, the upper world, the sea world and the sky world. I had never been in a Clan House, but I felt I understood it. Looking out on the scene before me I was already in the Clan House, or at least my spirit was, and I too was at a great intersection in my life, like the season, the sunset and the struggling salmon.

For the next few days we spent our time wandering around the National Historical Park. Often I was sure I could hear black bears grunting in the undergrowth of the foliage rustling and moving several yards from us. There were fifteen amazing native totem poles to be seen, and we chose to see them all. I was amazed at their height and girth, but more drawn to their naïve simplicity, their stoic forbearance and their reduction of a complex world into a collection of intimate symbols. You know just by standing and looking at them in the vast silence of the forest that these things are powerful beyond their sheer bulk. But they were never frightening. They were comforting and welcoming, like a family you have been too long away from.

Standing underneath the giant Sitka spruce and great western hemlock was like being in another world. I thought of Debra and her childhood belief in that other world. Lewis Carroll would have loved this place, and the Grimm brothers knew it well. Inside the forest you left life and the real world behind. It was as if you had passed through an invisible veil. Here the air felt different, and it was full of smells. We had to shelter at the foot of one of the forest's great giants as a squall of rain sheeted down. The downpour was somehow orchestral and had a diamond brightness that brought the forest closer to you, the way a magnifying glass does. Through the invisible swelter of vegetation, birds and animals called out in the green silence. After the rain had gone and we looked up to be sure, the trees exploded in a blizzard of foliage against the bright sky; for a few seconds it looked like fairy lights strung across the treetops. Inside the forest, time, too, had been blown away.

Under that dappled canopy, myth and legend awaited us. When we entered it, it was as if we had shrugged off the gaudy raiments of civilization and tattooed ourselves with primitive and carnal images—our camouflage and acceptance of belonging in this natural refuge. For now we were in the land of talking beasts and changeling creatures—Distant Time land. It was as if the oldest and most basic part of ourselves leapt out to meet us.

I am convinced you need the mind of a child to live in the wilderness. A child's imagination is untamed and unafraid. My first responses to the vast wilderness were like those of a caged animal—anxious, watchful, even afraid. I still remembered how my nervous system had been charged into high alert. As I wandered alone into the bush my skin was tingling from the heat of unseen eyes watching me, and perhaps there was cause.

Native tradition unfolds many stories about animals with human characteristics, and vice versa. This same folklore also speaks of an enigmatic human creature that inhabits the forest as a person who has crossed over from the world of men to the world of nature. This "woodsman," as he is called, is like a kind of missing link, the final affirmation that the view of man as a separate and superior being is an illusion. This wild man is like the raven, who mocks and jeers our human endeavor but is never malign. It is only our civilized conditioning in fear that makes him threatening. I was sure we all needed to find the "woodsman" in ourselves. A being who was utterly free, who could understand the wild and commune with it.

When I looked at the magnificent totem posts, I knew they were telling a story about a people and the incidents that made up their history. But the arresting blend of animal and human imagery hints at another story. They speak of another part of ourselves that the forest sets free, perhaps those half-crazed, half-unlived parts of ourselves that have been "civilized" for too long. Anyway, I thought to myself, who doesn't want to go mad sometimes? Maybe madness is the end of fear, and of prohibition, and of the sanctions we impose on ourselves. Madness is not about losing oneself, but reclaiming for a moment what has been lost and hidden away within us. The psychic cleavage between things of the flesh and matters of the spirit is healed and restored.

Alaska demands much of the person who comes here to understand it. Maybe you never really can. Like the extreme landscape that it is, the Final Frontier remains impregnable. But it reveals itself to you in momentary flashes, like the wolf in Denali, the moose in McCarthy, the night on the frozen lake, the healing on Oneson's hill. I was happy for it to remain so. It was there to question and confuse us, and to humiliate and humble us, just like the mythological trickster Raven. To come to any sense of what it could mean, you had first to prostrate yourself before it. I was convinced it would hear your petitions and prayers. I was also sure that spiritual, psychological and physical well-being could be found here. Maybe you have to find the changeling in yourself and live by rules that are more than human. You have to scent it like the bear and the wolf, scan it like the sea eagle and falcon, be prepared to live as lonely as the moose and with the resilience of the caribou. Like the whales, you have to echo-locate yourself without maps or guidebooks. The imperatives of survival and shelter must be your first compass bearings.

We stayed in Sitka longer than we had planned. I was sure that my sudden decision to come here had been directed to me by the land itself. I was sitting once more on our motel balcony watching the magical transformation of earth, sky and sea. It was like the high point of the mass where that which is sacred is revealed to you and you know for sure that there is another reality out there, invisible yet accessible.

As I trawled through my memories of these past months, I thought how the land itself and that profound sense of "the other" that emanates from it is like a colossal haiku, obscure yet profoundly coherent, and transcendent with a kind of power that elevates all of life. That's the real power of Alaska. It's hallucinogenic. It heightens perceptual experience to sometimes fearful dimensions, before you crawl back into your human skin for a sheltering place. The problem with trying to write coherently about my experience from all the haiku-like word pictures that laced the pages of my diary together was that it was like trying to construct a linguistic quadratic equation that would solve the riddle of this metaphysical environment.

For a moment I smiled, sick with apprehension at those other writers who had drawn words out of Alaska. For me, the fluency of language was pulled up short here. Whatever the moments of sheer pleasure, fear, dislocation and all the other half-baked notions that impel us to strange places, one thing is for sure: a line traced on a map is no measure. The original of the cartographer's blueprint is somewhere inside ourselves. My trek through Alaska was mirrored by a struggle in the heart to find my own spirituality, which had been lost, or which time had dulled. A renewal of faith, a belief in the spirit. Confirmation that love, beauty and freedom were still real and attainable. That life, whether man, beast or bird, is related in spirit. My experiences in Alaska proved to me the reality of something that had been hanging around in the shadowy corridors of my understanding: life is not a journey to a terminus, and even when we are gone from this world, we never leave it. There is a very real world beyond sight and reason that we can enter into. It exists to enrich and help us. Life is a rite of passage out of all the confines and limitations we sometimes fall into. It is not enough simply to pass through a place. I want to pass into it, for I am convinced that it is really the unseen that makes a place permanent to human perception.

A few days before our departure, I sat long into the small hours. The night was chilly and there was a noticeable drop in the light. I remembered that it had been like this when we arrived. Then it had been early summer; now I could smell winter in the air. I wondered how all those places in which I had stayed might already be in the depths of winter. As I thought about how the coming winter was signaling itself, I felt that part of the problem when it came to writing about Alaska was that the land and everything on it seemed to be in a constant dynamic: animals, birds and fish migrating and returning; humans working and surviving in constant response to the seasons; ice breaking up and glutting the rivers in summer, and seas freezing over in winter; the coming and going of whales; the still active volcanoes and the ever-present threat of tsunamis that could change the coastal landscape; the mad frenzy of summer and the dark, white silence of winter. Alaska never stays still long enough for you to get a hold on it. Maybe you have to have the psychological stamina of the hunter to live here. Maybe it would take a whole lifetime to track down what Alaska means.

I had spent many hours in the Sheldon Jackson library and museum in Sitka, with its thousands of books and magnificent collection of native artifacts. I had even bought a copy of James Michener's epic *Alaska*. Its historical sweep, from prehistory, the Ice Age and early hunter-gatherers through to various periods of occupation and exploitation with their different layers of cultural and religious beliefs, made it a massive tome. Throughout the book it is the land itself which dominates the affairs of men. The book ends where it started, with a hunting scene. Two friends, who are oil barons and among the important movers and shakers in Washington, are in Alaska to discuss oil development. One of the men, Jeb, has come to love the unspoiled wilderness and is determined to obstruct his friend Poley's ideas, which amount to turning Alaska into another Texas, an oil-dollar republic in which the only motivation for any endeavor is profit and Mammon is the new religion. The two debaters go to a remote "primeval area which few people ever saw." There they intend to hunt a magnificent specimen of a dall sheep. During their debate they ignore radio warnings about the intense volcano activity of the Aleutian Islands. At last they find their prey and Jeb kills it. But it falls down the side of the mountain and Jeb must follow it to reclaim his prize, while Poley remains on high ground preparing for departure. He watches his friend's descent, then looks out onto the fjord to see the sudden and persistent suction of water from the bay. Inevitably, Jeb is swept away by the rising waters of the tidal wave. Poley, the entrepreneur and exploiter, reaches high ground and safety. It is a kind of fable which at first glance awards the future to the capitalist. But then you remind yourself that it is the raging of the elements, the mountains, the seas and the rivers that determines the course of history. Mammon will be left shivering on a precipice.

I smiled as I thought of Michener sitting here in the library absorbing facts and creating characters to carry the huge weight of his research. I wasn't really interested in the factual history of Alaska; it was only a gloss on the surface. What intrigued me was the land itself as the immutable force behind history's cause and effect, and the unique power of transcendence that seems to breathe out of the land and can sweep all rational preconceptions away, just like the tsunami at the end of Michener's *Alaska*.

Before going to bed for our last evening, I searched my memory and leafed through the pages in my diary for a particular phrase or specific incident that would render up this invisible Alaska. But, like Moses before the burning bush, I was speechless. Like a child, I suppose, I wanted some fairy-story image to lullaby me during my last hours here; more importantly, something that would connect my spirit to the spirit of the place, which I had felt with me everywhere. Instinctively, I picked up Barry Lopez's book *Arctic Dreams* and copied these words from it as the closing note in my diary:

> *I looked out over the Bering Sea and brought my hands folded to the breast of my parka and bowed from the waist deeply toward the north, that great strait filled with life, the ice and the water. I held the*

*bow to the pale sulphur sky at the northern rim of the earth. I held
the bow until my back ached, and my mind was emptied of its cate-
gories and designs, its plans and speculations. I bowed before the
simple evidence of the moment in my life in a tangible place on the
earth that was beautiful.*

*When I stood I thought I glimpsed my own desire. The landscape
and the animals were like something found at the end of a dream. The
edges of the real landscape became one with the edges of something I
had dreamed. But what I had dreamed was only a pattern, some
beautiful pattern of light. The continuous work of the imagination, I
thought, to bring what is actual together with what is dreamed is an
expression of human evolution . . .*

*Whatever world that is, it lies far ahead. But its outline, its ad-
umbration, is clear in the landscape, and upon this one can actually
hope we will find our way.*

*I bowed again, deeply, toward the north, and turned south to re-
trace my steps over the dark cobbles to the home where I was staying. I was full of appreciation for all that I had seen.*

I recalled making this same instinctive act of supplication on
Oneson's hill. I knew, too, that in some confused way the pattern
and outline of my own dreams had brought me here. Even though
I would be leaving the next day, I knew those same dreams
would bring me back again.

I rose to go to bed and looked in on Jack and Cal. Littered
across their bed were toy sea eagles, bears, wolves, moose and
musk ox. I laughed, thinking of the racks of antlers waiting to be
shipped home with us. If my dreams ever failed me, my sons'
totem animals and my own "toys" would not let me forget.

Text Acknowledgments

The author and publishers are grateful to the following for permission to reproduce extracts:

To Barry Lopez and Sterling Lord Literistic, Inc., for lines from *Arctic Dreams*, published by Scribner, reprinted by permission of SLL/Sterling Lord Literistic, Inc., copyright © 1986 by Barry Lopez.

To Macmillan, London, for lines from *Into the Wild* by Jon Krakauer, published by Macmillan, 1998, used by permission.

To Thad and James Poulson, for an extract from *All About Sitka*, a publication of the *Daily Sitka Sentinel: All About Sitka* 2001 Copyright © 2001 *Daily Sitka Sentinel*, used by permission.

To Ned Rozell, University of Alaska Geophysical Institute, for a passage from his article "World's Oldest Mammals," in *Anchorage Daily News*, February 25, 2001.

To the University of Washington Press, for an extract from *Alaska's Copper River Delta* by Riki Ott, published by the Artists for Nature Foundation and the University of Washington Press, reprinted by permission of the University of Washington Press, 1998.

To Alfred A. Knopf, for an extract from *Going to Extremes* by Joe McGinnis, © 1980 by Joe McGinnis.

The author and publishers have made every reasonable effort to contact the copyright owners of the extracts reproduced in this book. In the few cases where they have been unsuccessful, they invite copyright holders to contact them direct.

BRIAN KEENAN is a writer and poet. *An Evil Cradling*, the story of his four years' captivity in Beirut, is recognized as a nonfiction classic. He is also the author of a travel book, *Between Extremes*, with John McCarthy, and a novel, *Turlough*.